THE KNIGHTS TEMPLAR
&THEIR MYTH

THE KNIGHTS TEMPLAR
&THEIR MYTH

PETER PARTNER

DESTINY BOOKS
ROCHESTER, VERMONT

Destiny Books
One Park Street
Rochester, Vermont 05767
Web Site: http://www.gotoit.com

Revised edition published 1990
First published by Oxford University Press 1981
First quality paperback edition 1987

Library of Congress Cataloging-in-Publication Data
Partner, Peter
[Murdered magicians]
The knights templar and their myth / Peter Partner.
p.   cm.
Previously published under title: The murdered magicians.
Includes bibliographical references.
ISBN 0-89281-273-7
1. Templars—History. 2. Occultism. I. Title
CR4743.P37   1990
271'.7913–dc20   90–2787
                                                                              CIP

Printed and bound in the United States

10 9 8 7 6

Destiny Books is a division of Inner Traditions International

Distributed to the book trade in Canada by Publishers Group West (PGW),
Toronto, Ontario
Distributed to the book trade in Australia by Millennium Books,
Newtown, N.S.W.

Distributed to the book trade in New Zealand by Tandem Press, Auckland

To Mark Hamilton
in gratitude for a long friendship

CONTENTS

ILLUSTRATIONS

ACKNOWLEDGEMENTS

For help with the revision of the text I am indebted to my wife, Leila May Partner, to Mr Peter Janson-Smith (formerly of the Oxford University Press), to my son Simon Partner, and to Miss Anne Stogdale. I am also grateful to my colleagues, Mr James Sabben-Clare and Mr Richard Wall, for help with some points of translation, and to Mr Andrew Maxwell-Hyslop and Dr Philip Khoury for their kindness in obtaining for me some out-of-the-way material.

INTRODUCTION

To modern men the idea of a Crusade is that of doing battle to defend the right. A knight bearing a bloody cross on his breast is a sign of preparedness for martyrdom; the white mantle on which the cross lies signifies innocence. This simple idea of the Crusade developed from less familiar origins. In the Middle Ages Christian soldiers 'took the cross' before they went on armed pilgrimage to Palestine. 'Taking the cross' was a legal act; the word 'Crusade' (from cross, *croix*, came *croiserie* and *croisade*) derived from the act. They called it a voyage (*passage*) to the Holy Land, and to take the cross was, at first, a promise to go on pilgrimage to the Holy Places of Jesus and of the Jewish history which he fulfilled. But in the later Middle Ages the idea of Crusade gradually became distinct from the idea of pilgrimage to the Holy Land. The Crusade was manipulated by political and religious leaders until it included a whole range of warlike acts which men undertook with the sanction of Church law, many of which had nothing to do with the Holy Land. When the last fragment of the crusading state in Syria was lost to the Muslims in 1291 the divorce between pilgrimage and Crusade became final. A Crusader no longer went to the Holy Land: he might, like Chaucer's knight, fight the infidel in Egypt and North Africa, in Lithuania and in Spain. A Crusader might also fight against dissident Christians, such as the Cathars of France or the Hussites of Bohemia; or he might even fight orthodox Catholics who happened to be the political enemies of the Pope.

So the *passage* or armed pilgrimage became obsolete, and what has survived in the idea of the Crusade is the concept of fighting unbelievers, the enemies of truth and right. Religious war preceded the Crusades and it survived them. 'Paien unt tort et chrestiens unt dreit' said the *Song of Roland* before the First Crusade ever left for Syria. Half a millennium later the English poet Spenser used the identical phrase of the *Song of Roland* to describe the combat in the *Faerie Queene* between the Saracen and the Red-Cross Knight: 'th'one for wrong, the other strives for right'.

The Crusades grew from that part of men's minds in which the boundaries between the real and the metaphorical, the signifier and the signified, are shifting and uncertain. They are evidence of man's idealism, but also of his cruelty and folly: like other episodes in the history of religion they tell us that religious metaphors can be turned into political realities by means of bloodshed and terror. In the *Song of Roland* the equivalence between the poetic language of vision and the military violence of ordinary life is simple and direct; in Spenser the same combat of Christian and 'pagan' is used as a subtle and complex allegory. Yet Spenser was a contemporary of the Battle of Lepanto in which the Turkish fleets suffered their bloodiest defeat at Christian hands; real violence stood behind the poetic violence of Spenser, just as it did behind the *Song of Roland*. In the first Crusades the vision of a Sion whose walls were built of diamond and lapis lazuli took men to the Holy Land; what they did when they got there was somewhat less than ideal. In the Holy Land today the stones of the city of Jerusalem – not the jasper pavements of the visionary city but the humble flags of the real one –can testify to a past and a present in which poetic and religious visions have materialized in forms of physical violence.

Symbols can root themselves in a culture and remain fixed there for very long periods of time; they can also migrate and transform themselves in a Protean manner, and travel under long tunnels of history to emerge in a changed form in quite different regions of time and space. The Crusade still lives in men's minds today: the writer learned this in 1960 from a group of French generals in Algeria who told him that the suppression of the Algerian nationalist rebellion was a Catholic Crusade against Communism and Islam. But if the Crusade and the historical agents which effected it have continued to work powerfully on the imagination of Western man, their meaning has profoundly changed.

The subject of this book is the history and mythical metamorphosis of a Military Crusading Order, that of the Knights Templar. Before approaching the transformation of this single crusading institution, it is worth looking at our modern attitude to the idea of the Crusade. If its primary meaning is 'fighting for the right', the term 'crusade' may commend itself to us as one which expresses practical idealism. Campaigns for great social reforms – sometimes even for small ones – tend to be described as crusades. Politicians in distress have been known to label themselves as crusaders. For a long time a great popular British newspaper has placed a sketch of a Crusader – of a red Crusader, which may be thought significant in view of what follows – on its front page, in order to emphasize the idealism of its editorial policies.

The bloodshed and violence of the historical Crusades are not, however, forgotten. It is well known that the taking of Jerusalem by the Crusaders in 1099 occasioned a terrible massacre of its inhabitants, in which the Crusaders walked in blood. It is not only the well-lit and rational parts of our minds which are stirred by the crusading idea; we may also find that it evokes Gothic fantasies of conflict and slaughter. The Crusades have bequeathed Western men a tradition in which they take idealistic pride, but on whose account they also may feel a certain guilt and shame. The idea of a knight vowed to the accomplishment of crusading ideals seems noble and praiseworthy, yet those ideals were dictated by a medieval Church which now seems to us to have been bigoted and obscurantist, and were put into practice in a manner which now seems barbarous and cruel.

The ambiguity of our approach to chivalry and to the Crusades is not new. From the time of the Protestant Reformation of the sixteenth century onwards, men have tended to feel for the chivalric ideals of the Middle Ages a mixture of sympathy and revulsion. The idea of nobility and gallantry in the medieval knightly life has attracted admirers even among those to whom the clericalism of the Middle Ages was repugnant. The survival of the Orders of the Bath and the Garter into modern times is not without meaning. Since the growth of humanism in the Renaissance period, educators have been very ambiguous in their attitude to chivalry. For example, when the great French comic writer, François Rabelais, in Gargantua's letter to his son, dictated his views on the ideal education of a Renaissance gentleman, he did not neglect to mention 'chivalry and the use of arms'. Long before the Gothic Revival of the eighteenth century and the sentimental chivalry of the Romantic Movement, men felt for the old chivalric and crusading ideas a combination of nostalgia and distaste.

Part of this book is concerned with the history of the Knights

Templar as it is thought to have occurred in fact, part with the beliefs invented about the Templars in modern and relatively modern times. Some of the origins of the Templar myth have to be sought in the tangled traditions of occultism, and are hard to drag to the surface. But the roots of the myth lie also in ambiguous sympathy for the old crusading chivalry. The myth is pinned to a single, sad incident in crusading history: the story of the trial, persecution, and fall of the Knights Templar. These were, as is more fully explained below, an Order of soldier-monks bound by religious vows of poverty, chastity, and obedience, and engaged in religious war in the Holy Land. After their withdrawal from Syria at the end of the thirteenth century the Templars became the apparently innocent victims of a terrible campaign of slander and persecution mounted against them by the French government. Many were dreadfully tortured during their judicial examination; others were burned alive in order to intimidate the rest into confession. At the end of a short period of crisis (1307–12) the Templar Order was dissolved for ever.

There are two very different ways of looking at the 'trial' and end of the Templars. One point of view is political: it views the Templar trial as a part of the history of political conspiracy and persecution. Interest of this kind was generated by a kind of fascinated horror at the ruthless way in which an absolute government can extort confessions of non-existent crimes and conspiracies from those whom it wishes to place under extreme pressure. That the Papacy, whose motives have been so deeply doubted since the Reformation, played the role of a passive or more or less complaisant observer during most of the Templar trials, has added a certain anticlerical spice to the story. It is significant that Voltaire, in discussing the Templar case, chose to blame the Church rather than the King for this deplorable act of injustice which took place during 'a time of ignorance and barbarism'. Napoleon encouraged a new academic investigation of the Templar trials; it does not seem to have occurred to him that the trial could be treated as an injustice committed by the same kind of government as his own! Voltaire treated the Templars, in a tradition already old by his day, as belonging to the category of political conspiracies invented or imagined by the government against whom they were supposed to have been directed. According to this view, which has obtained strong support down to our own times, the Templars belong to a short but important list of innocent conspirator-victims. They are strange bedfellows: the Bacchanals of ancient Rome; the Christians of the great persecutions; the Templars; the witches; the Jews of the great pogroms and of the Nazi holocaust.

On the other hand, many writers from the sixteenth century onwards have declined to assign to the Templars the passive role of simple soldier-monks betrayed and condemned by the government and the Church which they served. At the time of their trial the Templars stood accused of magical and diabolical practices. Though it has seemed unlikely to most historians that the Templars were, as a group, guilty, some people have sought to turn the Templar trial on its head, by asserting that the Templars were, indeed, the holders of real and important magical powers, powers even greater than they were accused of possessing. Far from being innocent and ignorant monks and soldiers, the Templars are supposed by these writers to have been learned magicians, rich and powerful not so much because they were well-endowed with church estates as because they enjoyed the control of hidden knowledge and hidden practices. Since the occult world is a continuum which in many ways defies time and space, the Templars are not in this view mere carrion for university professors to feed on, but a living tradition of hidden knowledge which may be shared by the elect. And, since the concealment of his great wealth is one of the typical acts of the worldly magician, the Templars may also, in this view, have secreted great deposits of riches which those who can decipher their mysteries may recover.

From the beginning of the Templar trials onwards, the unifying factor in the Templar story is magical accusation. We may, if we choose, take a rationalistic and 'political' view of the Templar case, and minimize or at any rate play down the importance of these accusations. If we do so, we share a sceptical point of view which was already in existence at the time of the trials themselves. Many contemporaries ascribed the whole sorry business of the accusations against the Templars to the unscrupulous greed of the French government, which wished to confiscate Templar lands and money. This sceptical view was held not only by cynical politicians but by the great poet, Dante Alighieri.

But when men of the eighteenth-century Enlightenment con-templated the Templar trials they were not all, as Voltaire and Gibbon were, content to ascribe the Templars' end to the bar-baric cunning of medieval Church and State, and to refrain from speculating on a possible concealed aspect of the Templar Order. Men of the Enlightenment did not all apply a uniform and pedestrian criterion of evidence to history. Many of them sought a new prophetic tradition which would correspond to the manner in which the poets of Greek and Roman antiquity had integrated the myths of the Gods into their own vision of life. When eighteenth-century men read the chronicles of medieval history, although these seemed to reflect monotonously the theo-cratic world-view of the medieval Church, they were alert for pointers to the stirrings of an alternative point of view. It seemed incredible to them that there was not, during the Middle Ages, some kind of covert opposition party to the reigning tyranny and barbarism. There was also a strong Gnostic trend in eighteenth-century thought, which tended to substitute for the idea of a general illumination cast by the principles of reason over all, that of a special illumination possessed only by a few. These sym-pathies with a mystical illumination had their roots in the her-metic traditions of Renaissance Neo-Platonism and Cabbalism.

Men of this cast of mind noticed the Templar story, and turned it into a paradoxical fable of a hidden wisdom which had set itself up against the reigning Christian orthodoxy of the Middle Ages. According to them the Templars were a secret society totally opposed to the medieval Church, but so skilful that they had installed themselves at the heart of Christendom; outwardly a Religious Order obedient to the Church, though secretly in every way opposed to it. A few hints in magical and hermetic works and in patristic writings on heresy provided pegs on which to hang this fantasy. According to this new version of the story, which utilized the Renaissance idea of the East, where the Templars had served, as the seat of hidden esoteric mys-teries, the Templars were indeed guilty of having treated the Christian religion with blasphemous contempt. Their spiritual independence of the Church was not based on any low or vulgar magical powers of conjuring, but on the possession of a veritable house of knowledge, a Temple of wisdom which was symbolized by the name of their Order.

In this context the metamorphosis of the Templars took place from their ostensible status of unlearned and fanatical soldier-monks to that of enlightened and wise knightly seers, who had used their sojourn in the East to recover its profoundest secrets, and to emancipate themselves from medieval Catholic credulity. In this version of the story the Ismaili sect of the Assassins ceased to be the murderous enemies of the Christians which crusading sources made them out to be, and became the secret philosopher-guides who instructed the Templars in the precepts of their House of Wisdom.

The vicissitudes of the Templar myth, which took shape between the time of the Masonic movement of the early eighteenth century and that of the early Romantic movement, are followed in the second part of this book. There is little doubt in the author's mind that the story of Templars endowed with occult powers is a kind of fairy tale, though this does not mean that the story is trivial. The Templar myth belongs to poetic and visionary experience, and has to be interpreted on this basis. The idea of finding a wise and noble myth of the Middle Ages was common to many great poets and thinkers from Milton onwards, and was especially attractive to the early Romantics. If somewhat far-fetched, the Templar myth is no more fantastical, for example, than the idiosyncratic mythology of William Blake. But the myth of the Templars never had the good fortune to attract more than the fleeting attention of any great writer, with the possible exception of Gérard de Nerval. It can be treated as part of the occult, magical humus which fertilized Romantic and, subsequently, Symbolist literature.

The Templars attracted the attention of the political contro-versialists of the French Revolutionary period, some of whom treated the occultists who disseminated the Templar myth as members of a seditious conspiracy. Such views played their part in the further propagation of the myth, but they are long dead. What still survives is a political tradition going back to the great political writer Jean Bodin in the sixteenth century, which includes the Templars in a list of innocent 'conspirator'-victims. Perhaps this view can now be revised, in so far as it exaggerates the part played by cold, rational calculation and *raison d'état* in the history of these false conspiracies and political panics. Governments do not usually launch savage attacks on innocent minority groups unless the governments themselves are a prey to paranoiac fears and suspicions, such as seem to have existed in the Templar case. The annihilation or extermination of a supposed internal enemy is a measure to which governments only turn under conditions of extreme uncertainty and mistrust. Magical and mystical attacks are not launched in a cold-blooded manner as an adjunct of *Realpolitik*; they are resorted to by people who at least half-believe in the reality of magically induced misfortune. The presence of the Templar case at the threshold of the great European witch-hunt of the Middle Ages and the Renaissance is an indication of the terrible way in which uncontrolled private fears can turn into uncontrolled public disasters.

One traditional way, therefore, of dealing with the story of the Templars is to treat it as a superstitious panic, perhaps cunningly engineered, which for political motives smeared people with invented crimes and conspiracies. On the reverse side the Templar story has appealed to some as a dream of secret wisdom and power, possessed by a favoured few who had acquired hidden knowledge of the principles of things, and who were treacherously slain by reactionary authorities who had half-understood the peril in which the Templars placed them. But there are also less intellectual, less high-flying aspects of the Templar myth. It is possible to view the Templars' end as a Gothic horror story possessing all the usual elements of the Gothic novel: sadism, sexual perversions of the clergy, treasure-trove, magic. Like most intellectual occultism, the Templar myth crumbles away at its edges into folklore. From this penumbra of Templar fantasies come stories of Templar hidden treasure which is still to be found, of Templar black magic; this is the world in which Aleister Crowley made himself the Master of a Templar Order which existed for magical purposes. Other offshoots of the myth can cast the Templars in almost any conceivable role of the mysterious guardians: for example, as the custodians of the Holy Shroud of Turin.

In this book I have tried to establish how a medieval act of political injustice grew into a modern fantasy. In so far as the magical elements in the original accusations against the Templars provided the material from which the myth of magical Templarism grew, it can be said to be a case in which medieval witch-hunting was the direct ancestor of modern occultism. But what is perhaps most striking in the Templar story, as it is also in the history of western witchcraft in general, is the power of literary texts to influence beliefs. From the twelfth-century Archbishop of Tyre to the sixteenth-century hermetic philosophers and so until our own day, the Templars were misrepresented through the spread of mistaken or forged texts. By this means they were transformed from the ignorant, obedient servants of an oppressive ideal into the enlightened magician-heroes of freedom and knowledge. It may be a transformation for the better, but it is not one which the Templars would have understood or approved.

PART I
THE TEMPLARS

THE ORIGINS AND FUNCTIONS OF THE TEMPLARS

The Templars came into existence in Jerusalem during the after-
math of the First Crusade. Their Order of Poor Knights of the
Temple of Solomon grew from a group of pious soldiers who
gathered in Jerusalem during the second decade of the twelfth
century. They undertook the duty of protecting pilgrims on the
dangerous roads between Jaffa, where they landed on the coast
of Palestine, and Jerusalem. They lived under the religious rule
known as that of St Augustine, and they had help and guidance
from the canons of the Church of the Holy Sepulchre in Jerusalem. Their leader was a nobleman from Champagne, a
member of a cadet branch of the Counts of Troyes, called
Hugues de Payns. They came to the Holy Land at a time when
the first wave of knightly immigration was spent, and when the
crusading state desperately needed not merely men but trained
fighters drawn from the military aristocracy.

King Baldwin welcomed the religious knights and gave them
quarters in the eastern part of his palace, which stood on the supposed site of King Solomon's Temple and adjoined the former
Al-Aqsa Mosque; in the same area the canons of the Holy
Sepulchre gave them stabling for their horses. In this first period
the Knights of the Temple were laymen who had promised to
live, as monks and nuns normally lived, in poverty, chastity,
and obedience. They said prayers at set times, and in their mess
they observed rules of behaviour which made it like a monastic
refectory. They wore no special religious garb. The king, the
Patriarch of Jerusalem, and the upper clergy fed them. An early
Templar seal shows two knights riding on the same horse, as an
emblem of the poverty and brotherhood which they professed,
but the shared horse cannot represent literal truth, as from the
beginning each knight needed two or three horses to fulfil his
duties. On the reverse of the same seal is a representation of the
Dome of the Rock, the great, glittering Dome built by the early
Muslim conquerors in Jerusalem, which stood to the west of the

Templar area, in the centre of the Haram-al-Sharif platform and on the supposed site of Abraham's sacrifice. This was the Dome, made into a Christian church, which was known to the Crusaders as the Temple of the Lord. It was quite distinct from the Temple of Solomon which was supposed to have once existed on the site of the Templar headquarters, a few hundred feet to the east.

At the beginning the Templars were probably under the command of the king and the Patriarch of Jerusalem. In an early letter Hugues de Payns speaks of the resentment which Templar knights felt because they were made to work humbly for others, unknown to the rest of the Christian world and without even the benefit of the prayers of Christian folk. At this early stage the Templars were evidently pessimistic about the role they had chosen. In a world in which the religious obedience of the monastery was reckoned the surest way to salvation, the obligation to shed blood instead of to pray seemed an inferior way to serve God: the poor knights seemed to be accepting the burden of a religious rule of life without obtaining its full benefits. From the tone of Hugues de Payns's letter they seem to have been on the edge of abandoning their task; only the campaign launched in western Europe by de Payns and his ally St Bernard seems to have rescued them from obscurity and to have launched them as an institution which enjoyed the support of Christendom.

In 1127 Hugues de Payns travelled from Syria to Europe to seek funds and support. At Troyes, near his place of origin, a church council was held in 1128 which was attended by French and Burgundian bishops and abbots, by a papal legate, and by St Bernard himself. Bernard, Abbot of Clairvaux, was a great spiritual leader, the inspirer of a fervent flight into the monasteries which swept over the men of his time like a wave. He was also one of the best-informed and most sensitive religious leaders of the century. St Bernard had an ideal of the religious purification of feudal life in which the Crusade already played a part. The new concept of a military religious Order fitted into his vision of a knighthood which would be cleansed from the bloodshed and ill-doing of feudal greed and conflict, and which would serve the new theocratic world order which he strove to bring into being. At the Council of Troyes in 1128 the association of Poor Knights of the Temple was given an official existence by the

Map of Southern Syria and Palestine

Church, and was prescribed a simple religious way of life. St Bernard certainly advised, and probably dictated, the new Templar Rule, and the Templars were influenced by St Bernard's austere Cistercian Order from this point onwards. Unofficially, at least, many of them thought their Order to be specially dedicated to St Bernard and to the Virgin.

At the Council of Troyes the Church accepted the Templars as a corporate organization of religious soldiers governed by church law. This was no simple or uncontroversial matter, though it was not immediately challenged. The Templars seemed to introduce confusion into one of the basic distinctions of medieval society, between the 'religious order' and the 'military order'. The split between the two lay at the root of the then recent dispute between the 'priesthood' and the 'kingdom', which had shaken the whole medieval political structure. Church reformers had determined to stop men whose hands had been stained with blood from touching holy things. Even when noblemen of knightly status repented, and in mature years sought the life of the cloister, those within the monastery who had been nourished there from childhood were often reluctant to welcome the recruit.[1] The life of a medieval noble was devoted to aggression, bullying, and bloodshed on behalf of his lineage. He might try to mitigate this conduct by founding churches or monasteries, or even by seeking the monastic life for himself, but on the whole the warrior nobles despised or at best disregarded the clerks, and were far from taking them as a model. Our modern idea, which has been influenced by the idealistic glow conferred on chivalry by the Romantics, is of harmony between sword and altar; nothing could be further from the medieval truth. The Templars were making a sharper break with tradition than is at first apparent to modern men.

Far from idealizing chivalry, religious leaders usually represented knightly life as lawless, licentious, and bloody. The clergy were absolutely forbidden to shed blood, and to combine the life of an active soldier, killing and plundering like any other soldier, with the life of a monk, was to go against a fundamental principle. On the other hand, the clergy had for a long time dreamed of harnessing the feudal machine for their own purposes, and the Crusades themselves can be seen as a part-fulfilment of this idea. The popes had conceived the idea of conscripting feudal knights into a 'militia of St Peter' under their command, but this had not come to pass. Though the general idea of the Crusade tended in the same direction, the institution had never fallen under the direct control of the clergy in the way that the popes wanted; for example, the project of a Palestinian vassal state directly subject to the pope had been frustrated by the realities of crusading politics. The Templars represented a revival of these clerical ideas, and thus though in some ways they went against medieval principles, in others they could be seen as favouring the new theocratic trends.

St Bernard used brutal and even cynical language about the lives led by the knightly class. He espoused the crusading movement with passionate fervour; following Pope Urban II's speech at Clermont in 1095 he called it a way of occupying and reclaiming a dangerous criminal sector of noble society. 'It is really rather convenient', he wrote, 'that you will find very few men in the vast multitude which throngs to the Holy Land who have not been unbelieving scoundrels, sacrilegious plunderers, homicides, perjurers, adulterers, whose departure from Europe is certainly a double benefit, seeing that people in Europe are glad to see the back of them, and the people to whose assistance they are going in the Holy Land are delighted to see them! It is certainly beneficial to those who live on both sides of the sea, since they protect one side and desist from molesting the other!'[2] *

The idea of a perfect Christian knighthood may have passed fleetingly through the minds of these early reformers, but essentially this ideal was a creation of the later Middle Ages and had little place in the earlier society, which was accustomed to the daily use of illicit force and brutality by the warrior class and was more interested in getting rid of knights than in romanticizing them. The Church wanted no truck with these undesirables, who broke all its laws, particularly those of marriage, and even in their diversions, such as the tournament or gambling, tended towards pursuits which could end in bloodshed. It is significant that not until the late thirteenth century was any church liturgical form devised whose aim was to bless the making of a knight with Christian rites. Until then knighthood was regarded as in most respects an illicit business which clerks should not meddle

---

* All translated quotations are the author's unless otherwise attributed.

with. The appearance of a literature of 'Christian knighthood' from the time of Wolfram of Eschenbach's *Parzifal* in the early thirteenth century did, it is true, represent the beginnings of a more civilized attitude among some members of the knightly class, particularly the courtiers. But for a very long time the clergy continued to view the idea of a 'perfect Christian knight' with well-justified scepticism. Knightly attitudes as preserved in the literature of the troubadours continued to testify to a class ethic which was essentially cruel, proud, and bloody.

When St Bernard wrote his exhortation to the knights of the Temple to persist in their vocation, he was trying to deal both with the doubts which Templar knights felt about their status and with the criticism of orthodox clerics that men pledged to bloodshed ought not to be treated as part of the clerical 'order'. To effect Bernard's purpose it was necessary to glorify the killing of unbelievers and to introduce an important exception to the unanimous teaching of the medieval Church up to that time, that a man consecrated to God may not shed blood. The manner in which St Bernard did this was typical of his disingenuous methods of argument.

Indeed, the knights of Christ fight the battles of their lord in safety, by no means fearing to have sinned in slaying the foe, nor fearing the peril of their own deaths, seeing that either dealing out death or dying, when for Christ's sake, contains nothing criminal but rather merits glorious reward. On this account, then: for Christ! hence Christ is attained. He who, forsooth! freely takes the death of his foe as an act of vengeance, the more willingly finds consolation in his status as a soldier of Christ. The soldier of Christ kills safely: he dies the more safely. He serves his own interests in dying, and Christ's interests in killing! Not without cause does he bear the sword! He is the instrument of God for the punishment of malefactors and for the defence of the just. Indeed, when he kills a malefactor this is not homicide but malicide, and he is accounted Christ's legal executioner against evildoers.

In the same vein Hugues de Payns assured the Templars that they must not succumb to the temptation of thinking that they killed in a spirit of hate and fury, nor that they seized booty in a spirit of greed. For the Templars did not hate men, but men's wrongdoing; and when they seized booty from unbelievers they did so justly, because of the sins of the unbeliever and also because they had won the booty by their own labour, and 'the labourer is worthy of his hire'. The last may seem a naïve apology but it reflects the fact that much Templar time and energy was spent in plundering.

St Bernard's argument was radical. It was better that unbelievers should be killed than that they should preside over the destinies of the true faithful. To the objection that a Christian does not kill he replied: 'What, then? if the use of the sword is not allowed in any circumstances to a Christian, why did John the Baptist indicate to the troops that they should be content with their pay [Luke, 3:14]: why did he not rather forbid them any form of military service? If it is right for all, so long as they have been divinely ordained and have professed no better [i.e. no monastic] objective, by whose hands and armed might better than theirs is Sion, the city of our strength, kept safe for the protection of us all? Once the transgressors of the divine law have been driven out, let the just people, guardians of truth, enter Jerusalem in confidence.'

The repute of the saint ensured the acceptance of the Templar movement in the highest Church quarters. A politician as sharp as St Bernard had been astute enough to secure the presence of a papal legate at the Council of Troyes in 1128, when the Templars had been launched into the official world of the Catholic Church. Papal authorization was not lacking for an Order which came with such impressive credentials. Nor did the popes hesitate, apparently, to approve the theory of a religious war waged by men under religious vows. In the papal bull, *Omne datum optimum*, of 1139, by which Pope Innocent II consolidated with papal approval and privilege the status of the Templars as a Religious Order, the pope referred to the Templar dead who had attained eternal life after the sweat of a battle in which they had 'consecrated their hands to God in the blood of the unbelievers'. This reference to Templar warfare was to its aggressive aspect: the defensive Templar duties of protecting pilgrims received no separate mention in the papal privilege. The Templar knights already wore, in imitation either of the Cistercians or of the Canons of the Holy Sepulchre, a white mantle; a few years later Pope Eugenius III gave them the right to bear a red cross upon it.

The Templars from the first had to take part in the daily armed struggle in the Holy Land, and it is most unlikely that they experienced any conscientious scruples about this. What did inspire them with doubt was the feeling that, though their work was allowable in Church law, it was inferior in the hierarchy of good to the pure contemplation and prayer of the professed monks. Why, when their contemporaries in Europe were flooding into the monasteries, should these knights accept the duties of Martha, and embrace a role which continued the dangers and hardships of knightly life without its temporal compensations, and perhaps also without the perfect assurance of salvation which could be found in the monastery? Hugues de Payns assured them that, like the peasants, they led an active life which was necessary to support the life of the monastic contemplatives. This comparison with despised boors touched them at their most sensitive point, their pride in their noble birth. A feeling of inferiority to the true religious monks who performed nothing but the 'work of God' recurred among some individual Templars as long as the Order lasted. Both the popes and the Temple repeatedly forbade Templars to leave the Military Order to enter a monastic Religious Order, but Templar knights constantly did so. The third Master of the Templar Order, Evrard des Barres (1149–52), returned to France from the Holy Land, left the Order, and entered Clairvaux, the 'true Jerusalem', as a Cistercian monk.

Within a few years of the Council of Troyes in 1128, Catholic Europe gave the Templars strong and almost universal approval. Some religious men expressed doubts about the bloodshed inseparable from their work, but Pope Urban II's letter to the monks of Vallombrosa, forbidding religious persons to bear arms in the Crusade, seems to have been forgotten by the time the Templars had come into existence. The biggest factor in getting governing-class support was the feudal nature of the Order. Thorough feudal gentlemen such as King Stephen were enthusiastic supporters in England. In Spain the possibilities of using Templars in the Iberian war against the Muslims were at once appreciated, and King Alfonso I of Aragon embarrassed both the Order and the Church by bequeathing to the Templars a third part of his kingdom; though this proved to be a bequest which it was politically impossible to accept in full. In Paris, in 1147, shortly before the departure of the French king on the

Second Crusade, a general chapter of 130 white-robed Templars was held in the presence of the king and the pope. Thousands of landed estates large and small were given to the Order, initially in England, France, and Spain, and then in most parts of Europe. A large organization soon had to be set up, not only to recruit new members for the Order but also to administer the huge patrimonies and to transmit money and supplies to the Holy Land. In a short time the transmission of funds gave the Order a new role as a banker not only for itself but for others. By the time King Louis VII of France went to the Holy Land on Crusade in 1147 the Templars were at least to some extent acting as his bankers. Since no system of deposit banking yet existed in Europe, and none was to develop for over a century, the use of the Temple for the deposit and transmission of funds gave it a new and unanticipated importance among the feudal princes.

The two Military Orders, the Templars and the Knights Hospitaller of St John, developed on approximately similar lines during the same period, though the Hospitallers were slower to assume a warlike role, and never assumed it exclusively. The two Orders acted in many ways as the poor-boxes through which Catholic Europe contributed to the running costs of the crusader states in the East. At bottom they depended on the generosity of the faithful, who gave them a secure income through the gift of estates, and a smaller precarious income through contributions, fraternity subscriptions, and the proceeds of indulgences. Their task was made much easier by the lavish privileges conferred on them by the popes. For the Templars the main effects of these were to exempt the Order from the jurisdiction and financial control of the bishops, and to confer on lay members of Templar brotherhoods a variety of other privileges. People of both sexes who had contributed to Templar funds acquired privileges from their status in the Templar confraternities: the knights in these were 'brothers of the Temple' with privileges not far short of those enjoyed by actual Templar knights. Often the associate brothers assumed the Templar habit as they died, or were clad in it after death. Almost all Religious Orders admitted laymen into fraternal relationships of this kind, but the Templar arrangements were especially resented by the bishops, whose authority and incomes they weakened. The bishops complained that where they had placed an area under church interdict and suspended all church services on account of some disobedience to church law, Templar priests and fund-raisers would rely on papal privilege to break the interdict, open their churches, collect money, administer the sacraments to men and women in the Templar brotherhoods, and bury the dead in their own graveyards. This ecclesiastical strike-breaking was bitterly resented, even if it only took place once yearly. The interdict was the last sanction available to the bishops, and its breaking occasioned anger, and even violence. The Templars connived in breaking the interdicts in order to make money. By receiving layfolk into its confraternities the Order profited, even if only to the extent of an annual payment of from two to six pence. Membership was available to all free men and women: in England not only did a humble parish priest in Templar service belong, but so also did his 'wife'.[3]

The privileged Church corporations of the Middle Ages all provoked similar resentments. But in the case of the Military Orders, the wealth conferred on them also demonstrated wide-spread social approval. The great effort of the Order was the transfer of funds and men to the east. They erected numerous buildings in the west – preceptories, churches, granges – for training and administration, but these were humble and utili-tarian in nature, with a few exceptions. There was no standard form of Templar church: a very few, circular or polygonal, recalled the shape either of the Dome of the Rock at Jerusalem (the 'Temple of God' of the Templar seal) or of the octagon of the Church of the Holy Sepulchre at Jerusalem. But most Templar churches were orthodox apsidal structures.[4] Templar castles were few in the west, and it was inconvenient to build a circular chapel within them; apart from that in Paris the only castles possessing such chapels are at Tomar in Portugal and at Chastel Pélerin (Athlit) in Syria. Very occasionally, where the Templars built with royal licence and approval, the European castles could be great fortifications which would resist a long siege. In Paris the Temple, which was probably the greatest financial institu-tion of the High Middle Ages, contained a great double *donjon*, which was by the thirteenth century one of the strongest in the kingdom. Part of the Templar Church in Paris, like that of the London Temple, was built to a circular plan. Immediately with-out the Paris Temple, and within view of the royal palace at the

Louvre, the area of exempt Templar jurisdiction was a sizeable village, called the Ville Neuve du Temple, surrounded by high walls.

Partly for reasons which are discussed later, misconceptions have grown up about Templar buildings. It would be wrong either to suppose that Europe was full of circular Temple churches built to meet the special requirements of their chapter meetings, or that it was well-stocked with great Templar fortresses. The first error arose because of the popular superstition that almost any round church is Templar-built. The second opinion is also without foundation. Templar organization was directed in a common-sense way to the financing, staffing, and provisioning of the Palestinian force, and little money was wasted on showy churches, still less on great European castles which would only be an economic and political liability. The only exception was the Iberian peninsula, where in Aragon and Portugal the Order was pledged to fight against the Moors, and needed castles just as it needed them in the Holy Land.

The main strength of the Templars lay in the ability of the feudal class to identify with them. They did not recruit much from the upper nobility; St Bernard was not entirely wrong in stigmatizing the knightly class in the Holy Land as formed from men who had many of them committed serious crimes. Great noblemen could purge their sins by founding monasteries; only small noblemen had to purge them in their own persons. The Grand Masters of the Templar Order were, all but a few, drawn from obscure families. Templar knights were as knightly as they purported to be; that is, they were from warrior families who practised the profession of arms freely, and not as mere mercenaries. In the beginning the distinctions may have been unclear, and it is also possible that in the Holy Land this Foreign Legion did not ask too many awkward questions. By the thirteenth century the enquiry was meant to be precise: an aspirant was required to be a knight, the son of a knight and his lady. Villein descent was a bar to entry as a knight; it was also a bar to the priesthood, so the Military Order was no exception. An excommunicated aspirant was to be brought first to the bishop, and he could be received into the Order only if the bishop would absolve him. It seems from the Statutes of the Order that recruiting went on among knights who had been found guilty of serious moral offences; a well-known rule in the French version directs the Templars to frequent and recruit from gatherings of excommunicated knights.[5] That the Latin version of the rule gives the directly opposite injunction, *not* to frequent such gatherings, probably shows the tension between the official clerical attitudes to the Order and the vernacular military culture which lay alongside it. Opinion was divided to the end; at the time of the trial and dissolution of the Order it was being said that it was a disgraceful thing that robbers worthy of death had been admitted to the Order. Evidently St Bernard's words had been forgotten by 1309!

The overwhelming need for trained troops in the Holy Land diluted the call for a strong ethical basis for the Order. In the Holy Land the Temple, besides its own knights, accepted others who engaged for a specific term of service during their presence in Syria. Below the rank of knights of the Temple, whose numbers were always small, there was another class of 'sergeants' or serving brothers, similarly armed and horsed but wearing brown or black mantles instead of white. In making this distinction the Temple simply followed the ordinary gradations of feudal society, as it also did in creating a further lower rank of 'esquires'. Lower again were the rural brothers (*frères casaliers*) who helped to run the estates, and the servant brothers (*frères de métier*) who performed all the menial duties of the house, including the important one of running the stables, smithy, and harness room. For all their mixed origins the Templar knights were thus a small military élite. It is unlikely that there were very often more than three hundred heavily armed Templars in the Holy Land, even when knights and sergeants are counted together. But these shock troops were surrounded by squires, servants, Turkish mercenary troops and other dependents, so that in the greatest Palestinian castles fifty or sixty knights and sergeants would form the nucleus of a garrison of four or five hundred.

Knights of the Temple, although under strict discipline, and expected to sacrifice their lives in battle without hesitation when the time came, lived in many respects a life which was more privileged, perhaps even more pampered, than that of many lay knights in Europe. Their equipment was splendid, their living conditions clean. At the time of the trial and the disgrace of the

Templars some captive Templar knights were above all unhappy because their money allowance did not permit them to have clean laundered clothes. Such expectations were not universal in the Middle Ages, even among the knightly class. On the other hand, like most members of the knightly class the majority of Templar knights – and the lower ranks were naturally no better off in this respect – were illiterate. In the disasters of 1307–12 many Templar knights, even important officials, described themselves as 'simple and ignorant'; this is backed up by the paucity of manual signatures on Templar documents and by the rarity of books in Templar houses.[6] The brothers who ran the banking operations of the Order were, naturally, literate, and a handful of knights at the time of the trials emerged as well-educated, but their number did not include the Grand Master.

Throughout their history the parallelism between Templars and the lay social order seems closer than the parallelism with the Religious Orders. Almost immediately after the spread of the Order at the time of the Second Crusade it acquired the great feudal offices of Marshal and Seneschal, and later it added the Drapier, a lesser officer who supervised the clothing of the Order. A Standard-bearer was responsible for the Order's particoloured black-and-white banner (*gonfanon bauçant*), which was carried in forces commanded by the great officers, and for whose custody and guard in peace and war there were precise rules. The spirit of aristocratic warfare lay over the whole: the typical expression of its regulations is the frequent command to do things 'smartly', *au plus beau*. As well as sharing the vows of poverty, obedience, and chastity, their general way of life was in many ways like that of other monks. Unless they had been on arduous duties they all attended the canonical offices of the liturgy which were prescribed by the Augustinian Rule. They were enjoined to silence in the refectory, and a reading of holy works took place during meals, though the reading must have been in French since none of them understood Latin. The 'Templar' translation of the Bible into French was made to fill this gap, but its use may not have been widely diffused. Unlike the monks, the Templars were enjoined to eat meat three times a week. The feeling which pervades their Rule is that of an élite cavalry corps rather than that of a monastery. The penalties for breaking the Rule were in some cases severe, and could include life imprisonment. The habits of a nobleman died hard: the Templars were supposed to hunt only 'lions' (by which 'ounces' or Palestinian lynxes are intended), but the Rule notes the case of a Commander who used a borrowed horse to course hares, and was expelled from the Order when the horse was lost.[7]

Above all, the Templars became the servants and companions of kings and princes: from the beginning they were trusted familiars in royal courts.[8] Henry II of England used the Templars in the shady deal by which he prised the French Vexin from the Capetians as a French princess's dowry; he also used the services of the Templar English Master in the Becket case, persuading him to go on his knees to the archbishop to ask him to accede to the king's wishes and to accept the Constitutions which Henry tried to impose on the English Church at Clarendon. Under King John the English Master was a royal soldier and a witness to Magna Carta. The financial dealings of the Templars led them straight to the royal treasuries, of which they were frequently keepers. From the early thirteenth century onwards the Temple in Paris was in effect the French Royal Treasury, and not until 1295, only a decade before the final agony of the Order, did the French Crown acquire an alternative Treasury. As late as 1303 the Treasury went back to the Temple, where it remained until 1307. The English Crown was less continuously dependent on Templar financiers, but it used them, and under Henry III of England a Templar brother had charge of the royal Wardrobe, the title used for the main household money offices.

The place that Templars found in the royal households as 'familiars' and courtiers was just as important as their financial role. They turn up as almoners, specially trusted servants, and as warriors of the kings of France and England. Templars came from that section of the lower nobility which supplied the kings with the household servants and officials who did their familiar business. As a result the kings were influential in the affairs of the Temple: both Richard I of England and Saint Louis of France nominated their own candidate to the office of Grand Master of the Temple. The Templar role in the courts of the popes was similar. From the time of Pope Alexander III (1159–81) onwards, the Templars fulfilled the same kind of household offices for the popes that they did for the kings; though the financial role differed, since the popes already had their own well-qualified specialists in money. Alexander III was the most lavish of all popes in privileges for the Templar Order, perhaps because he borrowed money from them. From his time onwards the Templars were papal chamberlains and almoners: they were also involved in the collection of crusading taxes. The popes held a feudal court and employed an army, and the presence of religious military men was especially welcome to them. They used Templar and Hospitaller knights as castellans in the Papal State, and caused them to build fortresses there. Knights of the Orders were often among the pope's bodyguards and intimates: when the wretched Pope Boniface VIII was assaulted by the King of France's troops at Anagni in 1303, his Templar and Hospitaller attendants stood at his side. It was the domestic intimacy with princes which made the Templars into such an accepted and influential body in feudal society. When Margaret of France, St Louis's queen, was delivered of a son in the great sea-girt Templar castle of Chastel Pélerin in the Holy Land, the Grand Master of the Temple stood as the child's godfather – and that in despite of a statute of the Order which forbade a Templar to act as a godparent. The apparent intimacy with the French royal family lasted to the brink of the final catastrophe: on the day before the general arrest of the Templars took place in 1307, the Templar Grand Master walked in procession and held one of the cords of the pall at the funeral of the French king's sister-in-law, Catherine de Courtenay. As the English courtier and gossip-writer Walter Map remarked of the Templars, they, 'because of their offices, are held dear by prelates and kings, and high in honour, and carefully see to it that means for their exalta-tion are not wanting'. But the Templars also had to bear the proverbial inconstancy of princely favour, an inconstancy which was to lead at the end to their destruction.

The vicissitudes of Templar reputation depended on the accuracy of western information about the Holy Land, and this was extremely poor. Popular judgement on the Holy Land was based on preaching and hearsay, on 'marvels' such as those later retailed by Sir John Maundeville, and on such references as that of Pope Innocent III himself to the Prophet Muhammad who was the beast of the Apocalypse, 'whose number is concluded in 666'. The main European governments usually received quite accurate reports of what went on in Syria, and so did some Italian cities. But most popular news was highly coloured or biased; a late example was the universal but quite mistaken conviction that in 1300 (the year of the Catholic Jubilee) the Mongols had made great conquests in Syria and had offered the Christians alliance and even the hope of their conversion.[9]

Catholic Europe was aware of the existence of the Military Orders as clerical estate-owners and feudal landlords; it also met them as itinerant fund-raisers and in a further guise as the servants of princes. Public opinion judged the Orders in Syria largely on the reports of great events, and unfortunately for the Military Orders most of the great events to be reported were the defeats of the Crusaders. As Walter Map remarked in the 1180s, after the Templars undertook military responsibilities in Syria the Christian boundaries shrank instead of expanding! No matter what powers of organization and what heroism are shown by soldiers in its defence, a society judges its armies by results.

From the beginning the crusading settlement in Syria was precarious, and the reputation of a special Order for its defence was bound to come in for some hard knocks. On the other hand, gifts and support continued to come to the Templars in Europe, even after the terrible Christian defeat at Muslim hands at the Horns of Hattin in 1187. Large estates still came to the Templars in Germany, and there were some new donations in Spain; in other parts of Europe they retained their possessions.[10] At the beginning of the thirteenth century Templar pride was resented, Templar efficiency respected; the Templar role in the defence of the far-off Christian boundaries was still accepted and approved.

Until 1187 the Templar establishment in the Holy Land was based on the Commandery of Jerusalem, the headquarters of the Order on the platform of the Haram-al-Sharif. Scarcely a trace now remains either of their conventual buildings or of the huge stables for a thousand and more horses which they built over the Byzantine basements against the south wall of the Temple area. Only a handful of Romanesque pillars and capitals in the room called the 'White Mosque' adjoining the al-Aqsa Mosque recall these once-great constructions. Whether the beautiful Crusader ironwork in the Dome of the Mosque can be attributed to the Templars is uncertain.

From the beginning the Templars must have manned forts, since their work of protecting pilgrims on the roads to Jerusalem could be done in no other way. On the roads leading to Jerusalem through either Lydda or Ramleh such forts as Chastel des Plains and Toron des Chevaliers were built at an early point in the Order's history. But both Templars and Hospitallers disposed of a formidable economic power which made them the obvious financiers and the obvious garrisons for much of the great system of castles without which the crusading settlement in the Holy Land had no hope of survival.[11] Both Orders could man the castles, not only with their own knights but with other knights hired for pay and with the local troops, termed 'Turcopoles'. Both Orders controlled not only the large sums and subventions in kind which came from the west, but also substan tial estates in the east which were given them by the governments of the crusading states. The growth of their responsibilities as castellans was slow, but their superior resources made it inevitable. By the fifth decade of the twelfth century the Counts of Tripoli could no longer raise the men or the money to defend the great March for which they were responsible. The most famous castle which the Orders built in the area is the Hospitaller one of Crac des Chevaliers, which dominates the valleys between the March of Tripoli and the River Orontes. But the large Templar castle of Chastel Blanc (Safitha) was built within sight of Crac, and there were other great Templar strongholds on the coastline of the County of Tripoli, at Chastel Rouge and Tortosa. Other Marcher strongholds belonged to the Templars in the far north of the crusading states in the hills between Antioch and Alexandretta. In the extreme south the key city of Gaza was a Templar fortress so long as the Christians held it.

The Military Orders operated not only on the Marcher frontiers of the crusading states in Palestine – and the Marches were never far from the heart of that narrow strip of land – but also in and near the Crusaders' main centres. The defence of the towns was originally a royal responsibility, but by the thirteenth century there were Templar forts within Haifa and Acre, and long sections of the urban defences were a Templar commitment. Other groups of Templar castles defended such main internal routes as the Plain of Esdrelon between Samaria and Galilee, and the approaches to Mount Carmel.

The watershed of crusading history was the collapse of the Kingdom of Jerusalem after the Battle of Hattin in 1187. No feudal monarchy could have emerged with its powers unimpaired after such a blow. The Military Orders, because of their key military functions, their external financing, and the continuity of their policies, became more important and independent than before. The advice and counsel of the two Grand Masters were sought at every great question debated by the Crown and the magnates.[12] The Orders were yet more central to crusading policy, in that unlike the crusading barons, or the kings before Frederick II of Hohenstaufen, they maintained permanent establishments in Europe and were consulted there by the intending leaders and organizers of crusading expeditions. As the crusading states weakened, the powers of the Orders increased, so that their maximum influence was exercised between the great Christian defeat at the hands of the Egyptian general Baibars at La Forbie in 1244, and the final catastrophe of the fall of Acre in 1291.

Jealousies and clashes of policy erupted spasmodically between Templar and Hospitaller Grand Masters from 1179 onwards, and the disputes grew more frequent and acrimonious during the last tormented half-century of the existence of the crusader states. It has been said that the Templars on the whole pursued a political policy which favoured the Palestinian baronage, and the Hospitallers one which favoured the monarchy. Be this as it may, the disputes were not continuous, and against the instances of open hostility between the two Orders, other instances of co-operation and compromise can be found. The Rules of the two Orders show that in the ordinary conduct of their lives in the Holy Land each Order relied on the other for help and support. Of course, the institutional egotism of all privileged medieval bodies was a factor in their relations, and sometimes was a negative factor for the crusading cause as a whole. Many internecine jealousies and rivalries – of the feudal barons, of the Italian cities, of competitors for the crown –played their part in weakening the crusading settlement. In this divided land the rivalry of the two Military Orders was one source of political weakness among many others.

With the thirteenth-century decline of the crusading king-dom, the building and manning of castles by the Orders became yet more important. Chastel Safad, which controlled the road between Acre and Damascus at Jacob's Ford, was rebuilt by the Templars in 1240 at a cost of well over a million gold besants.[13] It controlled a region with a population of about ten thousand, and in wartime housed over two thousand people, including a garrison of four or five hundred. Chastel Pélerin (Athlit) was built to secure the southern approaches of Mount Carmel during the Fifth Crusade (1217). It was constructed on the site of a Phoenician fortress, and coins from its long-vanished prede-cessor were found both by the Crusader builders and by the British archaeologists who excavated the site in the 1930s. The castle occupies practically the whole headland, and behind it on the beach a small settlement grew up, which in its turn was protected by a wall three-quarters of a kilometre long. One of the northern towers of the castle, looking towards Haifa, may still be seen, but there is little trace now of the labyrinth of medieval buildings which the French writer Lamartine found when he stumbled upon the site in 1832: he compared the walls to the Colosseum, and found the Bedouin Arabs living in the ruins as though in some giant necropolis. In the interior of Chastel Pélerin there is still a great vaulted room, but nothing remains now above ground of the octagonal church – visited by Lamartine – in which St Louis and the Templar Grand Master held the infant Count of Alencon at the font. The eastern defences of the castle, which secured the neck of the little penin-sula, are reckoned by R. C. Smail, the most expert British scholar in these matters, to have been a masterpiece of scientific design. In the stable located in the angle of the outer town the horseshoes, horses' bits, and equipment of the Templar farriers were uncovered by the archaeologists of the Mandate. It is a beautiful and sad place.

Elsewhere the thirteenth-century Templars acquired more castles which their feudal lords had become too poor to run, such as Sidon, on the Palestinian coast, and Beaufort, which com-mands the Litani valley south-west of Merdjayoun and which has been the scene of fighting between Palestinians and Lebanese recently, from 1978 onwards. In Beaufort the Gothic

Templar hall still stands in the midst of the fortress, or, at least, it was standing before the outbreak of the recent combats. Sidon was a coastal castle with its own harbour; after the final disaster at Acre in 1291 a small group of Templars elected the penultimate Grand Master of the Order here, and then embarked for Cyprus before the Mamluk armies arrived.

Too stately a list of fortresses gives a wrong impression of the power of the Orders, or indeed of the condition of the Crusaders, during the last unhappy years of the crusading settlement. In 1260 the Templar Grand Master said the Holy Land contained only seven defensible strong places belonging to his Order: three in the Principate of Antioch; two (Tortosa and Chastel Blanc) in the County of Tripoli; two (Safad and Chastel Pélerin) in the Province of Jerusalem.[14] The Christians held Acre and Tyre; the Hospitallers held two fortresses (Crac des Chevaliers and Margat); and the German knights two. And that, according to the Grand Master Thomas Bérard, was the sum of Christian active strength in Syria. From his gloomy description of Mongol and Muslim power and Christian weakness it seems that the final collapse of the crusading settlement, which did not occur until 1291, might easily have occurred at any time after the departure of St Louis from the Holy Land in 1254. It is true that the Grand Master's list of Christian fortresses was selective, and that more were in Christian hands in 1260 than he mentioned. When Baibars launched his big offensive against the Crusaders in 1265, Caesarea, Haifa, Toron, and Arsuf, all important Christian strongholds not mentioned by Bérard in 1260, fell to the Mamluk Muslim forces. The great Templar castle of Safad, which he does mention, fell to the enemy by a ruse in 1266. It may be that as early as 1260 the Templar Master knew that the strong places which fell in 1265 could not be effectively defended: it may be, however, that as he had Mongol rather than Muslim attack immediately in mind he mentioned the targets likely to be first chosen by the Mongols, who in the event never launched a general attack on Christian Syria.

Whichever interpretation we choose, the impression of Christian weakness is overwhelming. At first glance the tight internal discipline of the Military Orders and the concentration of their forces in well-designed castles seem to make them a kind

of consecrated exception to the general rot. But the Orders were
not really an exception. In 1258 Templars and Hospitallers had
taken opposite sides in the ruinous Palestinian civil war of St
Sabas, whose main protagonists were the Venetians (backed by
the Templars) on one side and the Genoese on the other. Templar feuds with noble families in the Kingdom also played a part
in this war, in which Templar and Hospitaller allies fought each
other bitterly, even if the knights of the Orders did not themselves come to blows. In this sour atmosphere of Christian dis-
unity old suspicions and jealousies of the Orders, especially of
the Templars, began to turn into a general feeling of alienation
and distrust.

2

CRITICISM AND ALIENATION

Theologically the criticisms of the Templars may be reduced to those of pride and avarice, the stock-in-trade of any medieval preacher's complaint. In practical terms they can be reduced to charges of greed and evil counsel; these are both violations of the feudal code, which required the distribution of largesse and the delivery of good counsel. However, most Templar violations of the feudal code were of a kind very frequently committed by others. In devoting a lot of attention to plunder, as they did from the start, the Templars behaved like other feudal lords. In exacting large payments of tribute from Muslim and Assassin rulers they again (in company with the Hospitallers) only complied with normal feudal and Syrian practice. But in one respect the Templars offended against all feudal ideas: this was in lending money and in accepting money to keep on deposit. Jean de Joinville's scornful account of his own seizure, in order to pay the ransom of St Louis, of the moneys the Templars held on deposit, shows the contempt of the nobleman for these low financial practices. Yet the Templars were no strangers to 'largesse': their Rule specifically defines the value of the gifts which the great officers of the Order could make to those whom they chose to honour. And by the thirteenth century, though noblemen like Joinville treated such matters with distaste, the Templars had for so long been employed by most members of the French royal family to run their financial affairs that the princely sector of French feudal society accepted their business functions without question.[15]

The most damaging of all the criticism made of the Templars probably comes from the pen of a single chronicler, William of Tyre. The importance of his text lies not so much in the specific allegations which it made as in its general tone, and in the almost universal diffusion which it achieved. William was the author of an important chronicle of the crusading states during the twelfth century, and perhaps because he was a Palestinian bishop who strongly resented their privileged status, he was strongly biased against the Templars. He was one of the few learned and able writers born in Christian Syria, and also a figure of political and ecclesiastical importance; he was Archbishop of Tyre and for a time the Chancellor of the Kingdom of Jerusalem. Although his chronicle does not quite extend to the Battle of Hattin in 1187, since he died in Europe before that date, he wrote the best-informed and constructed account of the Kingdom during the half-century preceding Hattin, and his work was well known during the Middle Ages and afterwards. He tells several much-quoted stories against the Templars which stress their greed and egotism.[16] An example is his account of the Templar part in the assault on the city of Ascalon in 1153. He says that when a breach had been made in the city walls by burning, the Templar contingent in whose sector the breach was insisted on attacking through it alone. The reason he gives for their rashness is their anxiety to take all the plunder in the city for themselves. The result was that some forty Templars, including the Grand Master, were cut off within the city and killed. The story is morally ambiguous; the attack was occasioned by greed, but executed with courage. It is a typical feudal complaint, on William's part, that the lust for plunder which the whole feudal army shared had impelled one group to try to forestall the rest.

Two stories in William of Tyre concern Templar greed in its relation to captured or apparently friendly Orientals. The first recounts how an Egyptian nobleman called Nasr-ed-din fell into Templar hands, and how he had learned Latin and was ready to accept Christianity, when the Templars sold him to his Egyptian enemies for a great sum and delivered him to them to be done to death. The second concerns Templar relations with the Ismaili religious dissidents or 'Assassins', the followers of the 'Old Man of the Mountains', famous for their political murders (which were ascribed to a technique of bemusing the intending terrorist executioners with hashish) and for their unorthodox religious beliefs. According to William the Assassins were under an obligation to pay the Templars an annual tribute of 2,000 gold pieces. His story is that Rachid-ed-din Sinan, the leader of the Assassins, was ready to embrace Christianity but that the Templars were so unwilling to renounce the money tribute which they would lose if the Assassins were converted that (in spite of King Amalric's supposed offer to replace the tribute from the

royal treasury) a Templar emissary slew the Assassin ambas-
sador on his way back from the King of Jerusalem's court.

These stories probably mix truth with falsehood: it is, for
example, quite possible that the Templars incurred Amalric's
displeasure by interfering in his negotiations with the Assassins.
It is very unlikely indeed, however, that Rachid-ed-din seriously
contemplated conversion to Christianity; the Muslim sources
make no reference to the possibility. Sir Steven Runciman has
concluded that the Assassin leader 'hinted' at conversion, but
the text will barely support this idea. However, both the story of
Rachid-ed-din and that of Nasr-ed-din passed into the common
coin of the western literary tradition of the Crusades: the latter,
for example, is repeated and embroidered upon by the twelfth-
century English writer, Walter Map, and both are repeated by
the thirteen-century St Albans chronicler, Matthew Paris. Map
includes Nasr-ed-din in his argument that out of cupidity and self-
interest the Templars preferred war to peace in the Holy Land.[17]
The story of Rachid-ed-din is the first reference to the supposed
Templar relations with the Assassins, and is the first frail thread
with which the most elaborate fantasies have since been spun.

Another damaging slur on the Templars was William's
denunciation of the Templar Grand Master, Odo de St Amand,
as 'a proud and arrogant man, with the spirit of wrath in his
nostrils, neither fearing God nor holding man in respect'. This is
a pale and mild criticism by comparison with many of the comments attracted by churchmen in Europe, and had it not been for
the odd circumstances of the Templars' end it would long ago
have been discounted as mere tittle-tattle. But fortune decreed
differently, and William's judgement lived balefully through the
centuries, perhaps to be reflected at a great distance in the novels
of Sir Walter Scott. In *The Talisman* Scott made Richard Coeur-
de-Lion describe the Templar Grand Master as a 'misproud and
amphibious caitiff', a grotesque epithet meant to emphasize the
mixed military and clerical nature of the Templars. Scott gave
the Templar Master in the novel the role of traitor and murderer, grafting Protestant prejudice to an older tradition which
represented the Templars as unreliable and morally tainted.

Inevitably, the Templars were accused of giving evil counsel.
For a century and a half no important decision was taken in the

Holy Land without consulting the Grand Masters of the Military Orders; though they shared the blame with the Hospitallers, the Templars had to take the larger part. The blame became part of a literary or textual tradition to which William of Tyre was by no means the only contributor, though he showed the way. In the thirteenth century the same or similar prejudices were taken up by the English chronicler, Matthew Paris. Matthew was a man to whom prejudice was the breath of life, one pleased to record the failings of any religious Order except his own. There were limits to his prejudice as there had been to that of William of Tyre; neither was entirely unaware of the existence of canons of evidence, though they sometimes seem to violate them. At the end of his life Matthew clearly felt he had been unfair to the Templars, and marked his most outrageously unlikely remarks with a marginal note that the passage ought to be suppressed, because of the offence it might give them.[18]

The behaviour of the Templar Grand Master during the fatal campaign of Hattin in 1187 was perhaps the most notorious occasion which exposed the Templars to the charge of being 'evil counsellors'. Gérard de Ridefort, the Grand Master of that time, is one of the most controversial figures in the history of the Order. Before he became a Templar he appears to have been a grasping and ambitious knight who had come to the Holy Land to make his own fortune there. In 1186 Gérard's personal feuds and ambitions led him, as Grand Master, to sponsor the coronation of King Baldwin IV's sister, Sibylla, as queen. In doing so he helped to create a dangerous division in the political leadership of the Kingdom of Jerusalem at a critical moment of its fortunes. In the great military confrontation with Saladin of the following year Gérard de Ridefort committed two disastrous tactical errors, both perhaps due to hot-headedness. First, at a time when every knight counted to the Kingdom, he overruled the Master of the Hospital and insisted, at Nazareth, on a suicidal cavalry charge which destroyed a large part of the forces of both Orders, besides leading to the death of the Hospitaller Master on the field. Then, when the Christian forces were camping above Lake Tiberias and debating whether to engage the enemy under unfavourable conditions, it was Gérard's advice, given privately and after the Council of War, which changed the prudent decision to retire to the fatal one to press on across the waterless hills, which led to disaster at the Horns of Hattin.

Matthew Paris, the St Albans chronicler, had no personal grudge against the Templars that we know of. But much of his information about the Holy Land came from the entourage of Earl Richard of Cornwall, and Richard, who was the brother-in-law of the Emperor Frederick II, was influenced by the latter's strong prejudice against the Military Orders. This tainted source led Matthew to tell several stories unfavourable to the Templars, notably that when the Emperor came to the Holy Land in 1228–9 they and the Hospital secretly told Sultan al-Kamil about his projected pilgrimage to the River Jordan, with the idea of facilitating an ambush. According to Matthew the Sultan chivalrously told Frederick of the plot, but there is absolutely no evidence that this was so. Other stories accuse Templars and Hospitallers of fratricidal jealousy. Matthew also blames 'Templar pride' for the final loss of Jerusalem in 1244.

Matthew also quotes a fierce denunciation of Templar policy said to have been delivered during the Sixth Crusade, that of St Louis IX of France. It concerns events in 1250 when the crusading forces had crossed the Nile beyond Damietta, and had charged and defeated the enemy in their camp. The Christian army then formed up opposite the town of Mansourah, and debated whether to pursue the enemy into the city. There was a quarrel between the Templar Grand Master and the Count d'Artois, brother of the French king. The Count was for immediate attack; the Templar Master advised obeying the king's orders to wait for the main army to cross and join them. Matthew blames the vanity and crazy bellicosity of the Count for the ensuing defeat. But both he and the chronicler 'Rothelin' claim that the Count delivered on this occasion a speech which was a compendium of the calumnies which had been circulating about the Military Orders for a generation. In his speech d'Artois is said to have referred to the 'ancient treason' of the Temple and the Hospital, and to have attributed it to the fear that, if the Christians finally gained the victory in the Holy Land, there would be no further reason for the existence of the Orders. To prolong their wealth and power, he said, they treated and plotted with the Saracens; he appealed to the Emperor Frederick for evidence of the 'mousetraps' which the Orders had set for Christian rulers. When this speech had been given, according to Matthew Paris and Rothelin, d'Artois charged into the town of Mansourah, the Templars following willy-nilly. The result was the cutting-off of the heavy western horsemen in the narrow streets, and their annihilation in detail. The Count d'Artois was killed, and almost the whole Templar force of some three hundred horsemen with him.

Like many reputed speeches delivered before battle, the speech of the Count d'Artois was probably a stylized invention written some time after the battle took place. It has been thought by some critics to have been a rhetorical inversion of the speech given by the Templar Grand Master, Gérard de Ridefort, when in 1187 at Nazareth he had taunted the crusading army as cowards and urged them forward to the charge. The close companion and biographer of St Louis, Jean de Joinville, produces a quite different and to my mind a more probable explanation of what took place before Mansourah. He says nothing of a speech by d'Artois, but says that while the Count and the Grand Master argued about what was to be done, the Count's bridle was held by a nobleman called Foulque du Merle. Du Merle, being deaf, misunderstood what the Grand Master was saying, released the Count's bridle, and thundered off against the enemy shouting 'Up and at them!' (*Or à aus!*). So the charge took place and the battle was lost, owing to a casual misunderstanding. Whether this is the true explanation or not, the Templars cannot have been too ashamed of their record at Mansourah, since fifty-odd years later when they were on trial for their lives in Paris, the last Templar Grand Master claimed credit for the prudence and bravery of the Templars at this battle. In reply the prosecuting royal Keeper of the Seals, Guillaume de Nogaret, did not refer to Mansourah at all, but produced a jumbled story about Templars doing homage to Saladin (eighty years before Mansourah!) and being accused by Saladin of being sodomites.[19]

Further criticism of the Templars came from the same source as their main sponsorship and protection, the papacy. Templar policy by no means always chimed in with papal policy; in addition, the popes were keenly aware of the criticisms which were continually made of the Military Orders by the bishops, and on many occasions issued orders which were intended to stop

Templar and Hospitaller abuse of papal privilege, in particular their abuse of the privileges of exemption from tithe payment and the breaking of ecclesiastical interdicts. The latter malpractice had been condemned as long ago as the Lateran Council of 1179, but Innocent III issued an especially vehement condemnation in a bull dated 13 September 1207, whose flowery rhetoric was, centuries later, to be the source of lurid conjectures about Templar reputation.[20] Essentially the bull was a protest against the practice of sending out Templar preachers to raise funds by publicizing the Templar privilege of breaking church interdicts in places where they had been imposed, so that in each successive church closed by the interdict the 'joyous entry' (as Innocent sarcastically says) of the Templar priests would be marked by opening the church and celebrating the divine offices. Innocent quoted St Matthew (18:6), 'whoso shall offend one of these little ones which believe in me . . .' and went on in a powerful rhetorical flourish to say that, 'exhaling their greed for money', the Templar preachers do not shrink from telling lies, 'while, employing demonic doctrines, they impose the sign of the cross on the breast of any ruffian, laden with the weight of his sins, who attends their sermons; and they assert that whoever is willing to pay two or three pence a year to join a Templar confraternity will never be denied Christian burial, even if he is excommunicate.' By this means, the pope complains, 'adulterers and usurers and similar people are buried, on account of this insolent behaviour, in Templar cemeteries as though they were faithful Catholics'.

There is no sign that this bull did the Templars any harm in the medieval period, even at the time of their trial and condemnation, though it has subsequently been often, because of its references to 'doctrines worthy of demons', wrongly understood as a strong papal hint that the Templars were guilty of magical practices. So far as we know, it was not so understood in the Middle Ages. While the popes frequently criticized the Military Orders, they seldom did so in a really radical manner. They occasionally made it plain to the Templars, as to the Hospitallers, that what the Apostolic See had given the Apostolic See could, in case of abuse, take away. Pope Clement IV (1265–8), while chiding the Templar Grand Master over his recalcitrance in protecting the former Templar Marshal Stephen de Sissy, referred to the envy caused among the bishops by Templar privileges, and told the Grand Master not to provoke the pope further by his 'insolence', lest papal protection be removed and the Order forced to answer for its breaches of church law.[21] But there is no evidence that the popes ever put the dire threats they uttered into effect: the numerous privileges in favour of the Military Orders were added to rather than reduced.

It is arguable that, so far from defying papal power, the Templars made an important political mistake in remaining loyal to the papal side during the great quarrel between the Papacy and the Emperor Frederick II (1227–50); the Hospitallers began by taking the same attitude, but later showed superior political skill in veering round to an understanding with Frederick, while keeping their formal obedience to the popes. In this way the Hospitallers perhaps avoided some of the opprobrium which the Templars incurred, when their independence marked them out as obstinately defiant of the power of great princes. Perhaps these decisions were taken by the Templars on grounds of their local political interests in the crusading kingdom, but the treatment they received at the hands of Matthew Paris shows that they paid heavily in terms of reputation for their intransigence.

The coolly explicit realism of Clement IV's warning to the Templars shows awareness of the fragility of the political and military structure which the Order had been created to defend. By the time Clement IV had become pope the penultimate act of the Christian military presence in Syria had been played out; most of the great castles had fallen, and Acre was the one populous and well-defended centre which remained. The situation of the Holy Land at this time can be grasped visually from one of the maps drawn by Matthew Paris to illustrate his chronicle. The whole centre of the map is occupied by a grotesquely large promontory, 'La Cité de Acre', whose dimensions on the map appear greater than the whole southern coast of Palestine. Jerusalem fills a modest space in the south-east of the map, not many times larger than the space assigned to 'Le Temple' in the city of Acre. Noah's Ark peers out over the north of the map from the peak of a mountain in Armenia. The Christian horizon in Palestine has shrunk to a single city.

Unlike his predecessor Urban IV, who had for a time been

Patriarch of Jerusalem, Pope Clement IV was a conventional French cleric who reflected the growing indifference of the clergy to the Crusade. Politically he was dominated by the French prince who had become King of Naples, Charles of Anjou, and in particular he was influenced by Charles's oriental policies. Charles, although he at one stage went to the trouble to procure himself the title of 'King of Jerusalem', was opposed to further French participation in a Syrian or North African Crusade; he planned instead to conquer the Greek Empire of Byzantium. Papal crusading policy was not vigorous; although papal lawyers had staked ambitious claims for the popes' right to control and dominate the Crusade, the popes themselves acted feebly in the matter. Flickerings of papal interest in a new Crusade in the Holy Land were visible at the Council of Lyons in 1274, but both in the papal and the royal courts the concept led only a rather ghostly existence. In the crusading kingdom the Templars were locked in the narrow-minded, selfish struggles of the Crown and the nobles: as Outremer hastened to its fall the Templar leadership became, if anything, more blindly partisan than ever. In Europe the popes and their followers became more deeply implicated in the ruthless *Realpolitik* of the Italian wars, and the Crusade was often proclaimed in order to enlist Catholics to shed the blood of other Catholics. Frequently men's vows to help Christians fight Muslims in the Holy Land were commuted by the popes to encourage them to fight other Christians in Europe. The attitude of Catholic Europe towards the crusading settlement in the Holy Land became marked by indifference and cynicism.[22]

It is not easy for modern men, who are accustomed to think of the Middle Ages as an age of steadfast faith, to think of the time of the building of the great Gothic cathedrals and of the writings of St Thomas Aquinas as one of cultural instability and neurotic tension. Dante's *Divine Comedy* seems to us to be the testimony of an age of balance and harmony; it is easy to overlook the elements of unease which it contains, and easy, too, to see the society which surrounded Dante as one in which earlier ideals were crumbling quietly, in a dignified sort of way. Yet, when we look at the conditions in which the crusading ideal declir ~d in the late thirteenth century, we immediately find ourselve   ` world of lost directions, of *Angst*, of failing nerve.

From the Crusaders' point of view this failure of nerve arose from the sour experience of defeat. The crusading ideal could not survive unchanged among an indefinite series of military disasters. One of its most important elements was the feudal one of a trial by battle between the champions of the lords of heaven and hell:

God has brought before you his suit against the Turks and Saracens who have done him great despite. They have seized his fiefs, where God was first served and recognized as lord.

God has ordained a tournament between Heaven and Hell, and sends to all his friends who wish to defend him, that they fail him not.[23]

The Latin Catholic world had always believed that the just judgement of God is mediated through history, and often directly declared through the issue of battle. In the mid-twelfth century Otto, Bishop of Freising, the author of a *Chronicle of the Two Cities* (meaning the city of God and the city of this world) had dealt with the 'new militia' of soldiers of Christ who under the impulse given by St Bernard had gone to fight in the Holy Land. These knights, he wrote, who 'seemed by their life and morals to be monks and not knights', had gone there 'by the just judgement of God'.[24] To men bred to these ideas it was monstrously unacceptable that God's soldiers should be decisively and finally defeated, and that Jerusalem, the heavenly city, should be lost for ever to the impious unbelievers. It seemed to amount to a judgement of God against the order which he himself had approved and established. A particular defeat might reasonably be visited on the believers because of their moral weakness and their sins. But it was inexplicable, intolerable, that the tournament with Satan should be finally and irredeemably lost, and that the sons of light should perish at the hands of the sons of darkness.

Perhaps the most reflective Catholics might be prepared to see this impending disaster as a manifestation of the tormenting problem of theodicy, which asks how to reconcile the experience of evil and suffering by the apparently innocent with the overarching sovereignty of God's providence. But medieval Christendom was not culturally equipped to view things in this humble way. Its view of Islam was ignorant, arrogant, and harsh. There was no complementary Christian tolerance, no Christian equivalent to the Muslim idea that Christians and Jews as 'people of the book' had been conceded a partial revelation of God's word. In so far as Muhammad had been vouchsafed some hints of revealed truth, medieval Christians considered that he had distorted them in the most wicked possible way. Dante, for example, viewed Muhammad as the most monstrous of all heresiarchs and sowers of schism, and portrayed him in the *Divine Comedy* as suffering the torments of perpetual disembowelment. There was such profound, wilful incomprehension of Islam in western Christendom that the monotheism of the Islamic faith, which above all other religions abhorred the ascribing of any partners to the one God, was casually dismissed in the west as 'idolatrous'. In the trial of the Templars one of the main charges was their supposed worship of a heathen idol-head known as a 'Baphomet' ('Baphomet' = Mahomet = Muhammad).

To a culture which viewed things in this manner the erosion of the Latin Christian presence in the Holy Land presented appalling emotional difficulties. Some idea of their nature may be had from a poem written in Provençal dialect by a troubadour who is thought to have been a Templar.[25] Referring to the disastrous fall of a number of the main cities and castles of the Crusader kingdom in 1265 (notably the town of Caesarea and the fortress of Arsuf), the poet correctly says that the power of the Christian kingdom of Syria has been destroyed:

Pain and wrath invade my heart so that I almost think of suicide, or of laying down the cross I once assumed in honour of he who was laid upon the cross; for neither the cross nor his name protect us against the accursed Turks. Indeed, it seems clear enough that God is supporting them in our despite.

At one stride they have captured Caesarea and taken by force the strong castle of Arsuf. O lord God, what a hard road have the knights, the sergeants and the burghers taken, who were harboured within the walls of Arsuf! Alas! the losses of the kingdom of Syria have been so heavy that its power is dispersed for ever!

Then it is really foolish to fight the Turks, now that Jesus Christ no longer opposes them. They have vanquished the Franks and Tartars and Armenians and Persians, and they continue to do so. And daily they impose new defeats on us: for God, who used to watch on our behalf, is now asleep, and Muhammad [Bafometz] puts forth his power to support the Sultan.

The poet concludes by saying that the Sultan has sworn to rid the land of every Christian and to build mosques where there are now churches dedicated to the Virgin. The pope, instead of helping, is interested only in selling indulgences to finance the wars of Charles of Anjou in Lombardy, and he is greedy to accept money so that men commute and abandon their vows to fight as Crusaders in the east, and fight instead in the wars of Italy. Because of these Italian wars the power of the Turks has overcome the Christians in Syria for ever.

There is nothing exceptional in the tone or the matter of Bonomel's poem. Other poets of the time, replying to the call for a new Crusade after the death of St Louis, replied by attacking the morals and the politics of the clergy. Austorc d'Orlac wrote that because God and Our Lady want our troops to be beaten 'against justice', he will become a Muslim! Another Provençal poet, Guillem Daspols, objected that the Temple and the Hospital had been founded to defend the holiness of God's Orders and to feed the poor; but the Orders were full of pride and avarice, and were asleep in their sins. The dispersal of papal resources on the Italian Wars of the Vespers instead of their being used in the holy enterprise of the Crusade was a continuing source of complaint: according to one chronicler a Templar called Guy, an envoy to the Holy See two or three years before the fall of Acre, made bitter reproaches to the pope on this score.

As the Christian lands in Syria were whittled away the doubts and unrest about Christian defeat became more nagging. It became impossible to ascribe Muslim victories merely to the sins of Christian folk.[26] Finally, the fall of Acre and the definite end of the crusading kingdom in Syria in 1291 brought these doubts to a head. There was nothing overtly unseemly or disgraceful about the fall of Acre. Everyone in the city, including the Grand Masters of the Temple and the Hospital, fought honourably to the finish. When the Mamluks stormed the city on 18 May the Templar Grand Master, Guillaume de Beaujeu, was wounded in the shoulder during the Christian counter-attack on the Accursed Tower. He was placed on a shield and carried dying to the Temple, where he was buried before the high altar while the desperate fighting continued outside. Except for the Temple, the city fell that night. After some abortive negotiations the Temple was stormed eight or ten days later, and all its inhabitants massacred. Only a handful of Templars managed to gain their castle at Sidon, from which after a short time they embarked to Cyprus. No Templar ever set foot in the Holy Land again. But their desperate and brave last defence did not excuse them in the eyes of Christendom.

'Where is their God now: where is the God of the Christians?' Not only Saracens, but Jews and Tartars seemed to mock at Christian weakness. Among the knightly classes the simple, old-fashioned crusading ideal which told a knight that the religious penalty for serious crime might be cancelled by fighting the pagans, was now dying out. Disillusioned anticlericalism was becoming almost universal. In such circumstances the Templars and Hospitallers who returned to the west, apparently unemployed and yet still enjoying their old moneys and privileges, seemed an offensive addition to the great class of clerical hypocrites and drones. An especially bitter poem by Rostan Berenguier of Marseilles, written at some time between the fall of Acre and the beginning of the Templar trials, taxes the returned Templar knights with idleness and cowardice, as well as with pride:

Since many Templars now disport themselves on this side of the sea, riding their grey horses or taking their ease in the shade and admiring their own fair locks; since they so often set a bad example to the world; since they are so outrageously proud that one can hardly look them in the face: tell me, Bâtard, why the Pope continues to tolerate them; tell me why he permits them to misuse the riches which are offered them for God's service on dishonourable and even criminal ends.

They waste this money which is intended for the recovery of the Holy Sepulchre on cutting a fine figure in the world; they deceive people with their idle trumpery, and offend God; since they and the Hospital have for so long allowed the false Turks to remain in possession of Jerusalem and Acre; since they flee faster than the holy hawk; it is a pity, in my view, that we don't rid ourselves of them for good.[27]

Its author probably knew when he wrote this poem that the Templars faced serious charges at the hands of the French government. But it is still evidence of the discredited state of the Military Orders after the fall of Acre, and of the scepticism and cynicism with which many knights now treated the remnants of the old crusading establishment. If the Temple and the Hospital had been rapidly reorganized after the fall of Acre to prepare them for some great new crusading initiative which could appeal to the imagination of Christian Europe, public opinion might have treated them more gently. But neither pope, princes, nor Orders had the energy and the vision, or indeed the resources, which such an undertaking would have required.

Those plans that did emerge for the resumption of the Crusade after the fall of Acre were rather cramped and disappointing. In Cyprus both the Templars and the Hospitallers were quickly caught up in local politics. The Templar occupation of the little island of Ruad, a few miles off the coast of Syria, led to nothing, and they withdrew a decade after the fall of Acre. In Europe the princely courts, and especially the French court, revived the demand for the merging of the two main military Orders of Templars and Hospitallers. Under the growing pressure for a commitment to a great military venture the Grand Master of the Temple, Jacques de Molay, wrote two memoranda in 1306–7 which constitute the last word to come from the Templar Order about the enterprise for which they had been founded.[28] The aim of the Order was not contested: de Molay admitted that while the Hospital had been founded for the charitable purpose of 'hospitality', the Temple had been founded for war. But when he came to discuss that war, de Molay showed an excessively conservative attitude: in opposing the union of the Orders he said that 'innovation is almost always very dangerous'. His military analysis of the problems of a new Crusade was sensible if discouraging: he gave an analysis of probable Muslim strength in Syria, and pointed out that a 'little' Crusade which joined up with the small Christian kingdom of Armenia would run the risk of disaster. In his view the only Crusade with a serious chance of success would be something on the lines of that led by St Louis, which is to say a force of between twelve and fifteen thousand heavily armed horse and five thousand foot, secretly levied in order to conserve the advantage of surprise. The idea of merging the two military Orders as a prelude to the Crusade was dismissed by de Molay on a variety of grounds, principally on that of tradition, and on the idea that healthy competition between the Orders encouraged efficiency: he also foresaw the danger of quarrelling and bickering over the details of a union of the Orders.

De Molay's memorials are not the blatherings of an elderly Blimp: they are serious and well argued, and they reflect a far more sober and realistic approach to the military problems of the Crusade than the feverish vapourings on the subject which were at that time being turned out by the propagandists of the King of France. It also has to be remembered that de Molay's advice was being proffered to the pope and not to the lay princes. The Templar Grand Master writes as the head of a Religious Order as well as a military commander: he shows himself conscious of the dangers which clerks were at that time running from the cupidity and aggression of laymen, and it is probable that at this time he knew that his own Order was in danger, though unlikely that he realized the gravity of his situation. The cautious tone of his memoranda was well suited to the timidity of Pope Clement V, the pope whom he was addressing. De Molay was not as defeatist as has been made out; the proposal to send a great new army to the east cannot be called defeatist. It can only be treated as such if we take account of the hypocrisy of the French government, and we are not sure that the extent of this hypocrisy was known to de Molay. When he wrote, the raising of a great army of fifteen or twenty thousand front-line troops for service in the east was practically impossible. If the King of France used crusading subsidies to raise a force of this kind, he was going to use it against the Byzantine Empire and not against the Muslims.

The Hospitallers were better advised than de Molay, in that they quietly began to raise and equip their own naval forces for service in the east. An Admiral was appointed to command the Hospitaller fleet, and the Order began to acquire a new kind of naval offensive capacity. With the aid of this fleet the Hospitallers seized the Byzantine island of Rhodes, thus giving themselves an alternative base to the unquiet island of Cyprus. Whether by luck or judgement the Hospitallers thus found a way out of the blind alley in which the Military Orders were penned after the fall of Acre. No such route of escape was found by the Templars, who under de Molay's conservative leadership did nothing but get further entangled in the internal squabbles of the Kingdom of Cyprus. As the Templars approached their last days their mood seems to have been passive and negative.

To earlier medieval man alienation had two meanings: on the one hand man was an alien in the world in which he made his pilgrimage: man the wayfarer was under a duty to recognize that he was a stranger and a foreigner in the landscape through which he passed.[29] On the other hand man had let himself become estranged from God, and had worshipped alien gods: in this sense alienation was to be feared and avoided. These feelings had grown in a world governed by the majesty of Christ, by Christ Pantocrator, who had chosen and redeemed his people. The monk was sustained by Christ in his pilgrimage through the world: the warrior revered Christ as the true, the powerful, the honoured one, who called his warriors to the Crusade against the infidel because he wished it – *Deus lo vult*. With the failure of the Crusade and with the crumbling of other parts of the clerical order, the confidence that God's will supported the Christian warrior against the pagan warrior was shaken. It is no accident that representations of Christ at this time begin to place less emphasis on Christ in majesty and more on the man of sorrows, on the passive Christ.

Loss of confidence in the divine order which supported the knightly class in their commitment to the Crusade was accompanied by a change in the idea of chivalry. The knighthood which had taken part in the first Crusades had been made up of acquisitive groups of warriors who hunted together, and who subordinated individual courage to the joint discipline of the pack. By the end of the thirteenth century this earlier knighthood, which had been taunted by St Bernard for its greed, its vanity, its evil violence, had begun to give way to the literary idea of knighthood as an individual quest, a kind of lay parallel to the divine pilgrimage of the monks. The knight-errant who sought 'adventure' in a personal search which was often connected with worldly, erotic experience had little in common with the violent sinners who sought to purge grave sins by taking the cross. Even when this new knighthood was explicitly Christian, it had little in common with the old. The Catalan knight, Ramon Lull, author of a book on chivalry which in the following century was to be printed in translation in England by William Caxton, was faithful to the idea of 'Christian knighthood'. But he no longer had very much use for the traditional Military Orders of knighthood, in spite of his passionate concern for the renewal of the Crusade against the Muslims.[30]

Ramon Lull had been in favour of merging the two Orders of the Temple and the Hospital. This did not mean that he entirely disparaged the two Orders: in his *Blanquerna* he had enquired what part the two Masters of the Orders would take in honouring the glory of God; he replied that they were already in the Holy Land to exalt the Catholic faith. But Lull's ideas for the conversion of the Muslims were very different from the simple policy of conquest of the old Crusaders. Lull conceived the idea of a kind of Christian taskforce which as the 'spiritual sword of Christ' would take the word of Christ to the Islamic countries. These men would include priests, doctors, artisans, teachers: they would all make themselves proficient in Arabic and travel to the Muslim lands as peaceful missionaries ready to discuss and reason with the Muslims and to work beside them. Such bold and radical ideas were very far from the simple and traditional ones of the Templars: it is not surprising that Lull proved ready, in the end, to listen to the accusations against the Templars.

The shift in values which was taking place round the late medieval Church can only be described as a process of alienation. The most alarming symptom of alienation in late medieval society was one which was profoundly to affect the Templar Order, but which extended its evil influence very far beyond it, into the fabric of feudal and popular life. This was the pathological fear of demonic possession which gradually took shape as the great European witch-hunt. No sharper experience of alienation from God's order could be had than the feeling that demons were threatening Christian people, and that the protection which the sacramental order had formerly given against these evil spirits was no longer effective. It was a commonplace of early Christian tradition that holy men could put demons to flight by the mere invocation of God's name. The ceremony of exorcism remained, enabling the priest to renew this power to banish unclean spirits: 'exorcist' was one of the minor ordinations conferred by the Church, and in the Roman liturgy the exorcist was termed a 'spiritual emperor'. In the late thirteenth century people came to doubt the efficacy of this protection against the demonic world.

Alienation between laity and clergy was one factor in this loss of confidence. Another, linked, form of alienation was the doubt which affected many of the knightly class who interpreted crusading defeats as a sort of withering away of divine power. Both kinds of alienation stemmed from the enfeeblement of the idea that God would always protect and sustain his people. It had been a commonplace of crusading tradition that God would sustain his people against the pagans. If he had ceased to do so, it was natural to look for scapegoats among the clerical class, and within that class the most vulnerable was the small section of the clergy which also had military status: the Military Orders.

3
MAGIC, HERESY, AND CONSPIRACY

The essentials of magical practice are concealment, plotting, and secrecy. A magical accusation almost always includes the charge, or at least the implication, of conspiracy. This conspiratorial secrecy could be represented as a plot which was directed not only against specific persons but against society as a whole. It was not necessarily so: for most of the Middle Ages magical acts were more usually treated as acts of malice directed against particular private persons and charged in the law courts as minor criminal offences. But the circumstances which had led to the persecution of Christians under the Early Empire could always recur when society was both politically and psychically unstable. 'Depraved religion – hidden knowledge, exclusiveness of admission, suspicion of monstrous practices – was the charge on which the government based the persecution of the early Christians in pagan Rome. When fear of witchcraft and its secret allies is married to social and political instability, the elements exist for public panic and for mass magical treason trials. Conspiracy against private persons merges, in these circumstances, into the wider idea of conspiracy against the state. Should this occur, the multiplication of suspects is almost inevitable: from being one or two the conspirators quickly become legion. Such a disaster-point may be deliberately planned by a few unscrupulous people for their own political ends, or it may be reached haphazardly as the result of a period of acute social tension. Societies which associate an internal with an external enemy are especially prone to such fears of mass conspiracy; it is only too easy to find panics of this nature in the records of the twentieth century.

The classical model for such panics is the Bacchanalia affair of 186 BC. This occurred at an early moment in the history of Rome's association with the Italian cities, when they were subordinate to her in the prosecution of the Second Punic War. The close alliance with foreigners produced acute fears of the dangers of imported magical superstitions. The worship of Bacchus was associated with wild private rites, which were protected by solemn oaths of secrecy. The Bacchic religion consecrated violence; its legend remembered the lynching and dismembering of the sacrilegious persons who refused to worship the god. Bacchus-worship was embraced by all classes in Rome from the lowest to the highest. It was neither the first nor the last belief to be taken by Rome from the eastern Mediterranean, and was probably no more immoral than many other: the secrecy of the rites was the main reason for their incurring suspicion. In 186 BC the religion suddenly gave rise to a grave political scandal, based on charges that the Bacchanals planned to fire the city and to seize control of the state. Six or eight thousand persons were prosecuted and many executed; the victims were drawn from all classes of society. The charge was not magic or immorality but treason against the state.[31]

The persecution of Christians under Nero in AD 64 is an obvious parallel to the Bacchanalian affair, and the best-known of all the great conspiracy panics which attributed monstrous and immoral practices to a secret sect thought to be conspiring against the state. 'Depraved religion' was inevitably a political accusation in Rome, where the religious institutions were so closely linked with the state. There is a less well-known parallel in later Roman history, under the Christian Empire, in the great sorcery persecution of Valens in AD 374. This was occasioned by the drawing of a magical pentagram by sorcerers close to the imperial court; the pentagram contained initial letters of the name of someone supposed to be about to supplant Valens in the rule of the Empire. Valens prosecuted all supposed magicians and their employers on suspicion of high treason. Anyone of note who was thought to have had the slightest connection with magical practices was summarily tried, his property expropriated, and his life often made forfeit. The historian Ammianus Marcellinus says that whole libraries were burned at Antioch and elsewhere from the fear that they contained magical literature. The charge of high treason removed all the normal legal safeguards for securing a fair trial for senatorial nobles; it allowed them to be tortured, a method of interrogation normally confined to slaves. Hundreds of high officials and rich men were condemned.

But fears and suspicions that magical action is being taken on such a large scale as to amount to a political conspiracy have at most times been the exception and not the rule. In western society magic has normally been the resort of individuals and not of groups. Magic is attempted as a protection against personal misfortune; it can also be used as a means of aggression and attack. We must also make a distinction between magicians and their clients. From Roman times onwards witches and magicians were low, vulgar persons with whom it was bad luck to associate. The second-century writer Lucius Apuleius related in the *Golden Ass* how he got himself turned into a donkey by his foolishness in becoming the lover of a slave girl who to his bad fortune was a witch's servant. The adventure showed the sordid straits into which a well-born young man could get himself from a taste for pranks in low company. For a very long time the Christian Middle Ages did not stray far from this view: the *Corrector* of Bishop Burchard of Worms, written at the beginning of the eleventh century, is virtually a treatise on the anthropology of popular magical beliefs, explained from the sceptical and detached point of view of a clerical aristocrat. The *Corrector* is essentially a handbook for priests who are to discipline the more outrageous superstitions of the peasantry.[32]

But if magicians were social pariahs, their clients were not. Fear of magic has never been confined to the ignorant, and the leaders of society have very often asked low people to practise low tricks for them. As Gibbon remarked of the superstitious Roman ruling class: 'They believed, with the wildest inconsistency, that this preternatural dominion of the air, of earth, and of hell, was exercised, from the vilest motives of malice or gain, by some wrinkled hags and itinerant sorcerers, who passed their obscure lives in penury and contempt' (*Decline and Fall of the Roman Empire*, Bk. II, xxv). Perhaps there was a point in Roman history when Roman literary circles were sceptical as a class about magic, but by the fourth century the most striking thing about magical practice was not so much the widespread belief in its efficacy as the social prominence of the people who used it.[33] Highly educated men, writers and powerful civil servants, believed themselves to have been the object of magical attack. Christians were virtually committed by their religion to belief in demons: the pagan gods were demons; the planets were governed by demons; rulers and politicians were naturally supposed to use magical weapons. Eusebius, Bishop of Caesarea, the official historian of Constantine the Great, complains bitterly about the use of witchcraft by the tyrant Maxentius in his struggle with Constantine. St Jerome tells without scruple in his life of Hilarion how a Christian horse-trainer had to compete in the circus races with a duumvir who was a pagan, and who employed a wizard to disable the competing team. Hilarion at first refused to assist, but was persuaded that a Christian victory in the Gaza races was a worthwhile exercise of his powers. The great Christian theologian, Origen, accepted not only the idea of planetary demons but magical names and spells, including the magical use of the name of Jesus to expel demons.

It has never been difficult to show that the intellectuals of this period lived in a world permeated by magical ideas. It has, however, been the particular contribution of the late-classical historian Peter Brown to show the extent to which the sorcery accusations which these men launched against one another came naturally to a highly competitive society in which parvenu intellectuals found themselves striving with one another and also with established aristocrats. In the top echelons of the late Roman civil service life was uncertain and promotion capricious. In such circumstances the 'man with a single image', the 'chaste' man or he who felt himself such, was liable to ferocious feelings of resentment against 'the man with a double image', who was believed to draw on unseen and murky forces to procure advancement and stem the advancement of others. In this world not only would great men hire their own sorcerers –Elymas was reported by the Acts of the Apostles to have been a wizard on the payroll of the Roman Governor of Cyprus – but men of middle status would employ wizards and dream-readers, just as today they would consult psychiatrists. Not all this magic was maleficent, and at the innocent end of the scale the consultation with a wizard was an alternative to consultation with a favoured or protected Christian 'holy man', who would be just as likely to enjoy the patronage of some great political figure. But the Christian holy man himself typically showed his powers by striving with and casting out demons. Sometimes the exercise of these gifts must to a non-Christian have looked remarkably like magical practice. Brown has pointed out that St Ambrose, who in the course of his career struck five persons dead, might have been the envy of any late Roman magician.

The relevance of this late Roman magical world to the world of the later Middle Ages is that both were societies with courtier-dominated bureaucracies, and that within these bureaucracies many men of humble origins but high intellectual attainment had found a means of promotion to the highest power and influence. In the long period between the end of the Roman Empire and the beginnings of the early modern West European state, there had been scarcely any society in the west which had been bureaucratically administered. It is perhaps not too fanciful to see, in the spate of witchcraft accusations which infested the late medieval courts and administrations, some return of the conflict between the man with a single image and the man with a double image, which had been so common in declining Rome.

The first thing to understand about any magical attack is that it is precisely that. People do not seek the use of magical powers out of disinterested scientific curiosity, but to gain certain personal and practical ends.[34] The Faust legend expresses a profound truth when it shows Faust turning from the intellectual curiosity of high magic to the vulgar satisfactions of low magic. Societies may treat magicians in very different ways, depending on the stability of the society concerned and whether it views witchcraft as an exclusively disintegrating force or one containing at least some positive social qualities. Witches may be spasmodically tolerated on the grounds that counter-measures can usually be taken against their witchcraft or that their prosecution is too dangerous to risk. Or they may be proscribed on the grounds that they are too dangerous to tolerate. Witches may be especially vulnerable to punishment where it is believed that their magical powers attach to their persons, and can therefore always be used for magical purposes whether they protest harmlessness of intent or not. A modern example would be the bad effects attributed to the evil eye in the Mediterranean, which are supposed to take effect whether or not their possessor intends them to do so.

We distinguish between the sorcerer who studies the use of occult powers and the magician who possesses them as a personal attribute. The sorcerer is a much less dangerous person than the magician: the former might be described as a primitive scientist, whereas the latter, the true witch, is a compulsive ill-wisher and ill-doer. Like the scientist – like Prospero – the sorcerer is powerless without his learning and equipment, and he always has the alternative of breaking his wand and burning his books, if he wishes to go out of business. On the other hand, the wretched Neapolitan *jettatore* goes on spreading ill luck as long as his eyes have life left in them. Perhaps the distinction between sorcerers and magicians is less prominent in European societies than in others, but there are some European contexts where it becomes important. For example, whole villages or areas were sometimes thought to be populated by witches, or some particular kind of person such as a Jew or a Templar was accredited with magical powers. When this happened, the persons accused of being magicians had no means of renouncing or denying their magical powers, since they attached to them from what they were, not from what they did.

Magical practices are infinitely varied. But magical attack normally took the form of an evilly intended act directed against a particular person or persons. So long as society feels able to contain magic as a practice confined to humble or otherwise impotent social groups, such attacks can be treated as a base criminal offence which does not attract undue attention or unusual punishment. Such is the condition of many present-day African societies, and such also was the condition of medieval Europe, perhaps from the sixth century of our era until the thirteenth. In the medieval Christian world no one doubted the existence of magical or demonic powers, nor did anyone contest that their use should be punished. Strict limits, however, were placed on the belief that misfortune can be ascribed to some kind of magical attack. If *all* ill-luck was due to devils, then the sovereignty of God was placed in question, and Christian orthodoxy would not tolerate this.

The extent to which a society feels itself damaged by magical attack depends on the attack's source. One of the most profound sentiments of Christian doctrine was the conviction that false gods or idols were not mere inanimate objects or mental delusions but the work of demons. A Christian who attached himself to these demons for his own selfish ends was cutting himself off from Christian society, from God's people. Here we may look for the origins of the idea, which later had such a startling development, of the pact between humans and devils. On the other hand, the merciful mildness of the penitential codes of the Church which were issued at the time of the conversion of the barbarian peoples to Christianity, mitigated the harsh effects of this doctrine. For example, though the missionary fathers described the lewd songs which were sung at some rustic funerals as being addressed to demons, they did not cut off those who sang them from the community of God's Christian folk but merely set them a penance which would reconcile them with the Church. The work of acclimatizing the rural masses to Christianity could not have gone on if rustic superstition and residual pagan custom had invariably been treated as a direct attack on the ruling religion.

Only in the most exceptional circumstances, like those of the supposed magical conspiracy under the Emperor Valens, had magic been felt to be a social danger which menaced the whole body politic. In medieval Europe the main fear of internal attack against the Christian people was from heresy, not from magic. Heresy was a permanent and acute danger to the whole fabric of Christian life. It was inevitable that 'there must also be heretics among you' (2 Cor. 11:19). It had been present in the Christian community almost from the beginning, and the struggle with heretics which took place in the early centuries of the faith left a profound mark on Christian consciousness. The heretic was an externally faithful person whose pride led him to twist the sense of the word of God in a wicked way which made him part of the city of demons instead of the city of God to which he outwardly belonged. He was likely to be mild, benign in aspect, of an outwardly good conversation, but inwardly hypocritical and proud, a wolf beneath his sheep's skin. Covens or nests of heretics were supposed to beckon the unsuspecting into their midst with seemingly godly words, double-talk that deceived the casual enquirer and concealed the lies which they revealed to the initiate. They preached their doctrine secretly and in hidden places, like the wizards, using night as the cover for things the day would reveal with shame. They deceived many, for 'Satan himself is transformed into an angel of light' (2 Cor. 11:14). Their description in the patristic texts was stereotyped and inflexible, and remained so in the medieval period, uninfluenced by the real heresies which actually existed in medieval life.[35] In their conventicles they were said to take part in monstrous, blasphemous rites. Heresy accusations were marked by a pattern of secrecy and blasphemy charges which closely resembled those brought against the early Christians, and in the early stage may have been modelled on them.

Heresy differed from magic in that the former was the supposed deformation of belief, whereas the latter was the degradation of moral practice. Witchcraft in the Middle Ages never amounted to a set of religious beliefs; it was never more than an incoherently grasped body of pseudo-scientific practices, used for motives of base personal interest.[36] In the fevered imagination of the late Margaret Murray the medieval witches were represented as the survivors of 'the old religion' and their covens as the chain through which prehistoric religious belief of a coherent kind was handed down to the modern world. There is not a shred of evidence in favour of this story, in spite of its survival in some of the popular witchcraft literature of the present day.

It is necessary to insist on the distinction between folk magic and primitive religion, since at no time in the history of Christianity before the mid-thirteenth century was magic even approximately equated, in the mind of the Church, with heresy. Magical attacks were treated as crimes, and sometimes even as evidence of communication with demons, but they were not treated as attacks on the whole people of God. The enemy *par excellence* of the Christian people was the heretic, whose lies were directed against the whole basis of faith and social life. The magician was vile, despicable, potentially of great danger because of his conversation with the demonic world, but in effect negligible. Negligible above all because in a world where education was confined to the narrow and largely aristocratic section of the upper clergy and to a still more modest number of laymen, magicians were thought ignorant. Their clientele was among the base people, and nobles who patronized them did so at the risk of getting not only their souls but their hands dirty. Some people today, bemused by talk about the myth of the magus and suchlike, may find this view of the medieval magician to be sordid and rather dull. But Merlin, the mythical Gerbert, Virgil the magician and their like are figures from medieval romance and not from the medieval police records.

Witchcraft, in short, was until the closing years of the Middle Ages of very little more than casual interest to important people. To bishops its control was part of the general moral hygiene of their flocks, not to be placed in the same category as the suppression of heresy. To feudal lords magical attack was a political weapon of a most unusual sort, either in attack or defence. The way in which magical attacks became common in medieval politics will bear detailed examination.

In some parts of Africa political sorcery is regarded as the delicate sport of princes, and is contrasted by these African societies with the sordid witchcraft which is practised by the lower orders. According to this view aristocratic sorcery is permissible, but the humble practitioners of witchcraft are rightly punished for their wicked acts.[37] Such distinctions did not exist in medieval Europe, but there was a comparable social distinction in that the elaborate practices which go under the name of 'ceremonial magic' were quite widely used in the late thirteenth century in the households of great persons. These practices were on the whole astrological or divinatory, when not concerned with alchemy. A typical one was the manufacture of the seal, carved with a lion and made when the sun stood in that part of the zodiac, which Pope Boniface VIII's doctor, Arnau of Vilanova, supplied for the pope's personal protection. This kind of astrological device had nothing to do with the magical attacks of witches, and it continued to be common in the courts of princes (including the papal court) far into the Renaissance period. It seems suddenly to have been observed at the turn of the thirteenth century that the practice of ceremonial magic in his household could expose the great man who allowed or sponsored it to charges of a very serious nature. The learned men who exercised ceremonial magic were commonly talked of as 'magicians' without people making the subtle distinctions between ceremonial and other kinds of magic which we may think appropriate. Arnau of Vilanova, for example, said that he was often referred to as a 'pythonista'. It was not too difficult for political enemies to represent astrology or alchemy as evidence for consorting with demons. Indeed, the attempt to establish a sympathetic magical relationship with the planetary demons was not very far from 'conjuring'. And the worship of an idol conducted in such a way as to disparage the Christian Trinity *was* construable as heresy; this was to be the intellectual basis of the case against the Templars.

The most important politician to attract charges of demonic practices was Pope Boniface VIII (1294–1303). The latter part of his pontificate was spent in a ferocious quarrel with the French monarchy, pursued both by the pope and by King Philip the Fair in a spirit of intense animosity. A Roman baronial family called Colonna was also involved in the struggle; having waged a fierce private war with the pope in the Roman countryside in 1297, they fled after their defeat and anathematization to exile in the French court. Pope Boniface was by then a far from edifying figure either physically or morally; in 1301 he was described as 'nothing but eyes and tongue in a wholly putrefying body . . . a devil'.

The quarrel between Boniface VIII and Philip the Fair of France involved many long-standing disputes between the medieval Church and the State. But in spite of its traditional nature the conflict was settled in a strange, radical, innovatory manner which can only be described as cloak-and-dagger. In 1303 the French government despatched one of its most influential figures, a civil servant called Guillaume de Nogaret, on a secret mission to Italy. Nogaret acted with the advice and help of the exiled Colonna family, who in Italy enlisted a small private army for him, and enabled him to descend secretly upon Boniface VIII while the pope thought himself secure in the heart of his own dominions. On 7 September 1303 Nogaret secured entry for his force within the walls of Anagni, the little papal-state town where the pope lay. The flag of the French lilies was hoisted over the town walls, and the pope was, after a short struggle, ignominiously arrested. The intention was to take him back to France to face trial by a French-controlled Church Council, but this part of the plan miscarried. Boniface was after a few days freed by a counter-stroke of his supporters, although only a few weeks later he died, a defeated and disgraced man (12 October 1303). His attackers were automatically excommunicated under canon law, although some were singled out for specific and public excommunication by Pope Benedict XI, Boniface's successor.

The shadow of Anagni hung over Franco-papal relations for a

decade. Succeeding popes were anxious to normalize relations with the French government, and they succeeded to a large extent in doing so; but the self-righteous government of Philip the Fair was unwilling to admit any degree of culpability at all in the affair of Boniface's capture at Anagni, in spite of the blatant violence and coercion which its agents had used. On their side the popes were tied by the strict legislation which made physical attack on priests a very serious offence in Church law. Although sanctions against the French king himself were soon lifted, the popes refused to lift the excommunication against Guillaume de Nogaret, the king's chief minister and the leading actor in the Boniface drama. On the French side the government refused to let drop the charges of illegality and moral turpitude which it had brought against Boniface. Far from modifying its position, the French government built up a huge dossier against the dead pope, representing him as a heretic, an unbeliever, a simoniac, and also as a magician and the patron of sorcerers. The most emphatically magical accusations were that Boniface had familiar converse with demons, whom he constantly called to his assistance and sometimes worshipped.

The compilation of this dossier against Pope Boniface VIII was complete, so far as the main charges are concerned, by 1307, the year in which the Templars were arrested. Other charges were added to the file later, as more witnesses were found, but the nature of the attack was by this time clear. It was not the first occasion at this time on which a clerk was charged with having had converse with demons: such charges were made against the English Bishop of Coventry and Lichfield, Walter Langton, in 1300. As with Boniface, the magical charges against Langton were mixed with other charges of a quite different nature. The accusations against Langton were, however, brought by a private prosecutor and not by the government, which on this occasion acted as Langton's defender rather than as his accuser. When Langton did in 1308 find himself the subject of an important political trial organized by the English government, magical charges did not figure in the case against him.[38] The trial of Boniface therefore remains the first important *political* one, apart from that of the Templars, in which charges of forbidden magical practices were mixed with other political and criminal charges.

The common author of the prosecution case in the trials of Boniface and of the Templars was Guillaume de Nogaret.[39] Nogaret was a bourgeois from Saint-Félix de Caraman, near Toulouse, a royal judge and a 'knight of the King of France', an honorific chivalrous rank granted to royal legists and civil servants. Some contemporaries suggested that he had had close relations who were burned by the Inquisition as Cathars, but the truth of these slurs is uncertain. The normal anticlericalism of a layman in royal service seems, in Nogaret, to have been sharper.

In the long wrangles of Nogaret with the Roman Church one of the main issues was whether he had acted against Boniface out of pious zeal (*bono zelo*) or whether he had been influenced by personal enmity. In Church law anyone who was known to be the mortal enemy of another was disabled from bringing a heresy charge against his foe. For this reason Nogaret asserted with passion the pure intentions which had led him to act against Boniface at Anagni, and subsequently to charge the dead man with heresy. But in spite of the protection of the King of France, Nogaret, who was one of his chief ministers, was formally excommunicated by Boniface's successor in the papacy, Benedict XI (1303–4). It was to be one of the great ironies of the Templar trials that the minister who was mainly in charge of their prosecution was for the whole duration of the trials lying under the formal ban of the Church. As late as 1310, in the midst of the Templar affair, Pope Clement V (1305–14) was carefully saying that even if he consented to engage in personal conversation with Nogaret, the act would not itself relieve Nogaret from his status as an excommunicate.

To Nogaret, whose passionate self-righteousness and prim religiosity shine through every word he writes, Boniface VIII is the man with a double image: the deceiving, heretical, conjuring sorcerer who is the natural enemy of the chaste and the good. In the dossier which he caused to be drawn up against the dead pope the pontiff's epicurean scepticism, his sophisticated assertion that fornication is no more than rubbing the hands one against the other, his sodomy, his constant turning to a private demon whom he kept in his chamber and consulted in all things, are all typical of the charges wont to be brought in envy against the wicked magician. The anger which breathes through the charges is typical of magical accusation; as Gifford wrote in the sixteenth century: 'It is no godly zeal but furious rage' which stands behind the accusation of witchcraft.[40] Nogaret went so far in his passionate hatred as virtually to threaten King Philip, in a memorandum which he wrote in 1305, with God's wrath which might end in the king's deposition, if he failed to act against Boniface's memory.[41] Social jealousy may also have sharpened the feelings of Nogaret against both Boniface VIII and the Templars. Neither the pope nor the religious knights were by origin great lords born to vast wealth; as members of a class they came from the sector of society just above his own. Most Templars had been small landowners or very minor noblemen, and the Caetani family, from which Boniface VIII came, was also one of minor gentry.

Quite suddenly, around the year 1307, magical charges became one of the standard methods of aggression among the jealous and competitive servants of King Philip the Fair. From the French court the fashion of denouncing other courtiers for the practice of witchcraft or sorcery spread to the English and papal courts, and so, in a sense, became one of the impelling forces of the great witchcraft hunt of the late Middle Ages. Nogaret was the central figure in the early period of this new mania. In 1308 a disgraced courtier called Guichard, Bishop of Troyes, who had been the household adviser of Blanche of Navarre and of her daughter Jeanne of Champagne, formerly Philip's queen, was accused of magical practices and incitement to murder by poison; he was also said to have caused the death of the former Queen Jeanne by having baptized and impaled a wax image which represented her. The prosecution case was added to by Nogaret, who appended other charges of sodomy, spitting on the cross, and so on, until the articles of accusation began to look like those drawn up against Boniface VIII. The charges seem to have stemmed from a small group of courtiers and civil servants who had resolved on destroying the bishop.[42] More rationally, he was accused of having lent money at usury. As with Boniface and as with the Templars, envy of ill-gotten gains is apparent in many of the accusations. In the event it proved unnecessary to go to the bitter end with the charges against Guichard. The case dragged on, some witnesses died, the pope was involved, and after some years it proved politic to release the bishop and quietly to drop the affair. But his enemies had been successful; by then Guichard was a broken and ruined man.

Towards the end of his life Nogaret again seems to have carried out a magical attack, this time against a great aristocrat, Louis de Nevers, son of the Count of Flanders. Louis claimed that he had been arrested and imprisoned by Nogaret, and charged with having committed treason by the most absurd magical means. He also claimed to have escaped from prison, but if his statements are correct proceedings against him must have been dropped as a result of Nogaret's death, which took place in the spring of 1313. But the death of Philip the Fair's malicious Keeper of the Seals did not end the run of similar magical accusations in the French court. Enguerrand de Marigny, the most powerful minister of Philip's last years, was after the death of his master in 1314 accused of high treason.[43] The charges were at first political, but magical ones were added. It was alleged that Marigny's wife had made wax images and had them consecrated to a demon so as to murder the king and his family. The wife was in the event spared, but he and one of his wife's attendant women were hanged.

These were the first of a long series of political trials in the French and English royal courts which included the accusation of magical ill-doing.[44] Such charges were periodically made in these courts for a further three centuries, into the early modern period of the seventeenth century. As late as the time of James I of England and Louis XIII of France such trials were still taking place.

In the papal court, the greatest bureaucracy of the medieval west, where promotion went to the strong, the able, and the unscrupulous, the fear of witchcraft was rife. Pope John XXII (1316–34) yielded to no one in his terror of the plots and devilish designs of magicians. His attitude was of especial importance, since he was the last of the great lawmakers of the medieval Church, and his views were to tip the scale in the decision to subsume the crime of witchcraft in the greater crime of heresy. John profoundly feared the plots of magicians, and also frenetically hated his enemies, to whom he readily ascribed devilish associations and practices. A great lawyer, and no mean theologian, he was also a good hater. When told, during the prosecution of his numerous and bloody Italian wars, to 'beware of German ferocity', the pope replied: 'By God, we will teach the Germans what ferocity is!'[45] He superstitiously sought magical protection against attack: for example, by accepting from the Countess of Foix the gift of a curved horn which was thought to be a defence against attempts to poison him.

Early in John's pontificate a conspiracy was said to have been detected on the part of Hugues Géraud, Bishop of Cahors, which was the area from which the pope himself originated. The papal police seized from Géraud's agents magical images which were supposed to have been designed for use against the pope. After questioning by Pope John himself, Géraud made admissions which also incriminated him in the murder of the pope's favourite nephew by the use of other magical wax figures. Whether the admissions were obtained under torture is not disclosed by the record. But Géraud was degraded and burned to death on the grounds of murder and attempted murder by magical means. In 1320 other magical charges were brought against the pope's political enemies in Italy. The great tyrant of Milan, Matteo Visconti, was accused of causing a silver image to be made which represented Pope John XXII and bore the zodiacal sign of Saturn, sign of melancholy and disorder, and the name of 'Amaymon', the 'demon of the west'. The papal court acted prudently about these assertions and no official case seems to have been made out of them, though Matteo Visconti was charged with heresy on other grounds. Similar magical charges were made on other evidence, which in one case named the poet, Dante Alighieri, as a suspect. A further political enemy of the pope, the Ghibelline feudal lord Federigo di Montefeltro, was accused of having erected an idol in a special temple in which he paid the demon divine honours. This was made an excuse for the papal publication of a Crusade against the Montefeltro clan in 1321. It is unlikely that there was a word of truth in the charges: the nearby Bishop of Urbino said he could find no reason to call the Count of Montefeltro a heretic. The charge was dropped, without explanation, after the violent death of the Count.[46]

John XXII issued a legal opinion which made his views on the connection between witchcraft, idolatry, and heresy fairly clear.[47] He was perfectly aware that the invocation of demons did not in itself amount to heresy. 'But', he said, 'as the worship of demons, the baptism of images and suchlike are grave sins which are at present pullulating everywhere', it would be quite reasonable for the Church to punish people as heretics for the commission of such offences, even if they did not fall within the strict definition of heresy. He argued that superstition was such a widespread social scourge that it ought to attract the capital punishment usually reserved for the more serious crime of heresy. That the pusillanimously superstitious John XXII argued in this way will not, by now, surprise the reader.

In this pattern of political trials and magical accusations one fact may be fortuitous, but cannot be passed over without comment. The two men who were most active and influential in forming the precedents for political witchcraft trials were Guillaume de Nogaret and Pope John XXII. Though one was a layman with an anticlerical record and the other the head of the Church, their origins and careers were strikingly similar. Both were bourgeois born within a hundred kilometres of one another in southern France, Nogaret in the area south-west of Toulouse, and Jacques Duèze (John XXII) in Cahors. In the period when Nogaret was Keeper of the Seals and chief minister in the government of Philip the Fair, Duèze was Chancellor of the cadet branch of the French royal house, the Angevin dynasty of Naples. Both men suffered from panic fear of magical attack, and their maniacal aggression against people whom they suspected of such attacks was typical of the insecurity and superstitious violence of court officials who lived in fear of the competitive plotting of others of their own kind.

Some historians have treated political witchcraft trials as peripheral to the history of witchcraft; perhaps this is because they tend to exaggerate the rationality of the behaviour of successful politicians. They feel that a politician who uses a mystical attack in the form of a witchcraft charge is probably doing so in a sceptical and cynical spirit, and that he brings the charge only because it is politically advantageous to do so. On this view a politician who brings a magical charge is trying to attain a rational end by a superstitious means. This disregards the fact that most other magical attacks can be described in the same way. The problem at issue is the rationality of magical behaviour.[48] If we try to understand what a political witchcraft charge meant to the men who brought it, we cannot interpret it merely as a rational political act which takes advantage of the existence of magical beliefs among other people. This overlooks the real fear of magicians which obtained among politicians, and which to them often made the supposed magical attack frighteningly real. Magical counter-attack, of the type of a witchcraft charge, can be inspired by either fear or hope. Magic may be, as some have thought, the world of hope and desire, but it is also the world of fear. Even John XXII and Nogaret, apparently secure in their power and dignity, were terrified of magical plots.

If the accusation of witchcraft can be considered as a form of mystical attack, so also can the accusation of heresy. The charges against Boniface VIII, against the Templars, against Federigo di Montefeltro, mixed magical matters with accusations of heresy in a way which suggested that those who brought the charges did not distinguish very clearly between the two. It is arguable that many of the 'political' heresy charges which various popes brought in the later Middle Ages against their enemies are better understood as mystical, quasi-magical attacks than as serious attempts to maintain religious orthodoxy. But this view is not essential to the present argument, which merely maintains that, in the minds of the people who brought them, the line between accusations of magical practice and accusations of heretical views was not always very clear.

Conspiracy was alleged by the prosecution in almost all the state trials involving magic or witchcraft. Only Pope Boniface VIII was thought powerful enough to take, in effect, sole responsibility for the wicked acts of magic and heresy which had occurred. The Templars, on the contrary, were claimed to represent a huge conspiracy embracing not only a vast number of living people but those stretching far back in time through the tainted history of the Order. In most other cases the accomplices were usually thought to be few, and of low social standing. But in all cases the peculiar thing about the charges is not the ruthless prosecution methods but the fusion of the idea of political conspiracy with the idea of magical attack.

4

THE TRIAL

In the early morning of Friday, 13 October 1307, the agents of the King of France arrested on suspicion of heresy every known member of the Templar Order in the kingdom on whom they could lay hands. The pope of the time, Clement V, estimated the whole strength of the Order in the country at roughly two thousand; but this would have included all Templars from knights to humble agricultural and household servants. A few weeks after the arrests the government told the University of Paris masters that over five hundred Templars had confessed to the charges; it did not disclose how many at that time still affirmed innocence but were believed guilty. In spite of the unexpectedness of the arrests some Templars did evade capture, though it is unlikely that many could have maintained themselves for long in a medieval world which was very hard on fugitives. Only a handful emerged from hiding during the trial, and the government's list of Templars thought to have been at large is a short one.

The main officials of the Order were at this time in France. The Grand Master, Jacques de Molay, had been negotiating there with the pope and the King of France since the spring of 1307. The Visitor-General, the Preceptors of Normandy, Aquitaine, and Cyprus, and the former French royal Treasurer were all taken during the arrests. However, the number of Templar knights arrested was fewer than has often been supposed. We know that there were only fourteen knights among the 138 Templars heard by the Grand Inquisitor, and only eighteen knights among the 546 prospective 'defenders' of the Order in 1310. Perhaps between fifty and a hundred knights were involved; this is a far cry from the army of 2000 knights which some have supposed to have constituted a military danger to the French monarchy.[49]

The charge was heresy. According to the royal letter ordering their arrest: 'Like beasts of burden deprived of reason, in fact exceeding the unreasonableness of beasts in their bestiality, they have abandoned God their maker and sacrificed to demons and not to God.' They were 'lacking in wisdom and prudence', and 'insane folk given over to the worship of idols'. The arrests differed in one important way from any ordinary heresy arrest of the time: though authorized by the papal Inquisitor in France, they were effected by the king and not by the Church. The usual procedure was for a Church court to arrest and to have custody of heretics, for it to try them under Church law, and at the end of the trial to release them for punishment by the secular arm if this was the verdict of the court. The claim of the secular prince to initiate action in heresy cases was not new; it had been made in the Empire by Frederick II of Hohenstaufen, and something like a rough-and-ready right of the prince to act against heretics had been vindicated by the French kings in the course of the Albigensian Crusades against the Cathars in the south of France under King Philip the Fair's ancestors.

For an Order enjoying papal protection such as that of the Templars the arrests must have come as a devastating shock. Church law protected the Templars from the most trivial legal action by bishops, unless papal authority had been obtained. Grants of privilege and protection from kings and princes, not least from the kings of France, filled the Templar archives. Philip the Fair had himself issued a comprehensive promise of royal protection to the Templar Order only three years before the arrests. The plight of the arrested Templars was a terrible one. The normal procedures for the examination of suspected heretics by Church courts were already very severe, and very unfavourable to the defence. The accused person in a heresy trial had no right to know the names either of his accusers or of the prosecution witnesses, nor did he possess the right to be defended by counsel. Torture could be used against him, though it was supposed to be applied according to a standard procedure and not taken so far as to cause mutilation or permanent injury. But the special circumstances of the Templar arrests made these already harsh procedures into an instrument of savage terror. The examination of the Templars was entirely in the hands of royal officials, and it is not even certain that Church officials were present at some of the interrogations. The torture of the accused was carried out with a barbarity which even medieval men found shocking: it was said that at some examinations the torturers were drunk, and that at others the accused, while under torture, were teased by young boys who had been allowed to be present at the spectacle. A peculiarly repulsive and cynical note was struck by the royal letter opening the enquiries, which remarked that, 'if some among them are innocent, it is expedient that they should be assayed like gold in the furnace, and purged by proper judicial examination'. In practice this meant that in order to obtain confessions the Templars were kept on bread and water for weeks at a time, isolated and in chains in their cells. The tortures were of such ferocity that on many occasions the victims died before confessions could be taken. An especially terrible treatment which the victim survived in one instance was that of having the feet rubbed with fat, and placed before a fire: in this case the accused lost several bones from his feet, which he produced in evidence at a later stage of the trial. Another accused said he would have agreed 'to kill God' in order to stop these torments, and in one of the few written defences of the Templars they feature prominently in the argument.[50]

Physical torture was far from being the only element in the Templar confessions. The Templars were soldiers who were vowed to braving death in combat; moreover, in Outremer they had been mentally prepared for sojourns in Muslim dungeons which would not have been dissimilar to their experience in the prisons of the King of France. Their worst trouble was not the harshness of their treatment but the complete overturn of their spiritual and social universe. They had spent their lives in what would now be termed by sociologists a 'total institution', entirely distinct from all other lay or religious institutions except the other Military Orders. In entering the Order they promised complete obedience, so that 'when you wish to sleep, you will be made to wake, and when you wish to wake, you will be made to sleep'. Though in some ways they had lived in an enclosed and cut-off world of a military élite group, in other ways they had been constantly reminded of the support of the rest of society. Papal privilege was from a legal point of view absolutely necessary to them, but noble and royal approval were just as much an important part of their lives. The Templar fraternities had kept them linked by bonds of brotherhood with a vast sector of noble and even of popular society. They were aware that their prosperity and arrogance aroused envy; they were aware that from time to time both bishops and royal officials could be hostile, as they were to other privileged religious corporations. But the sudden and complete cutting-off from the rest of the people of God, the absolute need placed on them to admit that they had by their unnatural and idolatrous practices all along belonged to the people of the devil, broke their pattern of life abruptly and cata-strophically. It is not surprising that some Templars lost their reason, and that at least a dozen committed suicide.

For men accustomed to the comradeship of the regiment and the fraternity of others vowed to a religious life, it was a severe shock to be separated from the other brothers and to have no means of knowing what was happening to them. Such isolation weakened their resistance to outside pressure; and it is signifi-cant that the only occasion during the trials when Templar morale seemed to recover, and 'defenders' were found for the Order, was the short period in 1308 when about five hundred Templars were assembled in the garden of the bishop's house in Paris. Information was passed from one to another; the phrase 'with the help of the brothers' was used; and the terrorizing effects of loneliness and ignorance were for a time reduced. To this loneliness in captivity we must add degradation, and the demeaning of status. For example, Templars had all normally worn beards, which made them a privileged exception among religious persons (to most of whom beards were forbidden) and also to some extent an exception among the knightly class. When a Templar in prison had given way under examination and con-fessed his sins of heresy, he was 'reconciled' to the Church. At this stage most Templars who had confessed guilt then shaved their beards and discarded the mantle of a Templar. They had thus been ritually humiliated, and made to undergo a sort of additional rite of renunciation which separated them from the Order. It was also peculiarly damaging to Templar self-respect that they were accused of carrying out debased and blasphemous practices in the conduct of the ceremony of admission to the Order, particularly in the insults said to be offered to the Cross. By dishonouring Templar initiation rites in this way, the accusers were nullifying the ceremony which had made the lives of individual Templars meaningful, and had once conferred on them an identity of which they had been proud.

Why did the French government try to annihilate a Military Order which enjoyed the special protection of the Holy See and which for almost two centuries had played a central part in the Crusades which were dear to the French monarchy? Only a decade earlier Louis IX of France, the companion in arms of the Templars in the Holy Land, had been canonized by the pope. In 1303 and 1304 King Philip the Fair himself had made specially binding guarantees of his protection to the Templar Visitor of France personally and to the Order as a body, in view of the support which the Visitor and the Order had given him against Pope Boniface VIII. Moreover, Philip had by no means abandoned the traditional interest of his royal house in the Crusade. In 1306–7 negotiations had gone on between the French monarchy and the pope, in which the military Grand Masters were also involved, for an attack by Charles de Valois on the Greek Emperor of Constantinople as a preliminary to a full-scale Crusade against the Muslims. An expedition by the Orders in the Levant was also being considered; and other projects in the Levant were being contemplated by the French Angevin dynasty of Naples.[51]

The French government protested religious zeal alone as the motive for its actions against the Temple. Announcing the arrest and confession of the Templars, the royal spokesman Guillaume de Plaisians referred to an affair in which King Philip acted not as accuser or prosecutor but as the hero of a battle for the faith, the victor of a spiritual conflict which had already been won by the spontaneous confessions made by the guilty enemies of true religion. But from the beginning some people were sceptical or incredulous about the supposedly pious motives of the French king. Three weeks after the arrests of the Templars had taken place, the Genoese politician Cristiano Spinola suggested that King Philip's real reasons for attacking the Templars were hopes of seizing their money and also of uniting the two Military Orders of the Temple and the Hospital into one Order which would be controlled by a member of the French royal family.[52]

Dante suggested (*Purg.*, xx, 91) that King Philip's action in lawlessly seizing the goods of the Temple was that of a 'new Pilate' who was impelled above all by avarice. Others down to our own day have accepted the idea that money was almost exclusively the real motive for the Templar prosecutions. But Spinola's letter, written so soon after the event, suggests immediately that scepticism about the declared public reasons for the arrest of the Templars does not at all commit us to the view that the French government was impelled merely by greed or by financial need. Nor is it necessary to view the religious zeal expressed by Philip and his ministers as mere hypocrisy.

Philip probably looked at the Templars first of all as an element in crusading policy. In this respect the Templars, the Hospitallers, and the pope had all opposed an irritating passive resistance to his policies. It appears that from the time of the Mongol victories in Palestine in 1299, which seemed to offer openings for a Christian–Mongol alliance against the Muslims, until the summer of 1307, discussions between the pope and the French king were still centred on the idea of a 'general passage' or a large-scale Crusade in Syria or Asia Minor, or, failing that, a 'particular passage' or a smaller-scale attack on a selected target. But more and more the idea of attacking the Byzantine Empire as a preliminary to a Crusade against the Muslims came to dominate discussion. The Hospitallers were representative of this trend in that the action they took in the Levant at this time was not against the Muslims but against the Greeks, from whom they seized the island of Rhodes in 1307. The idea of a 'particular passage' led by the Hospitallers against the Muslims continued to be pursued until 1309; plans were made for it in France and elsewhere and clerical subsidies were imposed for it, but in the autumn of 1309 the whole project collapsed.[53] The French court languidly played with the idea of an attack on Constantinople, and for a long time serious planning of a new Crusade in the Holy Land was tacitly dropped.

The French government had for some years been demanding the fusion of the two main Military Orders. It was discreetly silent in the diplomatic negotiations about what was to be done with the Orders when they had been merged, but from the writings of royal propagandists we know that the aim was to form a single Order headed by one of the sons of the King of France. The general atmosphere of crusading thought was not alien to such an idea. The Catalan zealot Ramon Lull, who has already been mentioned, had earlier launched the visionary idea of a Christian 'Warlike King' who would centralize and lead the whole Christian crusading effort. Ramon Lull spent a great deal of time in the French and papal courts in the early years of the century, seeking support for his projects. Until 1312 Lull was in and out of the French royal court, lauding Philip as the 'champion of the Church' and explaining to French academic and political circles the complicated theoretical grounds on which his own crusading theories were based. In the course of his stay in France Lull made some significant concessions to French royal policy.[54] He went along with the idea that the attack on Byzantine Constantinople ought to precede the 'general passage' against the Muslims. He also accepted the guilt of the Templars, to which he referred as a 'horrid revelation' of 'secrets' among the Christians which was imperilling the safety of the ship of St Peter. Lull had always been in favour of the merging of the Military Orders, and it may not have needed much effort to persuade him that the Templars ought to be suppressed. Certainly, however, Lull would have insisted that Templar funds and estates should be devoted entirely to the Crusade; he would not have knowingly consented to an arrangement which made them the absolute property of the French Crown.

It was common practice among late medieval kings to obtain very large sums of money from the clergy by promising to take the cross, or by actually taking it, and persuading the pope to tax the clergy of their land for a crusading tithe. In many if not in most cases the king concerned would somehow get control of these moneys, which he had promised with more or less sincerity to use on Crusade. On very few occasions was the money actually so used: once it came into the direct control of the royal financial agents it was usually made to disappear on one pretext or another into the general stream of royal finances. Philip the Fair himself acquired a great deal of money in this way, as did his contemporary Edward I of England. Arguably, the attempt of the French monarchy to get temporary control of Templar moneys and lands as a result of the heresy charges brought against the Order in 1307 belongs to the same kind of aggressive and acquisitive policies, carried out on the same excuse of religious and crusading zeal. Sharp though these methods were, it is doubtful if they were deliberately irreligious in spirit; exploiting Church revenues had always been one of the main aims of secular government.

It is unlikely that the French government accused the Temple in 1307 with the main objective of solving its own short-term financial problems, serious as these may have been. Naturally, while the royal agents had custody of Templar lands they exploited them ruthlessly, as was the custom when any government had temporary 'regalian' charge of Church lands. No doubt Philip the Fair would have hung on to the Templar lands for ever if he had been able, but in the end the pressure of the pope and of the Church establishment forced him to order the handing over of all the Templar lands to the Hospitallers, even though the lands had not been transferred by the time of his death in 1314. The French government invented a very large sum which it claimed the Templars had owed it since they had had charge of the royal treasury earlier in Philip's reign, and forced the Hospital to pay this, and some other similarly dubious claims, before it could finally get custody of the former Templar lands after 1318. As for the main Templar holdings in cash, the 'treasure' of the Order, about which some modern writers have become very excited, little is known either of its amount or of what became of it. One Templar brother who sought to attack the Order during the trials had heard it said that an escaped Templar, Hugues de Chalons, had taken with him all the treasure of his uncle, Hugues de Pairaud, the Visitor of France.[55] This is the hearsay evidence of a vacillating witness, and even if the report was true, we do not know if it refers to the main treasure of the Order or to some other fund. It may be that the Templars had accumulated a substantial cash reserve in view of the proposed new crusading expeditions: if so, Philip the Fair probably got his hands on this money. The figure of 150,000 gold florins was mentioned by another witness: this is about half the annual expenses of the King of England, or about four times the annual income of a rich English earl. But it is unlikely that the Temple in Paris held some vast treasure beyond the dreams of avarice; the heavy expenses of re-equipping and re-establishing Templar forces in Cyprus since the fall of Acre would alone have absorbed any big cash balance which it had been holding in reserve. Loans, moreover, took up much of the ready money.

Financial need alone will not account for the attack mounted by the French government on the Templars. Nor will the bare fact that the Templar officials refused to conform to the crusading policies which the French government wanted, particularly the fusion of the Orders. Both these factors may have weighed with Philip in ordering the attack, but if we leave the matter there we are certainly failing to do justice to the mentality of an epoch. The French king saw himself as God's representative among men; his ministers saw themselves as executing the work and the will of God. The shrillness and the grandiloquence with which they expressed themselves do not mean that they were lying. They had convinced themselves in some way that the Templars were the devil's agents, betraying and breaking down the house of the people of God. We need to look more closely to try to find how this came about.

When the king's minister, Guillaume de Plaisians, spoke before the pope to urge him to confirm the royal judgements and settle the Templar affair, he described its origins as 'awesome and terrible' in that the original accusation came from a person of humble conditions. This was Esquin de Floyran, a Templar comprior from southern France, who in 1305 had denounced the Order, first to the King of Aragon (who paid no attention) and secondly to the King of France. Two other Templars are also known to have participated in the early denunciations. Their exact content is unknown; according to Plaisians the king then despatched a dozen secret agents to enter the Order and report what they found, and these men also were said to have confirmed the charges. These were mentioned to the pope on a couple of occasions, but he took no action, and without further consulting him the king made his own arrangements for the arrests. The Templars were then examined by the king's agents, with some participation by the clergy, and the confessions, described by Plaisians as 'joyful and wonderful', began to roll in. Among the earliest to confess – there is a conflict of evidence whether with or without torture – was the Grand Master himself. Similar confessions to those of the Grand Master were made by the other chief officials of the Order in captivity; one of the main features of the trial was to be the complete failure of these officials to give guidance or leadership to their brother Templars.

Two of the main charges referred to the ceremony at which a Templar was received into the Order. It was said that at initiation a Templar was required to deny three times that Christ was the Son of God, to spit three times on a cross, and to promise to relieve his sexual desires by relations with other Templar brothers. They also, as postulants, had to bestow obscene kisses on the exposed back, the navel, and the mouth of the brother who received them. Strictly only the kisses on the lower spine and the navel could be deemed obscene, since kissing on the mouth was a recognized part of licit reception ceremonies. Finally, they bestowed worship in their chapters on a heathen idol, variously described as to its physical characteristics, but known as a 'Baphomet', which etymologically was the same word as 'Muhammad'. Like so many persecuted heretical groups of the past, they were said to hold their chapters only secretly and at night.

The questionnaires which elaborated the charges against the Templars were re-drafted at various points of the trial, and eventually came to include a large number of charges which were not in the original versions. But apart from a rather technical Church law charge that Templars, without priests's orders, bestowed a form of absolution in chapter on brothers who had confessed to faults, these were the main and the vital accusations. Templar confessions in very large numbers admit specifically, always in the same form although with many minor variants, to the charges which concern the initiation ceremonies. The standard nature of the confessions bespeaks the standard application of a questionnaire, which as in most subsequent witchcraft trials guaranteed a remarkable uniformity in details.[56] The worship of the idol was less commonly admitted, and the descriptions given of it varied wildly. The physical characteristics assigned to the 'Baphomet' seemed to come either from the *maufé* or demon of northern folklore, or from church reliquaries. It was often said to represent a cat, a beast traditionally associated with witchcraft and heresy. In spite of its oriental name, no one assigned it oriental characteristics.

Whether, as the French historian Michelet thought, the original charge of a perverted initiation ceremony arose from some genuine Templar mock-renunciation of the cross based on the scriptural precedent of the renunciation of Christ by Peter (Matt. 26:69–75), cannot with certainty be determined. Michelet's suggestion, which does not necessarily entail the conclusion that the Templars were heretics, remains the most persuasive one. Many historians have followed the conclusions of the German, Heinrich Finke, who at the beginning of this century published the classic examination of the 'guilt-question', and exonerated the Templars of all ritual or regular perversions and heresies. The most recent work on the subject by a British scholar, Malcolm Barber, in effect follows and confirms the work of Finke. Jean Favier, on the other hand, in his recent biography of Philippe le Bel, inclines to think that both the irregular initiation ceremony and the veneration of a strange image must have had some foundation in Templar practice. He ascribes the acceptance of these oddities by otherwise orthodox Templars to their mediocrity and ignorance. But Philip IV and his ministers did not have a team of disinterested scholars to assist them, and they were convinced that the machinations of perverted and corrupt clergy were already working within God's Church to undermine and overturn it with the help of devils. They also found themselves at grips with a grossly rich and over-endowed Church, which obstinately refused to grant all the money required by God's vicar, the King of France, for purposes which were good and holy. The Temple, which until recently had been the money-manager of the French crown, and to which French princes and barons were almost certainly still in debt, was one of the embodiments of this proud, rich, stiff-necked attitude of the clergy. This was at a time when the Church's own weapons were being turned against it, and the royal ministers were certainly aware of one of the favourite biblical quotations of Pope Gregory VII: 'rebellion is as the sin of witchcraft, and stubbornness is as iniquity and idolatry' (1 Sam. 15:23). Behind the Templars stood Pope Clement V, the Gascon pope, elected in 1305, who was resident in or near the French kingdom. One of the main aims of French policy was to profit from Clement's French origins and from his vicinity to the French king, and to bully him into complete compliance. If a previous pope, Boniface VIII, had been guilty of idolatry and witchcraft, then so could this pope be. Once such a terrible internal enemy as Boniface had been identified in the Christian community, perversion and heresy could be expected to appear almost anywhere within the Church's ranks. Thus Clement could defend the Templars only at his own extreme peril.

There is no doubt that Guillaume de Nogaret was the minister mainly responsible for the arrest and prosecution of the Templars. He received the royal seals on 22 September 1307, the very day when the instructions went out for the arrests.[57] His appointment was a slap in the face for the papal court; here was the minister responsible for the outrage committed against Boniface VIII at Anagni, still under sentence of excommunication from the Church, and working energetically to obtain the condemnation of Pope Boniface for heresy. To make such a man head of the French royal administration was a direct menace to Pope Clement V. How far Nogaret was henceforth personally responsible for royal policy is not easy to establish. Some historians have seen Philip the Fair as a casual, idle man, obsessed alternately by religious mania and by hunting, who only took an active deciding role in the affairs of his kingdom for a few years after the disastrous battle of Courtrai in 1300, and who in 1307, following the death of his wife, passed into a new phase of withdrawal and religious self-absorption from which he never fully emerged. Others have, by contrast, represented him as the alert and responsible author of most of the policies carried out in his name. It is notoriously a futile business to try to pin down responsibilities for given acts or decisions of absolute governments of the *ancien régime*. An alternative view of Philip is that he sheltered behind his ministers, thrusting them forward to take responsibility for policies which might either fail or draw down upon the initiator the sanctions of the Church.[58] When governments carried out anticlerical policies, the popes always purported to think that the kings were misled by evil counsellors: only at the very end of the day were kings put to the ban of the Church. Even Boniface VIII, though he drew up a bull of personal excommunication against Philip, never lived to publish it.

Both king and ministers shared the view that the king was Christ's vicar, responsible directly to God for his kingdom. When heresy or apostasy threatened the people of God, it was the monarch's duty to act, brushing aside any detailed prescription of canon law which might have imposed a fatal delay. Through all royal propaganda there runs a passionate, urgent, and almost hysterical note that insists on action being taken at once. There were political reasons for this, especially the desire to throw the pope into a panic and to get his assent to royal demands. But the inflated, grandiloquent style of the French ministers was also typical of the royal chancery of an absolute ruler of the time; the same windy rhetoric can be found in Frederick II of Hohenstaufen's chancellor, Petrus de Vinea, and the rhetorical style of France, especially of southern France, was at this time especially verbose and pompous.[59] Plaisians, addressing Pope Clement V, began his discourse: 'Christ reigns, Christ conquers, Christ rules!' Nogaret, addressing King Philip, began: 'Christ is truth, and whoso denies the truth, denies Christ, and who goes back on the truth, retires from Christ, and who goes back on either Christ or the truth, is no longer faithful but profane: he leaves the way of God!' This was the rhetoric of Philip's ministers; it was not the cold and austere reasoning of lawyers, but the pious bombast of zealots. They were not only pious but superstitious zealots. Belief in demons had been implicit in the whole case brought against the dead Boniface VIII by Nogaret, as in that brought by him against Guichard the Bishop of Troyes. It is not surprising that another royal propagandist, Pierre Dubois, was a strong believer in the power of evil demons to influence human affairs.[60]

The so-called trial of the Templars was not a single legal process but a succession of legal actions which involved a fundamental conflict of law. By pre-empting papal authority and arresting and examining the Templars by lay agents, barely covering his action with the authority of the French Grand Inquisitor (who was also his own confessor), Philip IV went against the basic precepts of Church law. The pope himself entered an energetic protest. In spite of the heavy pressure he brought to bear on his subjects, even Philip was unable to make the theologians of the University of Paris agree to his right to bring final judgement against the Templars. His right to arrest suspected apostates as an emergency procedure was not contested, but the obligation to hand over the suspects for final judgement in Church courts remained. As one pamphlet of the time remarked, in the way he treated the Templars Philip behaved like a doctor who gave the patient a purge so strong that it killed him![61] Philip called several assemblies of his subjects to inform them about the awful facts of the case against the Templars: he was especially careful to get a good attendance from lesser folk. He may not have been as successful in silencing scepticism as he hoped: though the tone of some of the contemporary chroniclers is dutifully horrified, that of others, including the well-informed Geffroy de Paris, is rather neutral.[62]

No matter how effective were the powers, the courts, the propagandists, the torturers of King Philip IV, he had to face the fact that the Templars were a Catholic Order spread through most of Christendom. Without the full support of the pope he had little prospect of achieving his aims in the Templar case. The pope had been born within the French kingdom. After his election he had been too ill and too timid to take the long road from France to the city of Rome of which he was bishop; he stayed in or near the French kingdom until his death in 1314. He had been crowned on the outskirts of the kingdom at Lyons; he was to hold a General Council of the Church just outside the kingdom in Vienne, and he took up occasional residence in Avignon, a city outside France which belonged to the French dynasty of the rulers of Naples, from 1308 onwards. The physical and political timidity of Clement V, and his willingness to accept the political outlook of the French royal court, made it possible for Philip IV to view the papacy as something which could be made into the political instrument of the French monarchy. But though Clement V was weak, he was not stupid, and he was aware that some legal and theological principles could not be conceded to the French king without endangering the basis of papal power. So he temporized and delayed, conceding one point and contesting another, playing a defensive and retreating game.

It is doubtful if anything could have saved the French Templars once the first crop of heresy confessions had been harvested within a few months of the arrests. But the stakes were higher than this, in that Philip the Fair's aims could not be satisfied by the condemnation for heresy of most of the individual French Templars: his policy required the condemnation and suppression of the Order as a whole. His agents insisted on the depravity of the entire Order: even if a few Templars were not technically guilty, their consent to the horrid doings made them guilty by association. The pope agreed to attend a meeting with the whole royal court at Poitiers in May 1308, at which a very vigorous attempt was made to persuade him to accept the condemnation of the French Templars as a *fait accompli*, and to proceed to the dissolution of the whole Order. A large number of

Templars were brought before him at Poitiers to make confession of their heretical practices; some of these were among the
great men of the Order, including the Grand Master himself.
The circumstances of the meeting at Poitiers were very
unfavourable to the pope: he was confronted with a very large
gathering of the French clergy and nobles under the king. It was
not what we would call a 'summit meeting', in that king and
pope had only the briefest political conference, perhaps of only a
few minutes. But the royal ministers went out aggressively to put
the maximum of pressure on the pope, and to hint that if he
failed to act promptly and finally against the Templar Order he
would himself incur a strong suspicion of favouring and abetting
heresy. Such a threat, when made in the heart of the French
kingdom, was not an empty one.

Clement V had admitted frankly that when the first accusations against the Templars were brought to his attention he had
not believed them. But this does not mean that it was ever his
political aim to save or to protect the Templars. Clement's aim
was to vindicate the principles of Church law and of papal jurisdiction. Only a couple of months after the first arrests of the
Templars he had written round the monarchs of Europe, urging
them to arrange secretly for mass arrests of the Templars on
exactly the same principles as the arrests which had been made
by Philip in France. The Templars, when they had been
imprisoned, were to suffer heresy investigations under the
normal procedure for such trials. The interesting thing about
this letter, which was dated 22 November 1307, is that it very
closely follows the wording of the procedures actually used in the
Templar case by the French court. The same policy was in effect
followed by Clement at Poitiers seven or eight months later. He
suspended the jurisdiction of the French Grand Inquisitor in the
Templar case, thus putting the legality of the earlier proceedings
in some doubt. But this merely indicated his dissatisfaction with
the nature of the legal proceeding employed; he was willing not
only to continue with the examination of the French Templars
but to order the mass arrest and examination of other Templars
all over Christendom. Besides the question of jurisdiction,
Clement V also worried about the threat to Church property; he
wanted the Templar lands and goods to be held by the French
and other lay governments on a merely temporary basis, and

then to be returned to the Church authorities. To some extent he had his way here.

The question of the Templar trials was only one among many political issues pending between the French and papal governments. It is true that the meetings at Poitiers had their moments of dramatic climax, beginning with the confrontation between the king's orators and the pope, and ending with the appearance of the long line of confessed Templar penitents. But the period of negotiations was long, and as the summer drew on the bizarre and nightmare charges against the Templars faded into the background, forgotten among the diplomatic bickering and bureaucratic fussing. The formidable resources of the legal specialists of the papal court were put to the task of organizing the trials of thousands of Templar suspects from Scotland to Cyprus. On 12 August 1308 no fewer than 483 separate papal letters were issued on a single day, in order to effect these arrangements. All over the Catholic world, governments, bishops, and inquisitors were mobilized for the enquiries. The methods to be employed, which included interrogation under torture, were minutely specified. A separate papal commission was to be set up to look into the Templar Order as a whole, and to hear a defence if one could be made. Examinations of the leaders of the Order were to be conducted separately; a small group of cardinals began this task at Poitiers.

Given the nature of the inquisitorial process, the action taken by the pope in August 1308 was bound to be fatal to the Order. The intentions of the pope were patent from the identity of the churchmen he appointed to examine the Templar leaders and to re-examine other Templars with a view to a possible defence: all of them were closely dependent on the French government. The president of the most important commission was Gilles Aycelin, the nephew of an important royal minister and himself a royal servant who took over custody of the royal seals from Nogaret during the latter's absence. It was Aycelin who during the tense opening scenes of the meetings with the pope at Poitiers had compared the Templars to the Midianites who had perverted Israel, and had intimated to the pope in public that anyone who refrained from rooting out such heresy must share the guilt of its authors. To make such a man guardian of the Templar goods in

France and head of the commission to control the proceedings against them was like making the wolf guardian of the flock.[63]

Not very much is known of the details of the enquiries made by the French bishops under the papal instructions issued in the summer of 1308, although they were long and extensive, and were carried out with a new list of no fewer than 127 charges. The papal commission which was supposed to consider a possible defence of the Templars, a defence which the French government had previously tried to forbid, did not begin to sit until late in 1309. When it did sit it only played a terrible game of cat and mouse with the prisoners. Though supposed to be independent, the commission allowed ministers of the French Crown to enter its sessions freely when important prisoners such as the Grand Master were being examined. It also kept in close touch with the French bishops who were continuing to interrogate Templars under the procedures issued in 1308. When Jacques de Molay and other leaders of the Order were brought before the papal commission they had little to say of any importance, and all sheltered behind the declaration made by the pope in 1308 that judgement on the leaders was specially reserved to him. De Molay did, it is true, show some signs – the first in his many recorded interrogations – of indignation at the charges, and he at least implicitly denied that some were true. It was on this occasion that the two highly placed French ministers intervened, first Guillaume de Plaisians and then Guillaume de Nogaret. In Nogaret's presence de Molay asserted the orthodoxy of the Templar Order in so far as it celebrated the liturgy in a proper manner and distributed charity generously; he also alleged its proved willingness to die in battle. But he did not specifically deny any of the heresy charges: it would have been hard for him to do so, since he had on several occasions in the past admitted to some of the most important ones. When de Molay asserted his own personal religious orthodoxy de Nogaret intervened in the presence of the commissioners, and told an extraordinary story which purported to come from the chronicles, that the Templars had done homage to Saladin, and that Saladin had remarked that the Templars had met with defeat because of their addiction to the vice of sodomy and their betrayal of their faith and law. So far as modern historians can establish, this tale was a pure invention; it is not surprising that poor Jacques de Molay was 'stupefied' by it.

The whole interview was bad-tempered, grotesquely confused, and quite irrelevant to the issues at stake; this kind of evidence is very familiar to readers of the 'Watergate' case.

Eventually, in the spring of 1310, a handful of literate Templars, one of whom had formerly been their diplomatic and legal representative at the papal court, tried to organize a systematic defence. This was the only occasion during the trials when such an attempt was made; potentially the move was threatening to the French government's case, but in terms of practical politics it was doomed from the start. However, since the papal commissioners were unable to deny the theoretical possibility of such a defence being entered, they allowed the assembly of over five hundred Templars in Paris, who for a short time were outside the prisons supervised by the French Crown. There was wrangling about the number of proctors whom these men could appoint to conduct the defence; in order to expedite proceedings the papal commissioners naturally wanted only a very small number. But while this wrangling was going on the Archbishop of Sens, who was the brother of one of the chief ministers of the French Crown, held a Church provincial Council which, instead of continuing the examination of Templars under the papal bulls of 1308, suddenly proceeded to their final judgement. On 10 May 1310 it was intimated to the papal commissioners (who in any case were certainly already aware of it) that the provincial Council, which was sitting in Paris not far from the papal commission, was about to proceed to final judgement against a number of Templars as relapsed heretics. The ground for the condemnation was simply that these Templars were going back on their earlier confessions which had been obtained under duress; under Church law rules, a heretic who admitted his guilt and subsequently denied it was 'relapsed'. Since most of the intending 'defenders' of the Order had made some kind of an admission at earlier stages of the investigations, the implications of the judgement of recalcitrant Templars as 'relapsed' heretics were fatal for any kind of defence. If the papal commissioners had possessed any intention of allowing a proper defence to be entered, they would have protested firmly to the Archbishop of Sens that he was acting *ultra vires*, but they did nothing of the kind. On being asked to take action the president of the papal commission, Gilles Aycelin, left the Sunday session of the commission 'to hear mass'.

Two days later, on the actual day fixed for fifty-four of the intending defenders to be burned alive by the provincial Council, the papal commission sent a mild remonstrance to the Archbishop of Sens. At the same moment the leaders of the putative defence counsel were rearrested by the Crown, and no more was heard of them. The defence of the French Templars promptly and finally collapsed. The probability of being burned alive is a strong discouragement to a witness, especially when the alternative of staying silent offers at least the possibility of a safe and a quiet life. The fifty-four Templars condemned by the provincial council were burned alive on 12 May 1310. To the scandal of some of the spectators, a few of them had the impudence to protest their innocence as they were led to the stake.

The only complete text we have of an official set of the charges against the Templars is that of the papal decree of the summer of 1308, which is very full but differs in detail from some charges brought in other investigations. But from a variety of sources we can piece together all the main accusations. It may be presumed that the most important allegations were those that most Templars were compelled, in France, to admit. Those that they were allowed to deny may be presumed to have been thought less essential. The vital points were denial of Christ, spitting on the cross, ritual kiss on the back and navel of the brother receiving the postulant, promise to commit sodomy with the brothers or else to obtain sexual relief only from such sodomy, and worship of an idol. Many denied the last three of these charges. Individual variants were countless, e.g. micturating on the cross, ritual kiss on the anus or penis, kissing the anus of the idol. One charge sheet referred to the worship of weird women or female demons who appeared near the idol. Apart from the weird women, the most lacking in verisimilitude among the main accusations was that concerning idol-worship; for instance, the prosecution never succeeded in locating a single example of the presumed idols. But the charge, however foolish, was needed in order to show that the Templars were guilty not merely of blasphemy but of apostasy. Many Templars denied the idol, but those that did not tended to let their imaginations run riot in describing it: it was like a skull, like a reliquary, like a cat, like two or three cats, like a painting on a beam or wall, like a head of a man with a long beard. A cord was supposed to have been placed round the idol and subsequently worn near his body by the Templar. The name given to the idol, 'Baphomet' (once or twice the form Mahomet is actually used by witnesses in the trial), is one of the most persuasive pieces of evidence that the charges were concocted to 'smear' the Templars. It was impossible for the Templars to have 'picked up in the East' the practice of worshipping an idol bearing the name of the Prophet Muhammed, since no such idol existed anywhere in the Levant, even among breakaway sects such as the Ismailis or the Druse. The idea that Muslims were idolaters was itself a part of another system of 'smears', the pejorative representation of the oriental world by western Christians.[64]

In the Templar trials, as in many heresy and witchcraft trials, the fantasies which were produced by some suspects in order to satisfy the inquisitors who had placed them under torture or mental pressure were then taken up by the prosecution and elaborated into new charges against other suspects, who then produced new fantasies, and so on. Some of the elaborated charges were more overtly magical than the main ones; for example, it was alleged that the Templars thought that their idol not only enriched them as an Order, but caused the trees to flower and the plants to grow.[65] The magical pursuit of riches was one of the most ancient of all gravamina against magicians, and was prominent in the Templar trials. They were charged with failing to make proper charitable gifts (which was denied by the Grand Master and by many others), and were also accused of not holding it sinful to increase the moneys and properties of the Order by any means, licit or illicit.

There were some attempts by the more articulate Templars to rationalize the accusations, particularly the charge of renouncing and dishonouring the cross. It is possible that the investigators pursued a policy of using all means to compel the admission of those charges they thought most essential while being slightly more permissive about others. Dishonouring the cross belonged to the former category. Geoffroi de Gonneville, the Preceptor of Poitou and Aquitaine, hazarded the guess that this particular charge was introduced into the Order either by a Grand Master whom the Saracens would not release from prison on any other terms, or by a rogue Master called Roncelin (there was never a Grand Master of that name, but a Roncelin de Fos was Master of Provence and later of England), or by the perverse doctrines brought into the Order by the Grand Master Thomas Bérard. Finally, de Gonneville produced a fourth theory, that this usage may have been based on the scriptural precedent of St Peter's denying Christ three times. Yet another theory was offered by a serving brother, who claimed that the priest who absolved him from the sin after he had confessed the illicit manner of his initiation into the Order had explained it by saying that the usage had perhaps been adopted in order to warn the brothers of the temptation to renounce God in the event of their falling into the hands of the Saracens. This priest imposed on the brother concerned a penance of fasting for three Fridays on bread and water, which seems quite a light penalty for the commission of blasphemy![66] It is hard to explain these rationalizations except by the assumption that the Templars who produced them believed *other* Templars actually to have practised illicit admission ceremonies, even if they themselves had been compelled to say they had practised them when they in fact had not done so. It is clear from the expressions employed by de Gonneville – 'some say that . . .', 'others say that . . .' – that he had discussed the alleged illicit usages with fellow Templars.

Secrecy, segregation, aloofness were the great Templar weaknesses. Their most pernicious effects during the trials were that they made it hard to answer the allegations that Templar chapters were held secretly, and that individual Templars were not allowed to hold copies of the Rule, or to show it to outsiders. Both these allegations were true, and could not be denied. But they could only be held to demonstrate apostate behaviour if it could also be shown that the chapters involved illicit behaviour, or that the statutes enjoined such behaviour. The only illicit behaviour in chapter which the French Templars, under pressure or torture, would generally admit, was the illicit reception ceremony; though some, a far smaller number, admitted occasions when the 'idol' was worshipped in chapter. As to the Rule, the prosecution may be said to have failed to have made its case, because although the illicit ceremonies of reception into the Order were frequently said to be 'the point' or stipulation of the Rule of the Order, no prosecutor ever succeeded in locating or producing a Rule which prescribed the illicit acts. Nineteenth-century Templarists forged a 'Secret Rule of the Temple',[67] but no such thing was ever found in France at the time of the trials, though half the agents of the French government must have been looking for it. One of the prosecuting counsel alleged that a Templar official had told him that there was a secret Rule, but that he could not produce it. On the other hand, in the examination of one of the Templar chaplains of Mas Deu, in Roussillon, the chaplain sent a young man into the Templar house for a copy of the orthodox Rule, which he then produced in court.[68] Perhaps the last word should be left to one of the witnesses in the English trials who, when asked the reason for Templar secrecy about their chapters and Rule, replied bitterly: 'Because they were stupid!'[69]

The examinations of Templars in countries other than France produced only a very weak and inconsistent confirmation of the truth of the charges. Only in areas which were strongly under the influence of the French Crown, like the Kingdom of Naples and Lombardy, was anything obtained which remotely resembled the kind of confessions which were extorted from the Templars in France. In Germany the prosecution came to a complete standstill, and one or two archbishops even found the Templars innocent, to the pope's irritation and displeasure. Pope Clement V continually exhorted the countries which normally did not use torture as a part of their judicial procedure, such as Aragon and England, that they must use torture against the Templars; these exhortations show that the pope knew perfectly well how the confessions had been obtained. But even in Aragon, where the Templars had actually opposed armed resistance to the royal attempts to arrest them, the examinations produced hardly any self-incriminating evidence on the French pattern. In England quite a few witnesses outside the Order were found to offer some testimony of a sort against them, but it amounted to little. Three English Templars, one of whom had been recovered after escaping from custody, did offer confessions about defiling the cross on the French precedent, but considering the close links between the French and English branches of the Order, the evidence was extremely thin. The English Master persisted in denial of all the charges; he died in prison before papal judgement could be pronounced on him. In Cyprus, where the biggest concentration of Templar knights outside France was to be found, some very confused hearings ended without any definite evidence being offered against them on the more serious charges: new hearings were ordered, but if these took place they left no surviving documentary evidence.

By 1311 the long agony of the Templar Order was drawing to a close. Even if the guilt of the Order had not been clearly proved outside France, defamation and ill report were recognized by medieval men as constituting a sort of irrefutable proof in some criminal cases. In England, for example, the Templars were held to be 'so vehemently defamed that they could not purge themselves'.[70] When the head of Christendom spoke against them so clearly, and when the interrogations required them to answer the fact that the Grand Master and chief officials of the Order had publicly made confessions of guilt, some before the pope and the cardinals, there was virtually no hope of proving innocence. The burden of proof clearly lay on the defence to establish innocence, not on the prosecution to demonstrate guilt. As this could not be done, the dissolution of the Order became practically inevitable.

But the manner of the dissolution, and perhaps also the possibility of a last-minute defence of the Templars, remained open and thorny political questions. Clement V had summoned a general Church Council at Vienne, in Dauphiné (which was technically outside the boundaries of the French kingdom), for the autumn of 1311, and the question of the Templars was one of three major items on the agenda, the others being the resumption of the Crusade and the reform of the Church. At the Council the assembled Church fathers proved unexpectedly favourable to the Templars, and the idea that they should be allowed to make a defence of the Order as a whole received support which to Pope Clement and to King Philip was frustrating and infuriating. Even the pope did not possess the legal powers to pronounce final judgement on the Templars without associating himself with the assembled bishops at Vienne. Since the bishops were proving recalcitrant, the pope was driven to act alone. It may be that he would not have summoned the resolution to do so had it not been for the appearance at Vienne of Philip in person, accompanied by his brother and his three sons, as well as by a small army. The matter of the Templars was not the only one in which Clement V had failed to give Philip satisfaction. The

French Crown was also extremely displeased with Clement because of his equivocal behaviour over French interests in Italy. Philip and the French princes came to Vienne to deliver an ultimatum to Pope Clement on both these questions.[71] They arrived in Vienne on 20 March 1312, and two days later Clement held a Consistory in which he announced his decision to suppress the Order out of his own 'plenitude of power'. He made an equally abject capitulation to French policy over the Italian question, only a week later; there are few more striking demonstrations that at this period the papacy was in the last resort no more than a tool of French royal policy.

The suppression of the Templar Order was greeted sulkily by the assembled Church fathers at Vienne, who had not been allowed to say nay or yea in the matter. Like the rest of the proceedings at Vienne, it was arranged entirely to suit the convenience of the French Crown; significantly, the only thing done in the prosecution of the Crusade at Vienne was to grant yet another Church subsidy to line Philip the Fair's pocket. But hardly a soul shed even a crocodile tear over the dissolution of a Military Order which had served Christendom against the infidel for almost two centuries. The kings took a considerable interest in the disposition of Templar possessions, many of which stuck to royal fingers in one part of Christendom or another, and never reached the Hospitallers who were supposed to inherit them outside the Iberian peninsula. The remaining Templars continued to be examined for heresy if the process had not yet been completed in their case. It is probable that the majority were in the end quietly pensioned off, to lead a more or less dignified existence as best they could. In the Spanish peninsula some were allowed to enter other Military Orders.

The final act in the drama, which cannot be denied a certain significance in the question of the innocence or guilt of the Templars, took place in 1314. The four main officials of the Order, the Grand Master, Visitor, and Preceptors of Normandy and Aquitaine, were brought for final judgement before a small commission of French cardinals and ecclesiastics, which included the Archbishop of Sens who had in so timely a manner burned fifty-four Templars in May 1310. The Church Council thus convened proceeded to condemn the four men to perpetual imprisonment, assuming that this would be the end of the whole matter. But on condemnation being pronounced, the Grand Master and the Preceptor of Normandy both spoke up at last, denied all the confessions of guilt they had ever made, and asserted the truth and holiness of the Templar Order. The churchmen were much put out by this contretemps, but took no action except to hand the pair over to the French royal authorities. Philip the Fair, acting arbitrarily and with dubious legality, as he had done from the first, had them both immediately burned to death on a small island in the Seine opposite the royal gardens; the burning took place on the same day as the judgement (18 March 1314). The question of the Templars had been finally settled, so far as the French monarchy was concerned.

It is notoriously difficult to bring people to the bar of history for judgement, since this tribunal is so very hard to identify, and the accused are unable to answer in their own persons. It can be said with approximate truth that most professional academic historians in this century have more or less followed Heinrich Finke in accepting that the denial of Christ, the dishonouring of the cross, the incitement to sodomy, and the worship of an idol were not normally practised in the reception of a Templar, nor in their chapters.[72] To accept Templar innocence in this sense is not to assert that the Templars were as pure as snow, nor to assert that one, some, or all of these offences were not practised by certain Templars on certain occasions. As is the case with so many supposed acts of heresy or witchcraft of this period, we cannot say that our knowledge of the motives of those who brought the charges, or of the methods they used to exact confessions, prove that acts of heresy or witchcraft were not committed. To assume, as Barber and Cohn tend to do,[73] that the parallels between the methods used to exact confessions in the Templar trials and those used to exact confessions in some modern instances of 'totalitarian brainwashing', *prove* that the charges against the Templars were false in all respects, is to make a judgement which goes beyond the evidence. Almost certainly the Templars were orthodox Catholics within the limits which their ignorance allowed. Some contemporaries, including some of the Church fathers at the Council of Vienne, thought that they were, as an Order, innocent. It seems, however, probable that the normal initiation ceremonies for Templar candidates included some unusual practices which lent themselves to the idea of a renunciation of the faith. There may have been a custom of fooling about with the candidate, or of bullying him. There may also have been a custom of venerating, in some chapters, a reliquary or image whose meaning was not properly understood by the brothers.

There were no Templar martyrs, as has often been observed. The aim of the examination of the Templars was to obtain confessions of guilt; so far as we know, once these had been obtained no Templar was ever made to suffer capital punishment on their account unless he went back on the confession. Both the fifty four Templars burned in 1310 and the two Templar leaders burned in 1314 died while asserting their religious orthodoxy and Catholic loyalty. There was every reason of convenience for Templars under examination to admit to the charges against them; in at least some cases they were promised exemption from severe punishment. The only real reason for denying the charges was their loyalty to an Order which they presumed Catholic and orthodox. Indeed, in this respect the charges resembled those brought in pagan Rome against the early Christians: what the judges really wanted was a declaration of loyalty to a specified ideological position. Once that declaration had been conceded, the question of culpability for past error assumed a minor place. The Templar examinations (many of which cannot accurately be termed trials) differed in this from most proceedings for heresy or witchcraft of that time. Both proceedings emphasized 'reconciling' the penitent deviant, but the Templar trials placed less emphasis on punishment.

That there were no Templar martyrs suggests that there was no unorthodox Templar religion. The charges against the Templars included the accusation of disbelief in the sacrament of the Mass, but virtually no Templar admitted to the truth of this item of the indictment. The charge may be connected with the wish of the prosecution to place the slur on the Templars that they were in some way connected with the Cathar or Albigensian heresy which was still widely present in the south of France. Convincing or specific evidence that the Templars were Cathars cannot have existed, or the prosecution would have used it, as it did use the rather technical charge that the officers in chapter absolved the brothers after their confession of sin as though the officers had been priests. It seems unlikely that the Templars would have pursued a way of salvation other than that offered by the Church, when the path to their life's end which was laid down by the official Order seemed to promise just that certainty of salvation for which men craved. Perhaps, particularly after the return from the Holy Land which deprived them of the chance of a martyr's death in battle against the infidel, some Templars strayed into unorthodox ways. But the evidence of the examinations outside France suggests that if there were such men, they were only a few, and that though there may have been irregularity, there was no real heresy.

What we do know about the Templar case is that, to quote the words of the indictment, 'great scandal has been generated against the Order in the minds of important people, including those of kings and princes, and indeed among the whole Christian people'. The ruin of the Templars probably came from the most fundamental of feudal motives, the king's anger at recalcitrance or imagined disobedience on the part of his vassals. It was incomprehensible to the ruling French politicians that these rich, stiff-necked soldier–monks should stand in the path of a king chosen by God to do his divine work on earth, unless they had been enabled to do so by the help of demons. To tread on the head of this serpent was to uphold the divinely inspired social order. Greed and envy may have influenced the accusers, but in the forum of their own conscience they felt that they fought God's fight against the Devil and his works.

PART II
THE MYTH

5

THE MAKING OF
A MYTH

The trial and the dissolution of the Templar Order were bewildering to most contemporaries. That the 'false hypocrisy', the pride and avarice of one of the Religious Orders should be punished, and even terribly punished, was not unwelcome to the numerous anticlericals. The Templars were unattractive and isolated, and they had few friends, as became only too apparent. On the other hand, medieval people were less credulous than is often supposed, and many were sceptical about the truth of the bizarre allegations made against the Order. The Italians tended to suspect that the charges were false, and that the King of France had been led on to bring them by his greed for Templar possessions. This view was expressed within a few weeks of the Templar arrests by Cristiano Spinola, and was shared in varying degrees by Dante, by the Florentine chronicler Giovanni Villani, and by Boccaccio. Some French clerics reserved judgement about the Templars, and some French chroniclers were impressed by the demeanour of the Grand Master and his companion when they went to the stake in 1314, and thought that such constancy suggested innocence. Other chroniclers swallowed whole the stories of Templar guilt, and even added traditional witchcraft embroidery to their accounts of the trial.[1]

Two distinguished contemporary writers expressed opinions on the Templar case. Dante, in the Canto of the *Divine Comedy* devoted to avarice (*Purg.*, xx), made no mention of the supposed greed of the Templars but instead, through the mouth of Hugh Capet, the founder of the French royal dynasty, charged Philip the Fair with this vice. Dante says in this passage that King Philip had not been content with the brutal capture of the Vicar of Christ (Pope Boniface VIII), but that he had also 'lawlessly brought his greedy sails into the very Temple itself'. Ramon Lull, the Catalan visionary and crusading propagandist, took a much less favourable view of the Order. Lull had been a strong advocate of union between the Orders of the Temple and the Hospital, and had expected the French Crown to lead the great new Crusade to which he looked for the renewal of Christian strength in the East. Influenced by the French court, Lull abandoned his earlier convictions about the honour and good faith of the Templars, and by 1308, at the critical point of the trial, he had come to accept their guilt as proven. He referred to a 'dreadful revelation' of secret and disgraceful things whose publication threatened to 'upset St Peter's bark'. Lull was perhaps impressed by the danger that Pope Clement V might be smeared with the heresy with which the Templars were charged; he was also perhaps ready to sacrifice anything in the cause of Christian unity in the Crusade. Having accepted Templar guilt, he attended the Council of Vienne in 1312 with the idea – which never came to pass – that a new Order would be set up to incorporate 'all military religious persons'.[2] Lull's countryman, the alchemist Arnau of Vilanova, also accepted Templar culpability.

For centuries opinion about the Templar trial fluctuated rather aimlessly. Dante's implied assertion of Templar innocence was shared by his countrymen: by the historian, Villani; by the writer, Boccaccio; by the theologian, Sant'Antonino. Fifteenth-century papal historians, on the other hand, cautiously upheld the guilty verdict which had been assented to by Pope Clement V, and talked of the 'pernicious blasphemy' of the Templars. But sixteenth-century differences between the popes and the French kings left their mark on papalist opinion, and by the time of the Counter-Reformation the historians writing in Rome no longer spoke with one voice on the subject. The Dominican Chacon ('Ciaconius') broke with earlier Roman verdicts and quoted the views of the authors who ascribed the condemnation to Philip's greed and ambition.[3] It cannot be said that there was a firm 'official' papal line on the subject. German chroniclers tended to follow the national tradition of maintaining the possibility of Templar innocence. English opinion was willing to see in Templar history an example of slack and self-indulgent religious men who had been overthrown by royal decree, a popular idea in England. 'For [i.e. Because] they held no religion, but lived after [their] liking; They were destroyed and brought down through ordinance of the king.'[4]

No doubt later generations were largely indifferent to the fate of the Templars because they had failed in their historic task.

They had not defended the Holy Land very successfully, and they had ended in a sordid and disgraceful way. The honour of the Military Orders was preserved by the Order of the Hospital of St John of Jerusalem, and, for a long time, by the Spanish and German Orders. Too much discussion of the misfortunes of the Templars might have embarrassed the surviving military monks. The papacy and the French monarchy, the two institutions which had brought about the Templars' fall, remained great and powerful. There was no profit in reopening a case which had been settled by king and pope, which by the sixteenth century was only interesting in the context of the continuing conflicts of jurisdiction between popes, French kings, and 'Gallican' Church. By the eve of the Reformation it must have seemed probable that the memory of the Templars would survive only as a murky footnote to crusading history.

A momentous change in the fortunes of Templar reputation was effected by a casual remark in a Renaissance handbook of magical theory, the *De occulta philosophia* of Henry Cornelius Agrippa of Nettesheim. The change did not take place, however, for a very long time, and because of the obscurity of the chain of occult transmission it is very hard to identify in an exact way. Agrippa was the best-known of the Renaissance magical writers, and his fame has spilled over from learned to popular lore; he can be found in Marlowe's *Dr Faustus*, in Mary Wollstonecraft Shelley's *Frankenstein*, and even in *Struwwelpeter*. He was a German humanist scholar whose interests were typical of the Platonist and Cabbalistic atmosphere of his generation. He was no vulgar conjuror, but a man of wide literary knowledge and attainment, whose tract *On the vanity of the arts and sciences* set a fashion in its genre. The aim of the *De occulta philosophia*, he said, was 'to distinguish between the good and holy science of magic and the scandalous and impious practices of black magic, and to restore the former's good name'.[5] Some have maintained that he published it in order to capture the popular market: if this was so then he was brilliantly successful.

The *De occulta philosophia* was written about 1510 but not published until 1531. In the book Agrippa examines various ways in which the powers emanating from demons and spirits may be attracted and controlled. He tries to distinguish between the good and holy use of such powers, practised by pious men who have prepared themselves by religious exercises, and the abusive binding of the powers of evil demons by profane men who use this magic for selfish purposes. At the crux of the argument he makes use of the doctrine, well known to Renaissance esoteric writers, that the sympathetic transfer of power from demons into figures or images could be used with a transitive magical effect. In order to distinguish between the good and the bad users of such practices he enumerates some examples of abusive and black magicians.[6] 'It is well known', he writes, 'that evil demons can be attracted by bad and profane arts, in the manner in which Psellus relates that the Gnostic magicians used to practise, who used to carry out disgusting and foul abominations, like those formerly used in the rites of Priapus and in the service of the idol called Panor, to whom people used to sacrifice with their private parts bared. Nor were they much different, if what we read is truth and not fantasy [*fabula*], from the detestable heresy of the Templars; and similar things are known about the witches and their senile craziness in wandering into offences of this sort.'

Agrippa's style is here, as often, rather evasive. Seeking witchcraft examples, he refers to the story told in the eleventh century by Michael Psellus, the Byzantine writer, about the heretical Bogomils, which alleged that they first took part in promiscuous orgies, then executed and burned the babies born of the unions which took place there, devouring the babies' ashes in a sort of bread.[7] Agrippa goes on to talk about the custom of sacrificing naked to Priapus or Pan; but there was nothing characteristic of later witchcraft rites in either of these cults, and the only reason for citing them seems to be to emphasize the salacious nature of witchcraft. Sixteenth-century occultist writers continually harped on the parallels between the sympathies involved in magic and those of sexual attraction; in fact a lot of magical writing of the period verges on pornography.

Why Agrippa chose to drag the Templars into this company is an unsolved mystery. He had perhaps met with assertion of Templar guilt in Ramon Lull, on a part of whose work he had composed a learned commentary. But he might equally have encountered the Templars in other writers who asserted their guilt, particularly in the *Grandes Chroniques de France*, which he could have come upon while studying at the University of Paris. The idea that the Templars practised promiscuous orgies such as those of the Bogomils comes into the *Grandes Chroniques*. On the other hand, while he speaks of the 'detestable heresy' of the Templars, Agrippa is not precise or definite about its nature, and he even implies that the whole business of the charges may have been a 'fantasy'.

But in spite of the reservation which he expresses, Agrippa does place the Templars alongside the witches. By his day Europe had been hunting witches for two centuries, and the *Malleus Maleficarum*, the standard textbook of witch-finding, had been published for a generation. Everyone knew the prevalence of witchcraft accusation against old women, none better than Agrippa himself, who had successfully defended an old peasant woman from such a charge. By vaguely coupling Templars with old women who practised witchcraft, and also with pagans and heretics who carried out obscene and (in the case of the heretics) murderous rites, he produced a strong impression in the minds of his readers that the Templars and the besotted old women had all engaged in black magic. There is no evidence that he was affected by ill will against the Templars. Agrippa's intention was to minimize the social dangers of interest in magic, and in this passage he may have wanted to skim lightly over the kinds of people who might misuse magical knowledge, and to suggest that such persons were either humble and impotent, like the aged female witches, or extinct, like the Templars and the Bogomils.

Agrippa's book was probably the most widely read and influential of all Renaissance magical texts. Though not too long or difficult, it included a great deal of scarce and recondite material, and it was much sought after by the curious in these matters. By placing the Templars alongside the witches as the two chosen examples of perverted Christian magicians, he thrust their already dubious fame into a definitely magical path. Magic and the fear of magic had pervaded the Templar case, but the main overt charge had been of blasphemy. Agrippa, as is emphasized above, had been none too definite about the matter. Nonetheless, the passage was potentially lethal to Templar reputation, because in the occult world qualities are transmitted by sympathetic contagion, not established by argument. Templar proximity to the witches was going to make Agrippa's less critical readers accept the Order as wizards. On the other hand,

Renaissance indifference to the Templars meant that for a long time this passage in the *De occulta philosophia* was to attract little attention. Not until the eighteenth century were those people who were interested in magic also interested in the Templars, and the insinuation had to wait over two centuries before it came into its own.

Agrippa was not the only Renaissance writer to ascribe magical activities to the Templars. A French chronicler called Guillaume Paradin published in the mid-sixteenth century a 'Chronicle of Savoy' which also followed the *Grandes Chroniques de France* in mixing the charges against the Templars with other witchcraft fantasies.[8] According to Paradin, Templar novices were brought into a 'cave' where they were compelled to worship an image covered with human skin and having two glowing carbuncles for eyes. Here they were made to renounce Christ and to blaspheme and desecrate the cross; then the lights were extinguished in the cave and an orgy took place with the women who had been – inexplicably – admitted. If a Templar died, his ashes were made into a beverage of which the sect partook; if a child was born to a Templar from one of the illicit couplings in the cave, it was passed from hand to hand among a circle of the brethren until the new-born child died; it was then roasted, and an unguent made from its remains was used to anoint the idol. These details, together with the accusation of sodomy and the charge that the Templars had been responsible for the capture of St Louis by the Saracens, were borrowed from the *Grandes Chroniques de France*. But the original source of the supposed orgy in the cave, and of the sacrificial murder of the new-born babies, was the Byzantine chronicle of Psellus, the same passage as that cited by Agrippa. Paradin added a learned remark that these things occurred in the manner in which they had happened in ancient Rome at the ceremonies of the Bacchanals. For good measure he observed that 'to drink like a Templar' was a tavern adage which had arisen from the drunken revels of the Order.

The most rationalistic treatment of the Templars by a Renaissance writer comes from the great political theorist, Jean Bodin. He discussed the Templars in the course of an argument which became the classic early modern discussion of the powers of princes to oppress minorities unjustly. Discussing princes who seek means 'how to fill themselves with other mens' wealth and blood' he instanced the persecution of the Jews, who were the particular objects of his solicitude. He also cited the persecutions of the early Christians under the Roman Empire, and the false accusations against the Gnostic heretics. And, to cite a recent instance of similar persecutions, he remarks that these ancient examples of injustice might seem incredible were it not for the condemnation of the Templars on trumped-up charges by Philip the Fair.[9] German scholarship, according to Bodin, had decisively demonstrated the innocence of the Templars; he says that the Grand Master of the Order and his fellows had been cruelly and unjustly executed on charges which had been fabricated merely to give an excuse for the confiscation of their lands and goods. This explanation was as old as the Templar trials themselves, but the Templar case had never before been used as part of a general argument which placed it among other instances of unjust persecutions by oppressive governments. Thus Bodin put the trials into a new context which was to be revived in discussions as diverse as those concerning the French persecution of the Huguenots (carefully ignored by Bodin), the Nazi oppression of the Jews, and the Stalinist purges.

The analogy of unjust persecution uppermost in Bodin's mind was that of the Jews. Philip the Fair had been their notable enemy and oppressor, and it is not surprising that Bodin, who strongly disapproved of anti-Semitism, should have pointed to Philip's equally malicious and unfounded actions against the Templars. Of Templar reputation in matters of magic Bodin breathes not a word, in spite of his own intense interest in magic and of his firm belief in its power. Though he believed in magic, he despised and loathed Cornelius Agrippa, whom he termed the 'master sorcerer'; and if Bodin had happened to notice the stigmatizing of the Templars as possible witches in the *De occulta philosophia*, this might well have convinced him of their innocence. By coupling Gnostics with Templars as the joint victims of unjust suspicion, he implied that the hackneyed quotation from Psellus about obscene Gnostic rites was only one more example of the unfounded smearing of an unpopular group. By instancing the Roman persecution of the Christians as another case of false charges fabricated by a hostile government, he underpinned the argument by an example whose force no one was able to deny.

The combination of early Christians, Gnostics, Templars, and Jews as the prototypes of unjustly persecuted and 'smeared' minorities was a powerful one which was taken up by Voltaire in the eighteenth century, and which has most recently been used by Norman Cohn in *Europe's Inner Demons*, published in 1976. The Bacchanals of ancient Rome have sometimes been added to this list, and they make an appearance in Cohn, though Bodin on the contrary regarded their suppression as having been justified by the 'abominable villainies' committed by the sect. Bodin was not free from what would now be regarded as superstition. He wrote one of the fateful books of his century, *De la démonomanie des sorciers*, to try to prove that the witches were real, as were their powers, and that it was the duty of all good men to secure their conviction and judgement. It is strange that Bodin, one of the greatest minds of his time, who invented the set of examples which enlightened writers have since adopted to show how evil fantasies have served the political ends of warped men, should himself have subscribed wholeheartedly to the most warped and evil fantasy of them all. It has been argued that the very rigour of Bodin's logical method drove him to these extreme conclusions about witchcraft. There is – alas! – no guarantee that scrupulously logical argument will lead us to tolerant and liberal conclusions. It is interesting that the contemporary Flemish Jesuit, Del-Rio, whose work on witchcraft was a handbook for persecutors, nevertheless came to the same favourable conclusions about the Templars as did Bodin.[10]

Thus the Renaissance was capable of seeing the Templars either as wizards or as the wronged victims of political malice. Both ways of viewing them had been possible from the time of the trial. But at the end of the sixteenth century a new tone is heard as men looked back and reflected on the Templars: the tone of literary nostalgia. As Renaissance men became accustomed to the smell of gun powder they began to look back to medieval chivalry with a kind of ironic romanticism. The noble chivalry of bygone days had been a theme of the Italian poet, Ludovico Ariosto; the deeds of the 'Knight of Christ' for the liberation of the Holy Sepulchre were the subject of his successor, Torquato Tasso; just as the Red Cross Knight was the hero of Spenser's great poem. Even in Protestant England the idea of crusading chivalry had acquired a certain romantic glow, especially in the royal court. Sir George Buc, Master of the Revels for James I of England and a former student of the Middle Temple in London, found much good to say of the Templars, whose piety it had been 'to make war against all infidels, and to preserve the Holy Sepulchre of Our Lord and blessed Saviour Jesus Christ from spoil and profanation by Turks, Saracens and other barbarous and cruel miscreants'.[11] According to Buc, Pope Clement V had been pressed to dissolve the Order by his old master King Philip the Fair of France, who feared the Order because they were 'mighty in force and favour' and because he envied the 'prosperity and flourishing estate of these brave religious knights'. Buc did not believe the Templars to have been guilty of any 'foul and heinous offence'. He saw the device of two knights on one horse engraved on their seal not as an emblem of poverty but as 'an emblem of love and charity and true Ieroglyph of religious kindness and noble courtesy of soldiers', recalling to him the 'noble chivalry of knights of yore' which had been sung by Ariosto.

Nostalgic appreciation of the Templars as knightly champions of the Christian cause survived in the English court after the Restoration of 1660. Elias Ashmole, the scholar and antiquary who was among the founder-members of the Royal Society of London, wrote about Templars in his *Institutions, Laws and Ceremonies of the most noble Order of the Garter* (1672) in rather the same terms that Buc had used at the beginning of the century. He described them, with the other Military Orders, as 'the principal Columns which supported the Kingdom of Jerusalem, for a long time; and therefore their valiant encounters with the infidels, and forwardness to sacrifice their lives for the honour of God and defence of the Holy Land ought to be had in everlasting remembrance'. Giving William of Tyre a Protestant twist, Ashmole suggested that when the Templars grew rich and proud they withdrew their obedience from the Patriarch of Jerusalem and transferred it to the pope; by implication he blames their papalism for their fall. But Ashmole terms them, even after their trial, 'a noble Order, no less famous for martial achievements in the east, than their wealthy possessions in the west . . . Which gave occasion to many sober men to judge, that their wealth was their greatest crime'.

Ashmole's sentimental affection for the Templars was fitting in an antiquarian who was Windsor Herald and the historian of the Garter. He was also an experimental chemist, or an alchemist if one chooses to term him so, and he was one of the first non-craftsmen (or so-called 'non-operatives') to become a member of a Masonic lodge. He was also interested in the presumed secrets of the Rosicrucians, which bordered on those of the alchemists. But the evidence of the nature of his interest in these matters is sparse, and it is hard to say how strong were the threads in Ashmole's mind which logically connected his apparently esoteric interests. The evidence for linking his membership of Masonic groups with esotericism is persuasive but not conclusive. His interest in the Templars seems to have been confined to their chivalrous merits.

There was in Ashmole a *mélange* of 'hermetical', experimental, and antiquarian interests, which amounted to a concern with both tradition and innovation. He lived in a milieu where curiosity about 'hidden' things coexisted with curiosity about experimental science. That the Templars should have been noticed by such a man shows how easily reconcilable historical and scientific pursuits were at this time.[12] Similar attitudes can be found in the Italian Jesuit, Filippo Buonnani, who was the interpreter and editor of the earlier Jesuit 'scientist', Athanasius Kircher. Buonnani produced a best-selling compilation on the Orders of Chivalry. In this early eighteenth-century anticipation of the modern coffee-table book, the Templar is portrayed wearing an imaginary armour which makes him look like a Roman soldier; the text refers to the Templars as 'this most noble Order'.

Not all antiquaries were sentimental about the Templars. The French official historians, Pierre and Jacques Dupuy, who were in charge of the Royal Library and documents in the early seventeenth century, published under the name of Pierre (but after his death in 1651) a collection of original documents intended to justify the actions of Philip the Fair against the Templars.[13] The Dupuy brothers were part of an apparatus of political propaganda whose controller was Cardinal Richelieu, the greatest minister of the absolute monarchy in France. The aim of their studies of Philip the Fair was to prove the rights of the French crown over the 'Gallican' church; they went back to Philip as the king who had originally defended and defined these rights. The documents of the Templar trial published in 1654 under Pierre Dupuy's name were the first of its original papers to be printed. It was a very selective publication which, for example, printed only a few pages of the evidence given by the Templars before the papal commissioners.

Both the way in which Dupuy selected the documents for publication, and the manner in which he discussed them, were partisan. His confessed aim was to defend Philip the Fair from the charge of having acted out of avarice and tyranny instead of from zeal for religion and justice. He maintained – the thought is not unnatural in a royal historiographer – that the generous actions of great princes are often twisted and misrepresented by interested critics. He examined the Templar record, allowing much weight to the worst insinuations made against the Order by William of Tyre. According to Dupuy the Templars had been depraved and sunk in corruption for at least a century before their discovery and fall. His account of the trial is incomparably the fullest attempted up to that time. There is some confusion in his chronology, which he tinkered with in order to put Philip in a better light. For example, at the appropriate place in the story he passes in silence over the first examination of the Templars following their arrest. This examination is later referred to as though it had taken place later in the trial, and with papal authority. His account also plays down papal dissatisfaction with the king's conduct until it almost disappears, and the existence of other sources of tension between the king and the pope is not mentioned. Dupuy eagerly grasps at hints that the pope consented in some way to the seizure of Templar goods by the government, in order to discount the idea that the prosecution was inspired by avarice.

In spite of its strong prejudice, Dupuy's tract on the Templars is a solid piece of academic work; for a century after him no one again studied the Templar documents with such precise attention. He read the Templar examination before the papal commissioners, even if he only published a small part of it, and it is to his credit that what he did publish included the Templar defence before the commissioners, with its references to torture by royal officials. The only serious gap in his knowledge was occasioned by the papal archives not being open to him; for this reason he could not see some of the papers which became available to scholars in the nineteenth century. From Dupuy's point of view this was no great loss, since some of the papal documents, had he known them, would have pointed to weaknesses in the French government's case against the Order. As he presented them, the arguments against the Templars looked very convincing. No one seriously attempted to reply to them during the seventeenth century.

At the end of the century the great historian Étienne Baluze, who, like the Dupuy brothers, occupied a privileged position in the official French cultural establishment, gave the Templars almost as short shrift as Pierre Dupuy had given them earlier. In the classic 'Lives of the Avignonese Popes', which he edited, Baluze went out of his way to defend Philip the Fair from charges of having attacked the Templars unjustly. He acknowledged that Philip had been the author of the assault on the Templars, but, he said, Clement V's bulls make the misdeeds and outrages committed by the Order so evident as to justify King Philip's policy of abolishing it. However, Baluze gave some signs of awareness that a less abjectly royalist interpretation was possible, especially in his book on the noble house of Auvergne, in which he defends the innocence of the member of that house, the Dauphin Guy, who was supposed to have been condemned for heresy as a Templar.[14]

In the early eighteenth century new ideas began to act on educated opinion in Europe, dispelling what were thought to be the mists and miasmas of over a millennium of credulity and false belief. The Enlightenment was a movement directed towards the critical renewal of all human knowledge. Since so much existing knowledge had been filtered through the organization of the Church, the Enlightenment emphasized its rejection of those patterns of knowledge which had been affected by superstition. The orthodox clerical accounts of Church history were among the first candidates for Enlightenment revision and it was in the renewal of this branch of historical science that Voltaire and Gibbon spent much of their great energies. But the Enlightenment was far from being the simple exercise of the rational faculties which some of its protagonists liked to suggest. The transformation of ideas about the Templars during the eighteenth century shows how far from stern scientific rationalism the men of the Enlightenment could wander. In the very body of Church history which was the prime target for rationalization and de-mystification eighteenth-century men found the Templars, and turned them into a wild fantasy which for mystagogy and obfuscation equalled anything that the old Catholic histori-ography could offer. So successful was the enterprise that to this day it is impossible to approach the Templars without encoun-tering the remnants, or even the full and gaudy robes, of eighteenth-century prejudice.

Literary nostalgia was not the only reason for early modern interest in the Orders of Chivalry. All over Europe men were fascinated by the idea of noble status, and even in countries like England which lacked the clear idea of a noble caste there was plenty of interest in the rank and privilege of knighthood. Governments had a financial interest in selling various forms of knightly rank, and a political interest in absorbing parts of the newly rich bourgeoisie into an established caste which would support their institutions. In the dictionaries of chivalry which proliferated at this period we can find the showy costumes of scores of knightly orders – of the Star, of Loreto, of St George, of St Lazare and so on – which supported the political establish-ments and the treasuries of the European monarchies. Success-ful lawyers, merchants, and civil servants made their way into these orders in large numbers, as did members of the entourages of princes. Outside the immediate vicinity of people who actually hoped to enter the knightly class at some future point of their careers, many clerks and middle-rank commoners were keenly interested in chivalry and its trappings, and were willing to spend money on expensive books which informed them about the subject.[15] An especially lavish publication was the eight-volume *History of Monastic, Religious and Military Orders* (Paris, 1714–19) of the Gallicized English monk, 'Pierre Helyot', which generously discussed and illustrated the Templars. In 1721 a four-decker history of the Orders was published in Amsterdam, leaning on the work of no fewer than five recent predecessors in the same field. The publishers were sure of turning an honest penny from these books.

In this middle part of society Freemasonry appeared, and grew with explosive force.[16] The 'craft' of Freemasonry was one of the more extraordinary manifestations of the Age of Reason, typical of its time not only because it stood for rationalism, deism, and benevolence, but also because of the ambiguity which turned one side of its affairs from rationality to mystery. It was in one way an emanation of that most British of institutions, the club. It took shape during the first three decades of the eighteenth century, and reflected the tolerance and the confidence of Hanoverian England. Its ideology, founded on the metaphors of the architecture of the universe and the building of the Temple, was deist and non-confessional. The Freemason obliged himself to submit to the civil power, whose benevolent nature was assumed; this optimism was typical of British Whig self-assurance. The Mason asserted a non-clerical ethos, and a middlebrow and commonsensical attitude to life. He claimed to be instructed and enlightened, but he did not set up to be learned; this distinguished his society from those of the contemporary 'academies'. Freemasonry encouraged the sociability of the table, and the songs and music which at that time went with it, but its strong ethical bent marked it off from mere eating and drinking clubs. It was a 'mystery' in the double sense of the old-fashioned English word: a craft of life which claimed the same protection of professional secrecy which the artisan-craftsmen had vindicated for the exercise of their trades.

Inside the Masonic lodge the brothers were all, in theory, equal; only rank within the brotherhood distinguished one from another. But in spite of this apparent egalitarianism the language of social status was used within the lodges. In England Masonic usage referred to a brother as a gentleman at a period when 'gentleman' was still an appellation which was supposed to be incompatible with, for example, that of 'merchant'. In France, too, brothers were often called 'gentilhomme', which for a commoner was a similar sort of misnomer. The idea of Masonic 'knights' was not an impossible one, therefore, in a society which had proved ready to use such terms of social distinction. The whole method of Freemasonry was to use historical fancy in the service of a new idealistic symbolism, and the historical symbolism of chivalry was quite an obvious system of metaphors on which to draw, especially as the taste for knighthood was shared by many who hankered after romanticized social prestige. In this matter, as in many others, the Masonic

movement betrayed an underlying conservatism which was at
odds with its apparently modernizing ideas.

However, there was no reference to the knightly Orders in the
early English Masonic constitutions: the author of this important innovation was a Catholic Jacobite resident in France, the
Chevalier Ramsay. He was a Scotsman of humble origins who
had become the secretary and literary executor of the great
French writer and churchman, Fénelon, and who had been
created a knight in an Order with historical connections with the
Crusade, the Order of St Lazare. In 1736 he delivered a speech
to the French Masons which surveyed the aims and principles of
the young movement, and which was strongly influential on its
subsequent development in continental Europe.[17]

From its beginnings, which only shortly antedated Ramsay's
intervention in 1736, French Masonry had been patronized by
the highest aristocracy; this may have owed something to the
Jacobite Scottish peers who had been Grand Masters of some
early French lodges. The craft was supposed to have grown from
'operative' stonemasons, but in addressing a noble audience
Ramsay naturally looked for something more dignified than a
lineage of humble British artisans. So he gave Freemasonry a fictitious crusading parentage, suggesting that some medieval
Crusaders had been both stoneworkers and knightly warriors.
He also related the internationalism of Freemasonry to that of
the Crusades: 'our ancestors, the Crusaders, who had come
from all parts of Christendom to the Holy Land, wanted to
group persons from every nation in a single spiritual confraternity. . . .' The 'innocent pleasure, pleasant music, and rational
gaiety' of Masonic meetings were also – somewhat mysteriously
– ascribed to Crusader precedent, and so were the secret symbolism of Freemasons and their private codes of recognition.
Both these last had been thought suspicious in the Masons;
according to Ramsay's quaint account, the Crusaders had made
use of secret signs of recognition in case Saracens should insinu-
ate themselves into their midst with the object of cutting Christian throats!

Though it has its naïve side, Ramsay's speech does not lack
subtlety. Its main drift is to suggest that the Freemasons had
access to ancient wisdom which was partly biblical in origin, and
connected with the Old Testament patriarchs and the builders of

the Temple, but which also reflected Egyptian and Greek mysteries, and other hidden secrets of the pagan world. These ancient rites and lore had been purified and legitimized by their transmission through the Christian Crusaders. Masonic meetings were not like those of the ancient Bacchanals – no doubt he knew what a sinister precedent he was quoting – but belonged to a moral Order of high antiquity, which sought to recall sublime truths in an atmosphere of innocent social pleasure. He did not refer to the Masons of crusading times as a class of humble artisans but as 'religious and warlike princes who wished to enlighten, edify and build up the living Temples of the Most High'. The metaphorical mode of speech is especially evident at this point; the apparent literalness of his earlier reference to the Temple of Solomon has been dropped in favour of a transparent metaphor for nobility of character and aims. The Masons of the crusading era are not represented as noble or princely in a literal sense, but as exemplars of human dignity and right. It is for this reason that they are justified in preserving secrecy among themselves: the 'Saracens' whom they wish to deceive are unrighteous and unenlightened persons.

To complete his historical justification for Masonry Ramsay traces a supposed history of the lodges during the Middle Ages. Kings and princes founded lodges when they returned from the Crusade, but all these lodges died out except for those in England and Scotland, which had at first enjoyed royal protection. 'Since then Great Britain has been the seat of our Order, the guardian of our laws, and the repository of our secrets.' Thus Ramsay explained and justifed to a French audience the process by which Freemasonry had come to present itself to them with British credentials. Since France was the historic heart of the crusading ideal, Freemasonry had, as it were, come home. It was also the more justified as a movement which could be at home in a Catholic country; as a Catholic convert, the favoured friend of Fénelon and the protégé of Cardinal de Fleury, Ramsay wished to present Freemasonry to the government as an organization acceptable to the higher echelons of French society and as a possible political tool. He failed in this immediate intention, though not in his wider aim of helping to introduce Freemasonry to the ruling French nobles. He clearly timed his intervention well; perhaps both his personal success, and the boom in

French Freemasonry which followed it, can be seen as part of the wave of Anglomania which broke over the Continent in the mid-eighteenth century.

Of Templars Ramsay did not breathe a word. On the contrary, he spoke of intimacy between the Crusader Masons and the Knights of St John of Jerusalem, who were said to have been the occasion of giving the Masonic lodges the title of 'lodges of St John'. The claim fitted with Ramsay's emphasis on the knightly and noble character of the Masonic movement. There was, however, a serious objection to the notion that the Masons were intimately connected with the Knights of St John. This was simply that the Knights of St John still continued in the 'Knights of Malta', who were well able, and perhaps quite likely, to deny that such a connection had ever existed. The Templars, however, were all safely dead and were in no position to make such a denial. In this respect, as in some others, they were well fitted for the role of mystical guardians. But it is most unlikely that Ramsay thought of the Templars at the time of his speech, since he was above all anxious for the approval of the French government, and the Templars had for centuries been viewed by French governments as a banned and disgraced organization. Masonic lore could not adopt the Templars without taking a further long step, and even when this adoption did occur, it was confined to one section of the Masonic movement.

Yet, once the myth-making process had begun, and the Crusaders had been pushed to the forefront of supposed Masonic history, the temptation to 'speculative' Masons to draw the Templars into their symbolic system was great. The Temple is the centre of the whole architectural metaphor on which Freemasonry is based. It is also an important part of the idea of a chain of tradition between an earlier secret wisdom and a later one. The concept of a continuously maintained tradition of spiritual knowledge was vital to Christianity itself, and the Freemasons did not stray far from the Christian pattern of mystically revealed truth. It is true that Protestantism had introduced the idea of a possible break in the tradition, to be repaired by returning to the original sources of knowledge. But Masonry, though born in a Protestant home, harked back to the concept of a continuously guarded deposit of truth. Ramsay, a Catholic addressing Catholics, laid emphasis on the transmission of the

Masonic secret from one generation to another. The Templars could be made to appear as though they had played a part in this tradition.

Masonic taste for a picturesque medieval past, in which the stonemasons of the Gothic period had prepared the way for the polite clubmen of the Masons' own time, sprang from an attitude to the Middle Ages which was typical of the eighteenth century. This was the seed-time of the vogue for the Gothic, which by mid-century was fashionable both in the visual arts and in literature. One of the main objects of interest in the Middle Ages was chivalry. The knight had been established as the main actor of romance by Ariosto and Tasso, who were still read. But taste now called for a more realistic, naturalistic approach to Gothic manners. The factual basis for this was supplied by the *Mémoires sur l'ancienne Chevalerie* of La Curne de Sainte-Palaye (1753). The Englishman, Richard Hurd, in welcoming them, wrote that what had formerly been censured in the writings of the Middle Ages as false, incredible, and fantastic, was 'frequently but a just copy of life, and that there was more of truth and reality in their representation, than we are apt to imagine'.[18]

But the approach adopted by eighteenth-century men of letters to the Gothic style was often subtle and ambiguous, and many contemporaries, including the Freemasons, found it hard to follow. Horace Walpole's preface to the second edition of *The Castle of Otranto* explained that he had wished to reconcile the improbable marvels of medieval romance with the naturalism of the novels of his own time. He had noted, and he had found that the theologians of his period agreed with him, that even in the presence of miraculous and wondrous events people do not cease to behave according to their ordinary human characters. In saying this he was adopting the same attitude as the Renaissance Italian poet, Ariosto, whose great poem is founded on a combination of extravagant fantasy and psychological realism.

The Masonic approach to the Gothic was inspired, in part, by the literary fashions of the day. But its psychology was relatively primitive; it resembled a view of chivalry which Richard Hurd had noted and criticized in the sixteenth-century popular tales. 'For it is to be observed, that the idolizers of these romances did by them, what the votaries of Homer had done by his. As the

Templar seal (1259), (enlarged), showing two knights mounted on one horse. See pp. 3–4, 97.

Templar seal (1214), (enlarged), showing the Dome of the Rock with two round-headed portals. See pp. 3–4.

Effigies of the First and Second Earls of Pembroke, in the Templar Church, London. These nobles were not Templars, but members of Templar fraternities. See p. 11.

Burning of the Templars, from the *Chroniques de France ou de Saint Denis*. For the
hostility of the *Chroniques* to the Templars, see p. 94.

Frontispiece of an anti-Masonic work, *Les Franc-maçons Ecrasés* (Amsterdam, 1747). The engraving represents a three-storeyed building falling down, while the Master-Mason stands by in distress.

Frontispiece to Louis de Gassicourt, *Les Initiés Anciens et Modernes* (probably published in 1796). The decapitated body may be intended for Louis XVI and the scene may be one of the Masonic vengeance. See pp. 130-1.

Supposed late classical figure illustrating Hammer–Purgstall's *The Guilt of the Templars* (1855). See pp. 160–1.

Supposed late classical androgynous figures illustrating Hammer–Purgstall's
The Mystery of Baphomet Revealed (1818). See p. 141.

Engraving by Alphonse-Louis Constant ('Eliphas Lévi') of the 'Baphomet of Mendes'. See pp. 164–5.

times improved and would less bear his strange tales, they *moralized* what they could, and turn'd the rest into mysteries of *natural science*. And as this last contrivance was principally designed to cover the monstrous stories of the *pagan Gods*, so it served the lovers of Romance to palliate the no less monstrous stories of *magic and enchantments.*' Hurd quoted a preface to a sixteenth-century edition of French romances, which could easily have been taken from an eighteenth-century Masonic author: 'See, reader, the fruit which can be culled from the mystical meaning of the old tales by enlightened minds [*esprits élus*], while ordinary folk have to be content with the simple and literal meaning.' Most eighteenth-century imaginative writers rejected this metaphorical attitude to the Gothic tales as obsolete, and even mocked it as naïve. But the metaphorical interpretation was very attractive to Freemasonry, in which the old popular attitudes were combined with a tradition of esoteric metaphor which went back to the Renaissance.

On the other hand, Freemasonry was very typical of its time in its attitude to the dramatic and the playful. The eighteenth century was passionately interested in drama, which especially in the cities was an essential part of the leisure of most educated people. People were also very fond of amateur dramatics, for which the big houses of the time gave plenty of opportunity. The extravagant language of some of the Masonic rituals, the blindfoldings and the dramatic closings of the entrances, the bloodcurdling oath of secrecy, were none of them so strange to a population which spent half its life in the theatre. The lodges were the resort of a new common species produced by the Enlightenment, the sceptical ritualist. In the sociability, the music, and the symbolism of the lodges he found a world midway between play and earnest, where the ambiguity of his feelings could find an outlet. In one way the lodges were toyshops where men played out their boyish fantasies, miming dreams of nobility and rites of power. In another way they were temples where men could take the first faltering steps in a new religious attitude to life. But they were also stages for the amateur drama, where men could enact pageants which seemed portentous but were essentially playful. Mozart's *Magic Flute* is not a complete representation of the Freemasonry of his time, but its reconciliation of the serious with the playful reveals the mentality of that world.

Another comparison might be made between Masonic attitudes and the point of view of a great contemporary novel. Lawrence Sterne's *Tristram Shandy* tells at enormous length the story of the birth of a child whom his father intends to name after the ancient philosopher, Hermes Trismegistus, the supposed author of the textbooks of hidden wisdom, but to whom he ends by giving inadvertently the unwanted name of Tristram. The novel thus treats esoteric philosophy in a comic way; it does the same for the idea of chivalry. The retired soldier, Uncle Toby, like so many eighteenth-century men, experiences his dreams through a veil of ambiguous emotion which causes him to represent them playfully. In his case the dreams are of martial valour; for this reason Uncle Toby and his man Corporal Trim fill the garden with miniature siege earthworks and melt down the household fittings for toy cannon. Masonry, too, was to be filled with mock-chivalrous pageants and to use dolls to represent some of its mythical figures. It is no accident that *Tristram Shandy* was translated into German by the future Masonic Templar, Christoph Bode, an autodidact who made his name by introducing Shandyism to Germany.

The idea of a connection between knighthood and Masonry led to a transformation of the idea of Masonic 'degrees'. The original three degrees of Masonic initiatory ceremonies were those of Entered Apprentice, Fellow Craft, and Master Mason; these were taken over from the practices, assumed or real, of 'operative' stonemasons of the earlier period. Ramsay's idea of knightly Masons of the crusading period led to the introduction of new 'higher' degrees (*hautes grades*) of Masonry, which were based on the concept of Mason-Knights who advanced in esoteric knowledge. These advanced degrees were, as it were, certificated by the lodge, and each degree was assigned a precise knightly title. The suggestion by Ramsay that Masonic secrets had in some way been preserved in an especially complete manner in Scotland, during the late Gothic period, led to the advanced degrees being referred to as 'Scottish'. This preference for Scotland was largely the work of French Masons. Another way of referring to the lodges which operated the system of Scottish degrees was as 'Red' lodges, to distinguish them from the 'Blue' Masonry which restricted itself to the original three craft degrees.

The esoteric element was more prominent in the 'Red' Masonry than in the 'Blue'. But Red or Scottish Masonry can also be seen as a return to more traditional ideas of hierarchy and social order. Freemasonry had been the intrusion into the stratified society of eighteenth-century Europe of a qualified egalitarianism. The nobles who entered the craft were aware of this, in England and France at least, even if they were occasionally irritated by having to treat gardeners or dancing-masters as their equals. The old concepts of status did not die as easily as that. It is true that the commoners in the lodges were not displeased to be termed 'gentlemen', nor were the nobles on the whole displeased to mingle with them. But the Scottish higher degrees meant the implied rejection of at least a part of the ideal of egalitarianism. The higher grades involved the subordination of the lower, and also the ignorance on the part of the lower grades of the wisdom enjoyed by the higher. M. Chevalier's exposition of this development has shown how in the Parisian lodges the growth of the higher grades led eventually to a social split between the aristocratic and bourgeois elements in the membership. Masonic knighthood thus proved an ambiguous idea, which could lead in either of two directions. By its means some nobles could retain their 'knightly' status in the lodges. But some commoners could also satisfy their desire for a romanticized noble title, usually by paying for the privilege. This can be seen as a transfer to the Masonic lodges of the social situation which obtained outside them.

One disadvantage of the higher degrees was that they encroached so far into the territory of the esoteric that they encouraged spiritual leaders of all sorts, some genuine and some mere charlatans and self-styled magicians, to concern themselves with Masonic matters. The pickings could be rich, especially for those who actually controlled a lodge and charged fees for admission to the various degrees; the multiplication of grades was a source of profit for the unscrupulous. The period was in any case prolific in seers, magicians, and thaumaturgic healers, who communed with spirits, sought out buried treasures, worked at the transmutation of metals. From Hamann, the magus of the North, to Lavater and Cagliostro, the magi of the South, a great network of spiritist contacts stretched across Europe. Not that the magi co-operated with one another: far from it. They were jealous, competitive, plotting, scheming, each fearful of being overreached by the others.

Not all magi were charlatans. Behind the many-coloured veil of eighteenth-century theosophy there lay a dream, shared by many far-seeing thinkers, of restoring man to his primitive innocence and dignity through the divinely accorded vision of the true seers. It was a dream which had haunted western consciousness since the time of the philosophers of the Italian Renaissance. It was a noble dream, even if it sometimes led men towards extravagant parables which melted away into paradox and absurdity; its significance was recognized by many of the greatest men of the age, including Goethe. But this noble vision could easily degenerate into trashy fantasies, even into nightmares. The Age of Reason was also a period of runaway superstition, especially in the Germanic lands, where alchemists were as common as bakers. Many unscrupulous men used the spiritist jargon for personal gain, especially in seeking to dominate the rich and powerful. Sometimes the charlatanry of such people was patent to anyone with a clear head; sometimes, as in the case of the Italian known as 'Count Cagliostro', the deceit was too well engineered and too confusing to be penetrated easily. The new Masonic 'high grades' which were accorded to 'the chosen' were a chance for charlatans to use their imagination and ingenuity to hoodwink and fleece the Masonic brethren.

The birthplace of Templarism was Germany, where the egalitarian and rationalist thrust of Freemasonry was resisted by an old-fashioned and rank-dominated society, and there was a demand for a version of the Masonic craft acceptable to conservative doctrine and Gothic taste. During the Seven Years War a French prisoner in Germany co-operated with a German pastor who went under the name of Samuel Rosa to concoct a Templar myth to serve the ritual needs of the Masonic lodges.[19] Whether their myth was the first of its kind is uncertain, as at least three were fabricated in Germany in the years on either side of 1760. A man who went under the assumed name of George Frederick Johnson, and claimed to be a Scottish nobleman with direct access to Templar secrets, invented another. And a third whose authors are unknown, is contained in a contemporary German manuscript written in

French and entitled 'De la maçonnerie parmi les chrétiens'.

The oldest ideas behind these parables appear to derive from a twelfth-century Calabrese abbot, Joachim of Flora, who had made the acquaintance of Richard I of England. According to Joachim the history of the world is divided into a number of epochs, each distinguished by its own spiritual characteristics. The concept was adopted by the Templar mythmakers, who changed the numeration of the Joachimite eras, and claimed that the open and operational epoch of the Templars in the East was the fifth in world history, the sixth commencing with the execution of the Templar Grand Master in 1314. According to their story the Grand Masters of the Order had been in possession of special spiritual illumination deriving from the Jewish sect of the Essenes. This had passed through the control of the Canons of the Holy Sepulchre at Jerusalem, and had gone thence to the Order of the Temple. Jacques de Molay, the last Grand Master, was by these story-writers given the Masonic name of Hiram, which according to Masonic lore had been the name of the murdered builder of the Temple of Solomon.

The new Templarism thus enshrined a story of the transmission of legendary secret wisdom. It claimed that on the night before his execution Jacques de Molay sent his so-called 'nephew', the Count de Beaujeu, to the crypt in Paris where it was customary to inter the Templar Grand Masters. He went, and returned with the shroud which had been put aside for the reigning Grand Master. Contained in its capacious folds were a coffer of silver containing the secrets of the Order, the crown of the Kingdom of Jerusalem, the seven-branched candlestick of the Temple which had once been seized by the Emperor Titus, and the four golden evangelists from the Church of the Holy Sepulchre at Jerusalem!

Buried treasure figures prominently in this story. De Molay was also supposed to have told Beaujeu that the two columns which decorated the choir at the entrance to the crypt of the Grand Masters were hollow, and that they held immense sums from the treasure of the Order. These are the columns of Jackin and Boaz where the members of the first two grades of Freemasonry are required by the ritual to assemble. But the 'secret' of the Order, it is suggested, will uncover great pecuniary wealth. The more high-minded of the brothers may have interpreted the hidden gold as a symbol of heavenly wisdom, but thousands of greedier and more literal-minded persons took the allusions to point to real gold and real treasure. Magicians have always been credited with powers of uncovering hidden wealth, and such a magus as Cagliostro purported to specialize in the discovery of buried treasure. The reports that the Templars had been falsely persecuted on account of their immense wealth made people wonder if the lost Templar treasure could not be recovered. All this was grist to the charlatans' mills.

The Templar myths supposed that after the execution of the heads of the Templar Order in 1314 the hidden wisdom was carried by some surviving Templars in exile to Scotland. This belief was exploited by George Frederick Johnson, who claimed possession of the secret knowledge in right of his being 'Knight of the Great Lion of the High Order of the Lords of the Temple at Jerusalem', and 'Provost-General of the Templar Order of the Scottish Lords'.

The invention of the Templar myths amounted to a patent to create new noble titles on a huge scale. In this new theosophical nobility the Knight of the Eagle, for example, was learned in celestial knowledge, and was symbolically received in mystic Jerusalem. He was concerned with spiritual rebirth and with natural magic. Johnson and Rosa, as 'Heads' of their Orders, created elaborate hierarchies with hundreds of such knightly titles. Rosa, for example, purported to appoint seventy-two Templar 'Heads' in various parts of the world under nine 'Knights of God'. This may sound very childish, but the concept of subordination and obedience in a secret society fascinated many men, and led them to accept the most foolish and absurd titles and duties. To Rosa and Johnson the fees for grades, banquets, and admissions in the new Templar lodges represented a rich income. To maintain their prestige they told boastful lies: Johnson told his followers that the British had shot their Admiral Byng only on the orders of the Templars, who were the real commanders of the British Mediterranean fleet! In this credulous atmosphere Templarism was born; it does not seem too severe a judgement to say that it was a belief manufactured by charlatans for their dupes.

The new Templarists did Freemasonry a very doubtful

service through the part they played in the elaboration of the so-called 'grades of vengeance'. The idea of vengeance to be exacted for a wronged and murdered magus was embedded in orthodox Masonic lore in the form of the myth of the murder of the Temple-builder, Hiram, and of the despatch by Solomon of chosen masters to avenge his death. There was originally no particular political context for this supposed murder and its atonement, though the paraphernalia of swords, skeletons, and decapitated dolls which was used in some lodges to represent the events was already alarming enough. But if the murder of Hiram was to be identified in some way with the murder of the Templar Master Jacques de Molay by Philip the Fair of France, then there was a political context for the Masonic myth. This had its dangers. If Clement V, Philip the Fair, and 'Noffodei' (the renegade Templar supposed by the legend to have betrayed the Order to the French king) were, as some Masonic rituals said, the 'three abominables', then some people might think the consequences of the betrayal to be still applicable during the eighteenth century, bizarre as the idea may now seem to us. It had been thought for centuries that the credit of the French monarchy was bound up with the justice of the charges brought by Philip the Fair against the Order; Dupuy's book bears witness to this. If it became widely believed that the charges had been inspired by royal greed, the prestige of the modern French monarchy was somewhat diminished;[20] if it was thought that a modern secret society was pledged to avenge this ancient act of injustice, then the modern French monarchy might be considered to be actually threatened.

The idea of the Masonic 'grades of vengeance' was that certain enlightened persons, each step in enlightenment being the object of a 'grade', were formally committed to avenge the sacrilegious murder of the Temple-builder, Hiram. The thirtieth grade, for example, was that of the 'Knight Kadosch', who played at being the medieval Justiciar or Chief Justice. If Hiram was to be identified with Jacques de Molay, certain Masonic Templar knights could be regarded as pledged to revenge the Order on the French monarchy. The whole thing suggested political meddling, and the deliberate acceptance on the part of the Masons of a pernicious Templar inheritance. Freemasonry had already incurred suspicion on account of its secretive ways, and governments and police had looked at it with a chilly eye, in spite of its highly placed membership. It could ill afford to give additional grounds for disquiet.

6

THE SECRET SOCIETIES

The course of this story may be mildly surprising to those who had supposed the eighteenth century to have been the Age of Reason. The 'Illuminist' trend of this period has been severely judged by its French historian A. Viatte: 'Rather than obey the dictates of the real, and adjust himself to his reduced limits, late eighteenth-century man took refuge among phantoms; satisfying his nostalgia with the marvels offered by impostors and necromancers, he fled matter and denied its existence. . . . A whole culture was collapsing.'[21] The psychology of this flight towards supposedly hidden knowledge, and of the perpetual struggle to seek protection against the unknown, was analysed at the time by David Hume in his *Natural History of Religion*:

We are placed in this world, as in a great theatre, where the sources and causes of every event are entirely concealed from us; nor have we either sufficient wisdom to foresee, or power to prevent those ills, with which we are continually threatened. We hang in perpetual suspense between life and death, health and sickness, plenty and want; which are distributed among the human species by secret and unknown causes, whose operation is oft unexpected, and always unaccountable. These *unknown causes*, then, become the constant object of our hopes and fears; and while the passions are kept in perpetual alarm by an anxious expectation of the events, the imagination is equally employed in forming ideas of those powers, on which we have so entire a dependence.

It would be hard to define more shrewdly the mentality which herded the 'Templars' into their lodges. Hume understood only too well the forces of unreason which pressed upon his age.

The great sociologist Max Weber, seeking to describe in a single phrase the decay of the ancient theories of the universe under the corrosive influence of post-Newtonian 'scientific' thought, used the expression *Entzauberung der Welt*, which he is said to have taken from Friedrich Schiller. The phrase means literally 'disenchantment of the world', and it may perhaps also refer to a famous Dutch book of the end of the seventeenth century which attacked the ideas of magic and the persecution of its supposed practitioners, under the title of 'The World Enchanted' (Balthasar Bekker, *De betoverte Wereld*, 1691). A rather expressive free translation of Weber's phrase was used recently by Albert Hirschman, 'the progressive disintegration of the magical vision of the world'.[22] But, as has been argued above, the disintegration of this vision during the Enlightenment period was only partial. Hermeticism in the sense of an interpretation of the universe based on occult premises had been a widely accepted part of Renaissance intellectual life, as Miss Frances Yates has been at pains to emphasize in numerous books. The Newtonian mechanistic view of natural philosophy tended to drive the old 'sciences' such as alchemy into disrepute, though Newton himself practised alchemy and may indeed have died of doing so. The way in which Newton's philosophy appeared to split the universe up into discrete units which were causally connected, so that it became a sort of machine, was distasteful to many eighteenth-century men; they still hankered after the ancient idea of 'the soul of the world' (*anima mundi*), in which nature was a kind of vital, organic whole. Natural philosophy or 'science' was no longer able to maintain this view of the world seriously, but in the world of the imagination the old ideas were still very much alive, both in theosophy and in the literary movement loosely known as 'Pre-Romantic'.[23]

It is not surprising that 'Templarism' obtained such a striking success in a milieu in which ideas of this sort were powerful. The Templar movement, like the rest of 'Scottish' Masonry, was more extravagant in spirit than the sober 'Blue' British Masonry of its origins; though this did not stop Templarism from being exported back to the Anglo-Saxon world. There were Templarist lodges in the United States by 1769, and in England by 1778.[24] The German Masonic Templars were led by men who tended towards aristocratic exclusiveness and fanatical mystery-mongering. They fell into the sphere of political influence of the German hereditary princes. They were deeply affected by alchemical and occult practices, and the hope of acquiring material gain from the transmutation of metals was a big factor in their recruitment. In the half-light of German theosophical circles the distinction between the traditional forms of esoteric science pursued by such groups as the so-called Rosicrucians and the supposedly more rationalistic Masonic 'Enlightenment' was easily lost to view. The question of disciplining the exuberant growth of the Masonic lodges, and of controlling their membership, was also approached differently in Germany than in France.

The most successful organizer of German Templarism, who came for a time close to controlling the whole apparatus of German Freemasonry, was Karl Gotthelf von Hund, a substantial landowner in north-east Electoral Saxony.[25] Hund was very different from the self-seeking charlatans such as Johnson and Rosa; he was much more of a self-deluded fanatic, said to have gone through life almost like a sleepwalker. He had begun his Masonic studies in France, and at about the same time as the invention of the other Templar myths he had produced his own. As a young man he was converted to Catholicism, a not infrequent occurrence among the Romantic ritualists. But Catholicism proved only a phase; once he had discovered or invented Templarism he spent the rest of his life, and a great part of his fortune, on propagating and organizing it. When he died in 1776 he was buried in the costume which he had invented for the Provincial Grand Master of the Order.

Like many theosophists of his time, Hund was passionately anxious to make what was in fact a loosely connected series of parables into something which could be described as a 'system'. This meant embroidering the Templar fairy story with even more imaginary details, such as the 'discovery' that Templar nobles called Aumont and the Wildgraf of Salm had, after the dissolution of the Order and the execution of its leaders, brought the secret doctrines to the Isle of Mull! But Hund's real gift was for organization, and his success in disciplining the growth of the lodges explains the great prestige he acquired. There were supposed to be nine Templar 'Provinces', of which two were German. Each province had a Master and a Supreme Moderator; among the brothers there were at first six and then seven 'grades', of which the highest was 'Eques professus', a 'professed knight'. Entry to the lodges was restricted to nobles and to commoners of 'suitable status'; it seems that in many lodges nobles were very much in the majority. At the summit of Hund's organization stood an authority which could never be identified, that of the 'Unknown Superiors'. To these mysterious and in fact non-existent persons Hund demanded complete and unquestioning obedience, especially as regards the delivery of scientific information about alchemical operations. Hund appears genuinely to have believed that the Young Pretender was the Unknown Head of his Order, and thought, erroneously, that he had met him when he had himself been 'professed' or initiated in France. In fact, so far as is known, the Young Pretender was unaware of Hund's existence, and the Comte de Clermont in France, to whom Hund also professed obedience, seems to have paid no more attention to him.

The attractions of Hund's Templarism did not lie entirely in the thirst for divine knowledge. His organization acted as a big clearing house for information about alchemical research, which included research into panaceas and elixirs of life as well as into the transmutation of metals. Bohemia had always been a great centre of curiosity about alchemy and similar matters; it was a Bohemian lodge which apparently sent to Jena, and then to Hund personally, a phial containing 'Elixir'. Hund sent it on for examination to a doctor (who was also a Templar knight) in Hamburg; the doctor very sensibly refused to try it on his patients, suggesting that he begin by administering it to animals; after this no more is heard of it. But other worldly hopes besides those of elixirs and transmuted gold attached themselves to Hund's Templarism. The hope of finding and enjoying the lost Templar treasure, the fabled riches which had been hidden from the prying hands of Philip the Fair, began to be mentioned as a practical possibility. The estates of the Templars had been conferred after the dissolution of the Order upon the Order of St John of Jerusalem, whose successors, the Knights of Malta, still enjoyed some of the remaining incomes. Perhaps the modern Templars could establish title to these revenues? It was a thin hope, but some thought it worth pursuing. Finally, there was the very concrete question of the revenues of the New Templar Order from admissions and promotions to masterships and 'knighthoods'. After Hund experienced difficulties in funding the lodges from his own revenues, a lieutenant produced an 'Economic Plan' for the Order, which promised to provide all the administrators of the Order with a lifelong revenue based on a tontine or chain principle, and funded from the fees for admission to the degrees of apprentice, novice, master, and knight.

The scheme met with the usual failure of such schemes, but for a time it may have added to the material advantages which Hund's credulous customers expected to gain.

Hund's passionate commitment to the revived 'Order', which he termed the 'Strict Observance', and his secure position as a nobleman, meant that he had little to fear from the competition of Johnson and Rosa, the sponsors of the rival Templar 'systems'. Rosa was cleared out of the way at an early stage after his conspicuous failure in a kind of magicians' duel with Johnson. Johnson was a skilful impresario, whose hold over the North-German nobles was such that Hund was at first willing to treat him as an ally. Johnson asserted, too, his knowledge of a great secret which Hund did not possess. In 1764 a meeting between the two Templar chiefs and their followings was arranged at the castle of Altenberga, in Thuringia. Johnson's troops, clad in armour, occupied and patrolled the castle in view of a supposed threat of attack by Frederick II of Prussia; though it is doubtful if their equipment would have been of much use to them against the Prussian army! When Hund arrived, also in full Templar harness, there was an exchange of medieval courtesies, and Johnson swore feudal homage to Hund on behalf of himself and his men. Hund then waited in vain for Johnson to unveil his great secret. After a few days it became apparent that Johnson had no secret to reveal, and Hund, unmindful of the parallel between Johnson's 'secret' and his own 'Unknown Superiors', denounced the 'Prior-General' and 'Knight of the Great Lion' as a trickster. Johnson had no stomach to fight the matter out, and the opportunity for a medieval battle in Enlightenment Germany was lost when he fled. Usually the charlatans who deceived eminent nobles with superstitious stories escaped punishment, because of the fear that they would make their prosecutors look ridiculous. But Hund's exceptionally good organization, which perhaps in Britain today would be called an 'old-boy network', had the better of Johnson. When the man was arrested a year later, Hund's influence obtained his indefinite imprisonment without trial in the Wartburg fortress, where the unfortunate fellow died in 1775.

For a time following the so-called 'Convent' or, rather, conference at Altenberga, Hund's 'Strict Templar Observance' dominated German Masonry, and he was courted by the princes who hoped to obtain transmuted gold and political influence. But magicians are competitive persons, and it was not long before a new star rose in the Templar firmament. Johann August Starck was the son of a Protestant pastor of Schwerin (Mecklenburg).[26] He was an able scholar who studied, perhaps not too profoundly, oriental languages at Göttingen. Here he was initiated into Templarist Masonry and met Masons with connections in Italy and Russia, notably the medallist Natter, and a Greek who went under the name of Count Melesino. With the help of this group he obtained a teaching appointment in St Petersburg. In 1766 he went to Paris in pursuit of oriental and Masonic secret lore, and appears, like Hund, to have been received as a Roman Catholic convert. As with Hund, the stimulus to conversion seems to have been Romantic ritualism and the search for quasi-Catholic 'Templar' rites, though with Starck there was perhaps a further inducement that Catholic priests who were Masons might show him 'secret' books. The conversion was to be an embarrassment to Starck, who later became a Protestant pastor.

On his return to Germany Starck turned with great energy to the setting up of a new 'Templar' rite, this time not of Templar knights but of Templar 'clerks'. The historical basis of the new Order was the citation of a passage in William of Tyre in order to suggest that there had existed alongside the Templars an organization of Canons or Clerks of the Temple; the inspiration for this was probably the Rosicrucian notion of a body of the crusading period called the Canons of the Holy Sepulchre, which had been (of course) in possession of secret knowledge transmitted by the Essenes. The most important fictitious element in Starck's version of the Templar clerks was the assertion that in the Middle Ages they had possessed a corporate existence separate from that of the Templar Order. The claim was mistaken, as in reality the Templar priests had been entirely subject to the Templar Masters. Starck's new 'clerical' Order reflected the split between noblemen and commoners in eighteenth-century Freemasonry; while he knew that financially and politically he could not do without noble support, Starck wanted a way to imply that chivalry was outdated and that its revival was socially absurd. It seems a pity that he could not have found a less tortuous and elaborate means of expressing this simple truth; one way of directing German Masonry towards a less caste-bound path would have been to return to the original, comparatively simple, 'Blue' Masonry. But the men of his time were too deeply committed to the search for the mysterious and the marvellous to turn back easily to the rationalism to which they paid lip-service. Instead of simplifying Templar doctrine, Starck embarked on a career of mystification which rivalled those of Johnson and Hund.

Starck's main conviction was that the sources of occult knowledge were to be found in the East, particularly in Persia, Assyria, and Egypt. This idea was drawn from the Renaissance occultists. It was also a generally distributed notion throughout the late eighteenth-century world, reflected in the graphic works of the Italian artist, Giambattista Piranesi, and in the Egyptian vogue of the Neo-Classicist style. It was not to be long before Cagliostro founded 'Egyptian Masonry'. Starck claimed that the Renaissance occultist Henry Cornelius Agrippa of Nettesheim had been a 'Clerk of the Temple'. There is little doubt that Starck was acquainted with the passage in Agrippa which denounces the Templars as wizards. His Templar ritual heavily emphasized the magical elements which he thought he could find in the Templars. Starck was apparently the first person to pick out the 'Baphomet' accusation, the charge that the Templars had worshipped a magical image of this name, and to imply clearly both that the charge was true and that the magical properties of the image could be repeated in modern practice. In the ceremony which he designed for the 'consecration' of a 'Canon of the Temple', the altar was occupied by the Bible and an object identified as a 'Baphomet', placed before seven candlesticks of which only three were lit. In spite of the superficially Christian nature of the ceremony, which included readings from the Old and New Testaments, the exorcism of the water, and anointment of the candidate with holy oil, it ended by the new canon's touching the 'Baphomet' on the altar, presumably in order to acquire some of its magical properties. It is the first suggestion that Templarism could be associated with something which looks suspiciously like Satanism.

Starck's claims that he had found the secret information for his new Order in the 'Province of Auvergne' in France, and in a

Templar chapter in Russia, had the right kind of exotic ring to make it sound acceptable to the German nobles, whose appetite for pompous and high-sounding gibberish seems to have been inexhaustible. Starck enjoyed the advantage of being a competent, if not a great, scholar, whereas the intellectual level of his magical and Masonic competitors was low. He found no difficulty in getting noble recruits for the new Order. It is pleasing to remember the support he had from a Swedish officer whose knightly title was 'Eques ab Hippopotamo'. Like the rest of the founders of 'Orders', he devoted a lot of energy to finding robes and costumes acceptable to his clients; his 'brothers' wore a violet robe resembling that of a Catholic secular priest, with a red collar, and the Canons wore a white robe of ground length with a Red Cross on the breast; they also wore a biretta of purple velvet.

Starck's new Order flourished. He was not, however, a fly-by-night charlatan who aimed to pluck his victims and to disappear, nor was he a credulous fanatic of the type of Hund. Starck seems to have been a serious and learned man who was willing to use Masonry in order to further his own academic and ecclesiastical career. He acquired academic posts in East Prussia, first at Königsberg and then at Mitau in Kurland. And although Starck's Order had gained adherents, the high tide of Templarism in Germany was beginning to ebb. The 'Swedish system', which grew partly because Gustav III of Sweden suffered from the illusion that Charles Edward Stuart controlled Templar Freemasonry, presented itself as a competitor in the Baltic Provinces. In 1772 there was a Templar conference, or 'Convent', at Kohlow in Prussia, at which the already existing arrangement between Hund's 'Strict Observance' and the 'Templar Canons' of Starck was recognized. But the more significant issue of the Convent was the enforced retirement of Hund to an honorary position in the Order, and the recognition by the brothers of the Order that Hund's 'Unknown Superiors' could not be traced, and were perhaps not worth looking for further.

German Templarism had always depended on the favour of the princes. At Kohlow in 1772 the Duke of Brunswick accepted the title of 'Great Superior' of the Order, and at Wiesbaden, four years later, he called a further 'Convent' which marks the end of the Order as conceived by Hund, who died a few months later. Starck saw that the hour had come for him to slide into another professorial position. When Carl von Mecklenburg-Strelitz approached him about a possible alliance of the North-German Masonic princes, Starck used this entry into the highest princely councils to secure himself a post as Court Preacher to Carl's brother, George Duke of Mecklenburg-Strelitz. In 1780 Starck went to Darmstadt to occupy this office, which he continued to hold for the rest of a controversial career. So the Strict Templar Observance began to fade in an atmosphere of princely manoeuvre and clerical jobbery. It continued to attract bold charlatans such as 'Gugumos', who had led German nobles by their noses in a costly voyage through France and Italy to seek the Unknown Superiors, or Schrepfer, who was flogged by his disappointed patrons and ended his life with a squalid suicide.

How is all this ill-directed activity to be judged? Starck himself pointed out some of the weaknesses of the anachronistic approach to life of Templarism and of the rest of Masonic neo-chivalry. 'What is the use of Masonry', he asked, 'if it is nothing but a continuation of medieval chivalry? If that is so, it becomes a purposeless, laughable institution. A knight in all his panoply was well enough in the dark and barbarous medieval times in which he served some purpose, but in our day he is simply ludicrous. If he goes out in public he is a figure of masquerade whose appearance draws the children into the streets, and the more gravely he manoeuvres his lance, the more they mock him! If anyone plays the knightly role in solitude, he shows himself to be mentally unbalanced. The whole nature of the world has changed, and to connect the old chivalry with Freemasonry is to think in a way which is no longer consonant with our times: it is like sending a Roman legion out into the modern world.'[27] It is a pity that these sensible sentiments did not occur to Starck rather earlier!

The strange episode of Starck's Templar Clerks shows how difficult it was even for a highly intelligent and learned man to place the theosophical parables in a proper perspective. Starck certainly had an eye to his own personal advantage, but it is doubtful if he invented his new Order simply for the sake of profit and advancement. He belonged to a generation which

wished to understand reality only through esoteric poetic metaphor. When we think of the conviction of Johan Georg Hamann,
the 'magus of the north', that he could come to a complete
understanding of the language of God, or of the insistence of
Novalis, the poet of mysteries, on 'riddles and metaphors' as the
only language he wanted to use, the way in which Starck accepted some of these extraordinary Templar stories and invented
others becomes more intelligible.

The Strict Templar Observance was not at its last gasp when
the Duke of Brunswick became its 'Superior', even if it was
becoming a little short of air. It still made converts in Italy and
Switzerland, and in France its doctrines were taken up by the
mystical brothers of the 'Élus Coëns' at Lyons. Brunswick sent
Baron Wächter on an expensive mission to Italy in search of the
Unknown Superiors.[28] In Florence Wächter obtained an interview with Charles Edward Stuart, who formally denied any
earlier knowledge of the movement. Unwilling to return empty-
handed, Wächter came back with some cock-and-bull stories
about Initiates who had conjured up horrid spirits in his
presence, and had intimated to him that the Unknown Superiors
were connected with the seven monks who worked in one of the
seven caves beneath a monastery in the Tuscan countryside.
These necromantic revelations were more probably due to
Tuscan wine than to the 'Spirits'. But they proved irrelevant to
the Order. The war of pamphlets which broke out when the
Clerks of the Temple separated from the Strict Observance
revealed publicly how threadbare and tawdry were the credentials of the latter. The Masonic groups continued to fragment; in
Lyons Willermoz and his disciples used a few elements of the
Templar theme to set up the 'Chevaliers Bienfaisants de la Cité
Sainte'.

Ferdinand of Brunswick and Carl of Hessen were aristocratic
dilettanti who lacked the fanatic conviction of Hund. Brunswick
showed his doubts about the Order by circulating a kind of questionnaire round the lodges. When this reached the lodge in
Chambéry it attracted a reply from no less than the young
Joseph de Maistre, the future conservative theorist. He replied
that the destruction of the Templars in 1312 had been of little
import to the world: 'Fanaticism created them; avarice

destroyed them; that is all there was to it.' In 1782 Brunswick decided to solve his doubts by holding a final Conference or Convent of the Order at Wilhelmsbad, near Hanau in Hessen. True to its aristocratic origins, the last gathering of the Strict Observance was a blue-blooded affair. But disillusion and decay were patent. The successively unveiled mysteries of the Order had yielded nothing but boring ritual; the alchemists had made no discoveries; the Templar lands would never be returned. No one expected to identify the long-concealed Unknown Superiors. The thirst for mystical illumination remained, but hope of quenching it at the Templar spring was over. The meeting decided that it was unproven that the Strict Observance was the legitimate successor of the medieval Templar Order, and it also decided to preserve the memory of the Templar knights in Masonry only in a very restricted way. The main thesis of occult continuity was thus abandoned.

At Wilhelmsbad various Masonic groups bid for recruits among the disbanding Templars. The mystical lodges of Lyons, led by Willermoz, gained much support. But beneath the surface the 'Bavarian Illuminati' were also secretly working to recruit new adherents. This quasi-Masonic association, soon to become notorious, was controlled by Adam Weishaupt, a professor at the University of Ingolstadt. He was a rationalist reformer with an ambitious plan for the modernization of German society. This he proposed to bring about by utilizing the secrecy and the social discipline of the Masonic lodges. By recruiting his own secret order he proposed to instruct and control an obedient body of enlightened adepts. What especially appealed to him in Masonic organization in Germany was the existence of defined grades of illumination, and the doctrine of obedience to unknown superior authorities. Weishaupt recruited a number of men who occupied responsible positions within and without the governments. His organization was perhaps a potential danger to conservative German society but it never became an actual one, as it never got out of the stage of ideological indoctrination and into that of political action. Whether Weishaupt possessed either the will or the political ability to make his society into a real revolutionary force is a question which cannot now be answered.[29] An enormous amount of rubbish has been written about the Illuminati of

Bavaria, from the time of their suppression down to our own day. Weishaupt certainly wanted to change the world, and he placed an emphasis on secrecy, on obedience, and on interrogation and inquisition of inferiors, which smacks of seminary tyranny. In making political use of Masonic secrecy he was only following the lead of the conservative German princes, and trying to turn their example to the profit of the radicals. It was all in vain; there was too much of the schoolmaster about Weishaupt, too little of the politician. When the Bavarian government became alarmed about the Illuminati in 1784–5 it identified and suppressed them without the slightest trouble.

There was no direct continuity between the Strict Templar Observance and the Bavarian Illuminati at all. The spirit and purpose of each were entirely different, even entirely opposite, to those of the other. The aristocratic mumbo-jumbo of the Templar lodges pandered to the confused conservatism of the German nobles and had a great deal in common with the mumbo-jumbo of the Rosicrucians, to whose ideas the Illuminati were absolutely opposed. The Bavarian Illuminati were an austere emanation of the spirit of the German professorate, inspired by a consciously bourgeois programme, irreligious and radical. It is true that several quite important persons were connected with both the Strict Observance and the Illuminati, notably the enigmatic and important Adolph von Knigge, who was prominent in the Illuminati interest at the Convent of Wilhelmsbad. Another such ally was the talented littérateur, Christoph Bode. But in the confusion of ideas at this period men moved from one Illuminist group to another in Germany with little clear notion of the ideologies which were involved, even when the men concerned were as clever and articulate as Knigge and Bode.

The suppression of the Illuminati of Bavaria in 1785 created a tremendous furore whose echoes reached as far as New England, drawing George Washington out in support of the suspect American Freemasons. In fact the Illuminati proved to be the unwilling occasion for the birth of modern conspiracy theory. Wildly exaggerated accounts of their supposed wickedness and of the imminent peril which they represented for society were published in a great epidemic of pamphlets. Their secrecy, their insistence on recruitment of important civil servants, their con-

cealment of the true aims of the society from all but a few highly
placed initiates, combined to make them into the bogeymen not
only of the German conservatives but of a wider European
public. Four years later, when the French Revolution broke out,
the mythical beliefs about the Illuminati of Bavaria were incorporated in a vaster and wilder conspiracy theory, which found
room also for the Templars.

Voltaire's contribution to conspiracy theory was, typically
enough, his denunciation of various cruel persecutions or 'proscriptions' of presumed guilty plotters as 'conspiracies against
the people'.[30] To Voltaire the 'conspiracy' lay in the cruelty of a
government which resorted to unnecessary and illegal atrocities
in order to exterminate supposed political enemies. The term
'proscription' he borrowed from the proscription of political
enemies in Roman history, first practised by Sulla in 81 BC. As
examples of such proscriptions he takes the massacres of Jews
carried out under divine instructions in the Old Testament; the
persecution of the Jews (but not that of the Christians) under
Trajan; the Manichaean purge under the Byzantines; the
pogroms against the Jews by the Crusaders; the Albigensian
Crusade; the Spanish massacres of pagans in the New World;
various oppressions of French Protestants; and the trial of the
Templars by Philip the Fair.

The burden of the charge which Voltaire brings against these
governments is unnecessary cruelty. There is a certain unsteadi-
ness in his approach to the subject; at one point he asks rhetori-
cally: 'Have I written the history of snakes and tigers in this
essay, or that of men?' But he also, apparently unaware of how
selective he has been in his choice of examples, suggests that this
kind of persecution is very unusual in human history, and that
there is real hope that the softening of human customs by
enlightened philosophy will make such atrocities obsolete. Of
the Templars he complains that the persecution was carried out
with the appearance of judicial process, though really it was a
premeditated scheme to exterminate an Order which had sinned
by being too proud and too rich. Voltaire refused to believe that
a Grand Master and a distinguished body of knights which
counted princes among their number could really have committed the foolish and base acts with which they were charged. He

doubted whether such an Order, which had fought in Asia for Christianity, and died in Muslim prisons rather than renounce the Christian faith, would have behaved in the way their accusers claimed. Their alleged worship of a pagan image he rejected as self-evidently false. Nor would the Templars who were burned have died protesting their innocence, had their claim not been well founded. His reading of the evidence was that the persecution of the Templars was due to 'the evil effects of a period of ignorance and barbarism'. This calm and serene interpretation of the Templar case did not survive the French Revolution.

Conservatives who reflected on the course of the French Revolution were much struck by the way in which moderate men had been led where they had no wish to go. The English political thinker, Burke, wrote: 'Men have sometimes been led by degrees, sometimes hurried, into things of which, if they could have seen the whole together, they would never have permitted the most remote approach.' These things had not taken place in some distant and dimly understood despotism, but in a country which the rest of Europe had admired and imitated. For a monster to be engendered by such a close relation, hidden powers must have been at work; a conspiracy must have secretly acted as the illegitimate begetter. Conspiracy theory was bound to become a propagandist weapon in the armouries of the post-Revolution conservatives, and in the growth of this theory the Templars played an unexpectedly prominent part. Voltaire had dealt with the Templars as an instance of conspiracy by the government against the people; the conservatives decided that the Masonic Templars were part-authors of a conspiracy of the people against the government.

The biggest error of the new Templars had been to hold the Wilhelmsbad Convent, which was the most-publicized Masonic meeting of the century. At the Convent itself the assembled brothers recognized that the Templar myth might bring them under political suspicion. The claim of continuity with the medieval Templars was admitted to be 'potentially dangerous in that it might cause mistrust of Masons among the governments; in any case it was out of tune with modern customs and opinions'.[31] These fears had been amply confirmed two years

later, when the scandal of the Bavarian Illuminati broke. Some
of the most notorious of the Illuminati brothers had been former
Strict Observance Templars, and this proved fatal to Templarist
reputation. From the seizure of Illuminati papers by the
Bavarian government, and the accompanying pamphlet wars of
Masons and ex-Masons, a cloud of spurious information was
released which could be used to prove almost any allegation,
however absurd, about the relationship between the two Orders.

The ex-head of the Order of Templar Clerks, Johann August
Starck, was well acquainted with the impostures and cheats of
the Strict Observance from the part he himself had played in
them. He exposed them in a bitterly satirical, anti-Masonic
novel, St Niçaise. Starck's line of argument was that the Masonic
Templars had acted as a kind of front or cover for the real political agitators among the Illuminati. The medieval fog which
surrounded the Templars led to wild theorizing, especially in
this period when the German intellectuals were looking for the
origins of modern beliefs and societies in early myth and religion. The German Masonic bookseller, Friedrich Nicolai, produced an idea that the Templar Masons, through the medieval
Templars, were the eventual heirs of an heretical doctrine which
originated with the early Gnostics. He supported this belief by a
farrago of learned references to the writings of early Fathers of
the Church on heresy, and by impressive-looking citations from
the Syriac.[32] Nicolai based his theory on false etymology and
wild surmise, but it was destined to be very influential. He was
also most probably familiar with Henry Cornelius Agrippa's
claim, made in the early sixteenth century, that the medieval
Templars had been wizards. Nicolai and Starck must between
them bear the main responsibility for the modern reputation of
the Templars for practising some form of sorcery and satanism.

At least these German controversialists had enough experience of the Templar Masonic groups to talk about them with a
semblance of authority. The unhappy Italian impostor, 'Count'
Cagliostro, in law Giuseppe Balsamo, of humble origins, was
finally brought in disgrace before the Roman Inquisition of
1789. To his captors he talked about the Templars in disjointed
ravings which suggested that they were lost in a bottomless pit of
guilt. According to Cagliostro, whose 'confession' was speedily
published, the Strict Observance of the Templars (which

included the Illuminati) was subject in its turn to a 'High Observance'. These modern Templar lords were said to be bent on avenging the execution of the medieval Templar Grand Master in 1314 by procuring the destruction of the Catholic religion and of all monarchical institutions. Cagliostro claimed to have been taken to a 'Temple' in Frankfurt-am-Main where he had been shown a quantity of secret documents in a chest. The most important of these – naturally written in blood – was signed by 'We, the Templar Grand Masters . . .', and contained promises by named prominent persons to take part in the destruction of all despots.

The French Revolution gave a new and sinister meaning to all these assertions about the Templars. In the preceding year a political radical and prominent revolutionary who was also a Mason, Nicholas de Bonneville, had published a bitter attack on Scottish and Templar Masonry, which particularly took to task the legend of the Unknown Superiors and the idea of a lost Templar treasure. De Bonneville was a Utopian Socialist of wild and woolly views, who claimed that the Jesuits were secretly the inspirers and organizers of Templarist Masonry. These allegations about conspiracy were passed from one publicist to another in an endless circle, so that de Bonneville and Nicolai were copied in Germany by Bode, in France by Luchet.

Templarist sensationalism reached its peak with Louis Cadet de Gassicourt, a pharmacist with radical political interests who was imprisoned during the Terror. In *Le Tombeau de Jacques Molay* he produced an hysterical theory that the medieval Templars had been the main link in a long chain of secret anarchist conspirators, whose evil beginnings stretched back to the Old Man of the Mountains in medieval Syria and forward to the storming of the Bastille and the instigation of the Terror. Like other pamphleteers of the first year of the Directory, Cadet de Gassicourt painted Philippe Egalité, Duke of Orléans, as the blackest of the Masonic Jacobin conspirators.[33] With Cadet de Gassicourt the theory of Templar vengeance against the French monarchy reaches a violent climax. The second edition of his book has a frontispiece showing the sinister tomb of Jacques de Molay, flanked by a mysterious Masonic inscription. It is possible that the decapitated body in the engraving is meant to be that of Louis XVI.

The culmination of all this pamphlet warfare came with the book of the Abbé Augustin de Barruel, a Jesuit writing in exile in England.[34] Barruel was a passionate controversialist who combined the skills of a medieval inquisitor with the mentality of an eighteenth-century occultist. His book became the great classic of conspiracy theory because he turned the occultists' own methods against them. In Barruel, as in the Illuminist Freemasons, everything connects; all thoughts are transmitted from one group and one historical period to another by magical contagion. In his mind the origin of all the ills (if we exclude Satan himself) was Manes, the founder-prophet of Manichaeanism. From Manes in the third century AD onwards the links in the chain are patent. 'It all connects, from the Cathars to the Albigensians, to the Knights of the Temple, and thence to the Jacobin Masons; everything points to a common parentage'. At the Templar Strict Observance Convent of Wilhelmsbad, to which Masons had been convened from all over Europe, the threads of the evil plot had been drawn together. In the minds of Barruel and Cadet de Gassicourt there was an invincible belief in a continuous historical conspiracy, through which anarchist beliefs had passed from the medieval heretics in the west and the Assassins in the east to the Templars, and thence through the four Templar lodges which were set up after the death of Jacques de Molay in 1314. From Naples, Paris, Edinburgh, and Stockholm the devilish doctrine was propagated. Cola di Rienzo, the Roman tribune of 1348; the English Cromwell; the Neapolitan revolutionary, Masaniello; the murderer of Henry IV of France; the conspirators of Portugal, Brazil, and Sweden; the Jacobins of 1789 down to Robespierre and Danton – all were agents of the same Templar society!

The later editions of Cadet de Gassicourt's book are, however, not quite so crazy as they sound. His imprisonment under the Terror had been the inspiration for the book, and to him the great enemies were not only the Jacobin extremists but political persecutors in general. Cadet de Gassicourt's aim was to stop further 'proscriptions', and never to allow the repetition of the suffering caused by the Terror. He saw mystification and the pursuit of the marvellous as the means by which the political radicals achieved their ends, and modern historians do not entirely disagree with this judgement. Recent historians have made us familiar with the idea that superstitious cults of Mesmerism in the period preceding the Revolution were used by the political radicals as ways of popularizing their ideas.[35] The same theory is clearly articulated by Cadet de Gassicourt, who mensions Mesmer, the alchemists, and the water diviners as being in one sense the precursors of the Jacobins.

With flagrant illogicality Barruel argued that it did not matter whether the medieval Templars were guilty or innocent, *or* whether they were or were not the fathers of Masonic doctrine; it was enough, to establish the guilt of the Masons, that they claimed the Templars as ancestors![36] However, Barruel did argue in favour of the guilt of the medieval Order; he also adopted Nicolai's suggestion that an evil doctrine had been passed down through the Gnostics of the early Christian centuries, to reach the Templars through the allied heresy of the Albigensians. Barruel seized with joy on the modern Masonic 'oaths of vengeance', on the rituals denouncing Philip the Fair and Pope Clement V as 'abominable', and on the childish Masonic practice of decapitating doll-images of pope and king. To Barruel, in whom the medieval stereotypes of the heretics in their dark and secret lairs were very much alive, the modern Templars fitted perfectly into this ancient category. It seemed quite natural to him that groups of such wicked folk should pass their seditious learning from one coven to another, through every land and every age. Anglo-Saxon empiricism found this hard to swallow. In his essay on secret societies Thomas de Quincey described how, even at ten years of age, he was puzzled by Barruel's logic as well as impressed by the sublimity of his thoughts. 'How men, living in distant periods and distant places – men that did not know each other, nay, often had not even heard of each other, nor spoke the same language – could yet be parties to the same treason against a mighty religion towering to the highest heavens, puzzled my understanding.'

Barruel's reasoning may have been blatantly false, but the documentation of his charges seemed overwhelming, and his book was bought and believed all over Europe. The Templars played only a subsidiary part in his argument, which sought to convince by the piling-up of confused evidence, and not by logical persuasion. But the influence of his book has been so great that he must bear considerable responsibility for the diffusion of the Templar myth. The strength of Barruel was in the pains he took to translate and interpret books about Masonry which were hard of access, and turgid reading even when they had been obtained. The best guardian of eighteenth-century German Masonic secrets was the vile prose in which most of them were expressed. When Barruel put them into readable French and English he made them accessible to the common reader of the early nineteenth century. De Quincey remarked of his own translation of Buhle's tract on Masonry: 'No German has any conception of style. I therefore did him the favour to wash his dirty face, and make him presentable among Christians.' This uncharitable remark could be applied to what Barruel did for Nicolai and Starck and Knigge and the rest of the tribe of Illuminati and ex-Templars. He translated – or more often mistranslated – their views, and fed them into the general consciousness of his time. Through Barruel the idea of political Masonic conspiracy became a commonplace, and the Templars became finally stamped in the popular imagination as a suspect group who smelled slightly of the pit.

7

THE ROMANTIC DREAM

The Masonic Templars had in effect been reproached because they had bad dreams. That dreams refresh and revive, and may tell us something of our fate, are beliefs which men do not easily give up. Dreams come to the poor man as easily as to the rich, a fourth-century bishop remarked, and no tyrant can forbid them unless he abolishes sleep. In the early nineteenth century men were not to cease dreaming of the Middle Ages – quite the reverse: the Templar myth still had a lot of life in it. It did not possess the creative power of the great myths which restore and heal; its history was too closely linked to personal vanity and to charlatanism. On the other hand, the direction taken by the myth at this time is interesting, since it marks one of the few occasions when a branch of Freemasonry seemed to be about to renounce its ambiguous status and to become a religion. Neo-Templarism failed, finally, to make the transition; it proved to be a short-lived sect. But its history is worth following, especially as it stirred up currents which still reappear spasmodically in the stream of French popular religion.

Templarism had been a German phenomenon, but by the turn of the eighteenth century it was dead on the east bank of the Rhine. Under Napoleon the Templar myth returned to its native soil, where it put down new roots. The origins of the revival of the myth are not at all clear, and are connected with the obscure status of Freemasonry under the Napoleonic regime. The government encouraged Masonry with the idea of using it for political purposes, though little came of this. Probably the revival of chivalrous Masonic orders was encouraged because they were likely to attract aristocrats whose spare-time pursuits could thus be easily placed under surveillance by Napoleonic agents. The littérateur Charles Nodier said of the Freemasonry of the period that in spite of their numbers the Masons were no danger to the regime, because the movement was negative, powerless, and frivolous. Nodier had a Masonic past, and his judgement was not unbiased, but he was right in thinking

Freemasonry to have become politically harmless. The Utopian, revolutionary Masonry of de Bonneville and the Bavarian Illuminati was finished.[37]

Like the German 'systems', the new Temple depended on a mixture of fantasy and forgery. The appropriate documents seem to have been concocted by two doctors, one called Ledru who was the former family doctor of the Duc de Cossé-Brissac, and another called Bernard Raymond Fabré-Palaprat, a former seminarist of the pre-Revolutionary period (possibly even a Constitutional priest) who after the Revolution had taken medical qualifications at Caen and Paris. Ledru is an obscure figure who may even have executed the forgeries without the knowledge of Fabré-Palaprat. The latter was a man of some talents, a rather distinguished doctor who is sometimes referred to disparagingly and misleadingly as a 'chiropodist'. Like so many men of his period, he longed for a heterodox religious solution which would reconcile mystical illuminism with 'science'. Like others before and after him, he swallowed obvious forgeries and fabrications with avid credulity. Once he had found the Templarist story he pursued and elaborated it passionately, and, like von Hund, he proved to be a capable organizer.

The differences between the new Templarism and the old were at first slight. Ledru's innovation of 1804 was to solve the problem of the link between the medieval Templars and their Masonic successors by boldly composing a new 'medieval' charter, dated 1324. This purported to emanate from the then Grand Master of the Templar Order, one 'John-Mark Larmenius' (presumably 'the Armenian'), who owed his appointment to Jacques de Molay and who passed on the succession to one Thomas Theobald of Alexandria, anathematizing the 'Scottish Templars' and the Knights of St John as he did so. The document contains a long and equally fictitious list of the subsequent Grand Masters of the Order, different from the equivalent list of 'Scottish' Grand Masters which had been fabricated formerly by the German Strict Observance Templars. Ledru's Grand Masters obligingly left their autograph signatures on the document, which is an obvious forgery. Its language is that of eighteenth-century Masonry and not that of the Middle Ages; the reference to the 'Scottish Templars' is especially revealing. Everything in the list of the supposed

'Grand Masters' is garbled, even to the names and titles of the early eighteenth-century Grand Masters who were Bourbon princes. How such poor stuff managed to persuade noblemen whose family hobby was genealogy is very mysterious, but persuade them it did, perhaps because vanity makes men blind. Not to omit any childish device, the charter referred to a secret writing by which the Knights were to communicate with each other.

The new Templarism was associated with a Masonic lodge, that of the Chevaliers de la Croix, which was affiliated to the Grand Orient de France. Many of the Chevaliers de la Croix belonged to the highest French nobility; in appealing to the romantic medievalism of the old nobility the new French Templars followed their German predecessors. But Napoleonic France was driven by forces very different from those which had affected the stuffy German nobles. The government may perhaps have encouraged the Neo-Templars, in order to confer a spurious aristocratic gloss on Masonic associations which might be politically useful. One characteristic of the Neo-Templars which sharply distinguished them from other Freemasons was their taste for public display. In March 1808, on the anniversary of the execution of Jacques de Molay, the new Templar Order celebrated a public requiem for the 'martyred' Grand Master in the Church of St Paul in Paris, near the place of his confinement. The officers of the Order wore medieval costume; they were led by the Grand Master, Fabré-Palaprat, and by an elderly and respected Norman cleric, the Abbé Pierre Romains Clouet, who was described as a Canon of Notre-Dame and also as the 'Primate' of the Order. A detachment of troops is said to have taken part in the ceremony, conferring on it a sort of quasi-official character. And the trappings of spurious medievalism were also provided: the brothers displayed 'relics' such as bones and weapons of the 'martyred' Grand Master and of the Dauphin d'Auvergne who was supposed to have perished with him. Under the new Templars the piebald banner of the Order was again solemnly carried.

Jacques de Molay's sword and Guy the Dauphin's helm were acceptable ornaments in a Paris in which Gothic antiquities were becoming very fashionable. In the former Convent of the Petits-

Augustins on the left bank of the Seine, Alexandre Lenoir had just installed the first Parisian collection of medieval objects.[38] Men of the early nineteenth century were very willing to look at life through a stained-glass window. Templarism was, it is true, too specialized to appeal directly to the imagination of many literary men. The German poet Lessing, who was interested in Freemasonry, made rather unkind fun of the modern Templars. The dramatic possibilities of the Templar trial were apparent, but they did not attract any very successful dramatist for some time. There were a couple of German verse dramas about the Templars in the 1790s, and in the same period the Templarist myth proper attracted its one and only poet, the German Zacharias Werner. Werner wrote a long verse drama about the trial, of bloodchilling tedium, 'The Sons of the Valley' (*Die Söhne des Tals*), in which he used the Masonic symbolism of the Templar story as the basis of the play.

In France a peppery and independent-minded Provençal lawyer and literary scholar called François Raynouard was attracted to the Templars and wrote a verse play, *Les Templiers*, which was performed with great success at the Théâtre français early in 1805. He was a better scholar than he was a dramatist, and the play is rather stilted and slow, moving ponderously to its tragic end. Napoleon showed considerable interest in the play, but was disappointed by Raynouard's insistence on the innocence of the Templars and the injustice displayed by Philip the Fair. According to Napoleon, who was hardly without a personal interest in the matter, modern political tragedies occur not because politicians commit crimes but because political necessity, or 'the nature of things', involves them in trains of events which lead to catastrophe. If Raynouard had taken account of this principle, he would have given Philip the Fair the heroic lead, and would in Napoleon's opinion have written a much better play. Napoleon was also rather put out by the open threats of torture and the stake which Raynouard allowed Philip to make. In the Emperor's prudish view, rulers use the executioner but never mention him.[39]

That the Emperor should have taken the trouble to compose this piece of literary criticism in his bivouac in the Polish mud of Pultusk, and to send it to his chief of police, shows that the Templars occupied a modest corner of the great Napoleonic canvas. Later in the reign, when he had compelled the pope to send the whole papal Archive to Paris to take its place in the great projected Imperial Archive, Napoleon again thought of Raynouard and the Templars. It had always been conjectured that the most astonishing information about the Templars had been jealously concealed by the popes in their Secret Archive; when the papal records had arrived in Paris in 1810 Raynouard was one of the few French scholars who were encouraged by the government to burrow there. Raynouard did indeed find and publish important new material on the Templar trial, but it was neither scandalous nor spectacular. The new papal documents which he located tended to reinforce historians' doubts about Templar guilt, but afforded no conclusive proof of their innocence. Equally, they gave no support to those holding dark suspicions of Templar magical practices or of their Gnostic religious rites.

Raynouard's labours to preserve a rational view of the medieval Templars were not entirely in vain. But Masonic myth-makers were not the only ones to concern themselves with the Templars at this time. One of the deepest convictions of German thinkers of the early modern period was of the historic continuity of culture expressed through language, and of exchange between cultures which leaves linguistic traces. This was ground common to Friedrich Nicolai, who has already been mentioned, and to his great opponent, Johann Gottfried Herder. Nicolai had already spread the idea that the Baphomet idol of the Templars did not take its name from Muhammad, although the medieval French word for Muhammad was 'Baphomet', as any competent scholar in Old French could have told him. Instead Nicolai maintained that Baphomet was a composite of two Greek words meaning 'colour' (or by extension 'baptism') and 'spirit'. By this simple linguistic fiction Nicolai was able to shift Baphomet from the Crusaders of the thirteenth century to the Gnostic heretics of the third. He thus launched Baphomet on a long and picturesque magical career, which seems to be far from over.

The central figure in the making of the magical Baphomet was an Austrian orientalist called Hammer, known at the end of his life as Joseph von Hammer-Purgstall.[40] Joseph Hammer was an able and industrious orientalist who spent his Middle-Eastern apprenticeship in British service in Egypt and Syria. For part of this time he worked under the flamboyant Sir William Sydney Smith, the hero of the siege of Acre, who protected Hammer when other British officers wanted to get rid of him from Alexandria in 1801. William Sydney Smith was a passionate romantic and a keen Freemason, who will reappear in this story. He claimed that a cross dating from the Middle Ages and belonging either to the Order of St John or the Temple had been given him by the Archbishop of Cyprus when he freed the island from the Turks in 1799. Whether he interested the young Hammer in the Templar story while they were together in 1799–1801, I have not managed to discover; but Hammer was working on the Nicolai 'Baphomet' thesis by 1806, when he mentioned it in a book published in London.

Hammer's main publication on the Templars was a long work of 1818 which denounced the Order as 'convicted by their own monuments as guilty of apostasy, idolatry and impurity, and of being Gnostics or even Ophites'. The tone is one of political delation, and this is confirmed by Hammer's book on the oriental Order of Assassins, published in the same year. To Hammer the Assassins, with their House of Science in Cairo, were a kind of Freemason, and 'as in the West, revolutionary societies arose from the bosom of the Freemasons, so in the East, did the Assassins spring from the Ismaili sect'. Hammer was not employed by Metternich, the greatest conservative minister in western Europe, for nothing. The whole drift of Hammer's argument is in the sense of that used by the ubiquitous Abbé Barruel. Everything connects, from the Gnostics of the early Church, to the Albigensians in the west, the Assassins in the east, thence to the Templars, thence to the Freemasons, thence to the revolutionary anarchists. In 1818 the political order of European conservatism was making its greatest effort to master the threat of radical ideology and radical sedition. The centre of that effort was in Vienna, where Hammer was employed by the Austrian Chancery.

It would be foolish to treat Hammer's *Mystery of Baphomet Revealed* as a piece of disinterested scholarly research.[41] Hammer had had some experience of Freemasonry through Admiral Sir William Sydney Smith, for whom he retained much personal esteem but whose principles he thought to be pernicious. His work was clearly aimed at discrediting Templarist Masonry and, through this, Masonry in general. He introduced it with a sinister quotation from Horace's Ode on the Civil War: Freemasonry was rising like a phoenix from the ashes of Templar heresy, and it represented a dangerous gamble for society.

The arguments and evidence used by Hammer were quite as wild in their way as those of de Bonneville and the revolutionary enthusiasts had been in theirs. Following Nicolai, Hammer took up a suggestion by the patristic theologian Origen that the Ophite sect of the early Christian centuries forced its members to 'curse Jesus', and he accepted the Templars as successors of the Gnostic Ophites. Like the Ophites, the Templars had forced their members to renounce Christ; Templar doctrines therefore proceeded from the Ophites. He also accused the Templars of having adopted a form of phallus-worship from their Gnostic predecessors. As evidence of these claims he produced an elaborate collection of coins, medals, and monuments of dates ranging from the late classical period to the Middle Ages. The apparatus of learning and the Latin in which it was written reinforced the impression of great erudition. The weakness of the argument was the frail nature of the connections which he alleged to exist between his monuments and the Templars; his reading of the inscriptions was also very arbitrary. A few of the archaeological exhibits may have been forgeries from the occultist workshops; there is an especially suspicious pair of so-called 'Templar caskets', found after the publication of Hammer's first article, which were supposed to have been medieval artefacts of Templar provenance. The Gnostic 'orgies' depicted on these supposedly medieval caskets are uncannily like the late classical objects which had a few years earlier been published in the original 'Baphomet' thesis. The 'medieval' caskets had come into the possession of the Duc de Blacas. Since Blacas was a leading figure in the reactionary French government, and a close personal friend of the renegade Freemason Joseph de Maistre, it is not impossible that they were forged on his behalf. Whether they were forged or not, Hammer failed to prove that they had anything to do with the Templars.

Like Barruel, Hammer returned to the medieval idea of a fixed, wicked, recurrent pattern of heresy, which hardly changed in time. The sexual elements in his text illustrate this well. There is no proof in the early sources that the Ophites indulged in sexual depravity. They got their name from their veneration of the serpent in the Garden of Eden, whom they elevated above the 'accursed God of the Jews'; no doubt the idea that Eve conceived the Word from the serpent assisted in the growth of the sexual suggestion. But the notion that they were sexually debauched was an unwarranted extension of charges brought against other groups.[42] Hammer connected the depravity of the Ophites with the two sexual accusations made in the course of the Templar trial: that Templars kissed the private parts of the brother who received them into the Order, and that they were ordered by their superiors to commit sodomy. But this was only the beginning of his speculations. Basing himself on supposedly late classical statues and vases, he worked out a great theory of an androgynous deity called Baphomet or Achamoth, which had from early times been the patron of a phallic cult requiring orgies for its celebration. In Hammer's mind the revival of medieval heresy-hunting began to be transformed into an early modern theory of comparative religion. He speculated, as many did after him, that the truncated cross or 'tau' is a phallic symbol. The idea was not definitely proved, but was pursued by folklorists throughout the nineteenth century. The application of this to the Templars was doubtful in the extreme; the Templar cross was regular in form, and was not truncated. Hammer's fertile imagination pursued 'tau' crosses which he thought he could see on coins or on the faces of buildings, but without proving one to be Templar in origin. Like Barruel, Hammer is a master of the circular argument. Either the monuments are Gnostic, and therefore concern the Templars, or they are Templar, and therefore Gnostic.

Finally, Hammer launched a theory which, unlike the rest, was based not on archaeological but on literary evidence. He claimed that the medieval legend of the Holy Grail was Gnostic in origin, and that the Templars took a direct part in the Gnostic acts of worship to which the Grail legend was supposed to have given rise. His evidence was rather trivial, but the story was destined to exert a long-lasting influence. The German medieval poet Wolfram of Eschenbach had attached the name of *Templeisen* to his knights in the service of the Grail in *Parzifal*;

such a hint was irresistible. Hammer not only claimed Wolfram's Grail knights for the Templar Order, but annexed Arthur and his Round Table (which numbered the 'Templar number' of twelve) for Gnostic heresy as well! The 'hyghe order and mete whych ye have so much desired' in Malory's *Quest of the Holy Grail* (bk. xviii) was identified by Hammer with the Greek word *meta* which was also a component of 'Baphomet' and which meant 'spirit'! He also found *meta* in Wolfram of Eschenbach, though in this case only after a dubious emendation of the text. The Grail itself was to Hammer a Gnostic vessel, the symbol of Gnostic illumination, and without Christian meaning.

To Hammer, Europe was strewn with the monuments which showed Baphomet idols and Grail-beakers, and which thus recorded the classical and medieval existence of these Gnostic beliefs. He also thought that the beliefs which these monuments enshrined had been adopted by the Masons, whose symbolism was more or less the same as that of the Gnostics. Hammer also thought it natural that the Freemasons should have assumed the beliefs which their artisan or 'operative' predecessors had actually recorded in stone (as he thought) during the Middle Ages. He accepted without demur the Masonic legend of a tradition of occult knowledge which passed from the Templars through the 'Scottish' masons.

Outwardly Hammer at first appears to be another Barruel, though wilder, more learned, and madder. Like Barruel, he piled one mountain of dubious 'proof' on another, never stopping to ask himself whether one argument was compatible with the next. Hammer never makes it plain, for example, whether the Templars drew their wicked doctrines from a guilty association with the Assassins, or from the Grail knights, or from the Albigensians, or from the Canons of the Holy Sepulchre at Jerusalem, or from memories of the original Ophites. But this vagueness is not at all surprising, since his underlying preoccupation is not exclusively with the Templars. Hammer's book sets out to show that Templar Baphomet-worship derives from Gnostic antecedents, but he ends by expounding a thesis that the Templars represent only one branch of a wider medieval Gnosticism. Like so many early modern students of religious origins, he sought to establish a pattern of a primitive pagan religion which had survived Christianity in various deviant ways.

Hammer's Baphomet, his half-female Achamoth or Sophia who holds the tau, the phallus, or the serpent, is the prolongation of the old nature-religions into the Christian Middle Ages and beyond. By locating such survivals in the Grail legend and among the Templars and other heretics, Hammer was blazing a trail which was later followed by scores of folklorists and mythologists, and which has still not become entirely overgrown. The Saint-Simonian myth of the Great Mother, Bachofen's exposition of the ancient mother cults, Margaret Murray's theories of the 'old religion' prolonged into modern times by an historic chain of witches' covens, all reason in the same way as Hammer.

The Romantic movement was passionately addicted to such theories of primitive religion. Close contemporary parallels to Hammer in Britain were the wild theories of the poet Edward Williams, and the philologist Edward Davies, on the origin and the survival of the Druids.[43] Williams's ideas on the 'deep Druidic lore' of metempsychosis, his speculations on the immemorial origins of the Druidic religion and its foreshadowing of Christian doctrine, and his feverish misreadings of Welsh bardic texts, all have a familiar ring to anyone fresh from Hammer.

Hammer's main arguments were based on archaeological evidence. He said that his predecessors had used only literary texts but that he would not use the witness of words where stones could be made to confess the truth. He was here helping to set a new and important precedent. It was true that folklorists and the students of religious transmission could find important evidence in the monuments and the archaeological remains: in Hammer's time Stonehenge was an example. He had not, however, realized how exacting the scholarly requirements were for this kind of work; he was a learned man, but his orientalist skills were only a part of the academic equipment he needed. His method, above all, was confused, and beset by poetic dreams.

One troubling question remains about Hammer. How was it that a writer enrolled in the service of rampant conservatism, whose duty it was to demonstrate that advanced radical thought was subverting the foundations of Christian civilization, ended by seeming to show that Christianity had always existed alongside another, more primitive and perhaps more powerful, religion? *The Mystery of Baphomet Revealed* seems at first an anti-

Masonic tract in the tradition of Barruel, but ends as a romantic rhapsody of religious primitivism. Hammer may have given the clue to the solution of this paradox in his explanation of the psychology of the medieval Templars. At the end of the *Baphomet* essay he offered to answer the question often asked by the partisans of Templar innocence: how a body of men entirely committed by their way of life to one theory of belief and conduct, could in their hearts profess a quite contradictory one. 'Easily,' answered Hammer: 'a man may easily divide his external conduct from his internal beliefs, and contradict the one by the other.' Perhaps he was speaking here for Joseph Hammer. His career in Austrian service up to the time of the publication of the *Mystery of Baphomet Revealed* had been far from what he had hoped.[44] By temperament Hammer was not the cool, calculating diplomat whom Metternich wanted for his oriental department, but a passionate, romantic dreamer, full of the *Schwärmerei*, the ardent longings of his time. In allowing his bold musings on primitive religion to run away with him, as he did in the *Baphomet*, he was perhaps mutely protesting at his lack of preferment, besides indulging in the poetic fancies which lay not far below his apparently arid orientalist learning. It was in appearance a very discreet self-indulgence: a long essay written in Latin in an obscure orientalist periodical does not invite the attention of the great public. But it achieved wide posthumous influence; no one can now pick up a popular work on the Templars or the Grail without meeting his theories.

The spirit of Hammer's work is to be found in an eloquent passage of Johann Joseph Görres, the expositor of the ancient Asian myths, published a year or so before *Baphomet* appeared.[45]

And so we stand before these tombs and their mysterious images; long ago the hand which made them departed, and the sight which has been fashioned in us to contemplate them did not exist when they were made. A dark presentiment grips us with wondrous force when we strive to decipher their secret meaning; it is as if our powers of recollection had found their proper mother; it is as if the stars once more shone for us which shone in the darkness when our childhood emerged from the night. We have nurtured the spirit, we feel in our innermost hearts, which formed those features; we ourselves have set up our own memorial in the stone; it is our own dark, veiled past which greets us. The first light of dawn sees the last glimmer of dusk still hanging in the

western sky. . . . Herein lies the basis of the religious feeling which
ancient times arouse in us; we were born on the funeral barrow of the
past. . . .

It is in the light of these ideas and feelings of his contemporaries that we must understand Joseph Hammer's theories of
ancient religion. He was not an isolated eccentric, located outside the mainstream of German intellectual life, but an insider
who shared in some of its principal trends. His translations from
Hafiz were the inspiration for Goethe's *Westöstliche Diwan*; he
was carried along currents of thought which led to German
Naturphilosophie, to Schopenhauer, to Nietzsche, to Marx. In
judging the exaggerated theories of adventurers in comparative
mythology like Hammer, we would be foolish to treat them as
the work of irrational mystagogues whose proper place is at the
fringes of Western intellectual tradition. Hammer and his like
were convinced that the foundations of man's spiritual and
social life are grounded in myth; this conviction is not dead, but
very much alive in the ideas of Northrop Frye, of Lévi-Strauss,
and of other figures to whom votive lamps are lit in modern
university seminar rooms.

Hammer's mythomania was very different from the milder
eccentricities of decadent French Masonry. Perhaps Fabré-
Palaprat's Templars were not, strictly speaking, Masons; in
1811 they replied to the Grand-Orient Lodge that they were
independent of Masonic organization and no longer connected
with Grand-Orient de France. However, their connection with
the Chevaliers de la Croix remained, and the definite nature of
their break with Masonry is in some doubt. Like Hund, Fabré-
Palaprat sought to dominate the Order in a masterful way. The
elaborate constitution of the Order, which envisaged Grand
Priories of Japan, Tartary, and the Congo, not to mention other
less remote points on the globe, also provided for four 'Lieuten-
ants-General' or 'Grand-Vicars'. It may be that Fabré-Palaprat
found it hard to control the aristocratic elements in his Order, as
he found it necessary to remove the Grand-Vicars, to quarrel
violently with the Duc de Choiseul who supported them, and to
fulminate bulls of interdiction and excommunication against all
and sundry. The opposition set up against Fabré-Palaprat a

rival Grand Master, Count Lepeletier d'Aunay, and for over a decade after 1814 the Order was divided by this schism.

By comparison with the German Strict Observance, the French Neo-Templars were a very modest body. They made almost no progress in proselytizing the Masonic world (there was some activity in eastern France, but it amounted to little), and remained hardly more than an exotic Parisian lodge of somewhat doubtful credentials. There were some British connections, notably with Admiral Sir William Sydney Smith and with the Duke of Sussex; principally with the former, who may have belonged to the associated body of Chevaliers de la Croix during the war, and who certainly joined them after its conclusion in 1814. While he was a British hero of the Napoleonic war, Smith was also a devoted and Francophile chivalrous Mason, who believed in Ramsay's idea of the knights who recognized their shared secret signs during the heat of battle to the extent that he aided French prisoners who were Masons to obtain their release. After the end of the war Smith tried to get support for the idea of a new international Christian chivalrous Order, which would replace the moribund Order of St John of Jerusalem and perhaps obtain Malta from the British government as its seat of operations. These new Christian knights would then carry out joint naval operations in the Mediterranean in order to suppress the Barbary pirates, and would work elsewhere for the suppression of the slave trade. Both the Chevaliers de la Croix and the Neo-Templars attracted Smith as possible helpers in the establishment of his new Order. On the other side, from the time of their beginnings the Masonic Templars had dreamed of making the Order of St John disgorge some of the wealth they had acquired from Templar lands after the dissolution of the medieval Order in 1312. A few of the Knights of St John had been or had become Freemasons, and one, Vié-Cesarini, according to Grégoire became 'Primate' of the Neo-Templar Order.[46] But Smith's was a vain dream: the British government sat firmly in Malta and was stubbornly unsympathetic both to the Hospitallers and to anyone who thought to succeed them. Smith's new Order never even reached the stage of serious political discussion.

Fabré-Palaprat was taking the Neo-Templars in a very different direction. He somehow came into possession of a manuscript written in Greek entitled the *Levitikon*; according to one version he picked it up from a second-hand bookstall. The *Levitikon* contained a heavily modified version of the Gospel according to John, in which the orthodox presentation of Christ had been excised in favour of a version which eliminated the miracles and the Resurrection, and presented Christ as an initiate of the higher mysteries, trained in Egypt. God is understood as existence, action, and mind, and morality as rational and benevolent conduct. The cosmos, in the ancient Gnostic tradition, is viewed as a hierarchy of intelligences. The part played by privileged initiation in the transmission of divine knowledge is central. Christ conferred the essential knowledge of this Gospel on John as the best-loved apostle, and it was transmitted thence through the Patriarchs of Jerusalem until the arrival of the Templars in 1118, after which the secret teaching was kept by the Templar Grand Masters. The esoteric doctrine was passed down through the official medieval Order until its fall in 1312, and then through their successors who extend the chain down to the present time. The part played by 'Levites' in this religion is essentially secularizing. Knights who were also initiates were 'Levites' with the power of pronouncing the words which declare the pardon of the Spirit to the repentant sinner. Since Levite-knights could create other Levite-knights the religion is in the hands of the initiate laymen; there is provision for 'Bishops' or 'Primates', but the function of these prelates is very different from their function in Christianity, since the part played by apostolic succession has been usurped by the Johannite succession of the initiates.

Fabré-Palaprat's doctrine of the *Levitikon* was reorganized after 1828 under the name of the High Initiation, or the Holy Church of Christ, or the Church of Primitive Christians. It was a secular religion of the kind which was peculiar to this period,[47] though it put down some roots, and still influences some French esoteric circles. Essentially it was an academic, didactic faith which became more and more bookish as it tried to leave the Masonic lodge and establish itself in public precincts. So long as the restored Bourbon monarchy persisted, setting up new secular religious places of worship was difficult. But once the July Revolution of 1830 had taken place – and Fabré-Palaprat himself took an active part in the July days – the way was clear for movements such as those of the Saint-Simonians and of Fabré-Palaprat's Church of Primitive Christians. He needed, however, a 'Primate' of some kind, and found him in the advanced radical clergyman, Ferdinand Chatel, whose 'French Catholic Church' proclaimed freedom from papal authority and the preaching of the liturgy in French, rejected clerical celibacy and the practice of auricular confession, and asked for the popular election of bishops. Chatel was seeking an authority to consecrate him as Bishop of this new Church, and he found it in the doctrines of Fabré-Palaprat's *Levitikon* and in the Neo-Templar chief's willingness to consecrate him 'Primate of the Gauls'.

In the New Year of 1831 Chatel established his new French Catholic Church in some former shop premises in Montmartre. He decorated it with black drapes hired from a local undertaker, with a bust of King Louis-Philippe placed under the tricolour flag, and with a poster announcing the names of the three greatest benefactors of humanity: Confucius, Parmentier the apostle of the potato, and the Orleanist banker, Lafitte. The Neo-Templar Johannite Church had its own premises in a former bottle shop in the Cour des Miracles, near the Porte St.-Denis. The place-name was utilized by the Neo-Templars to locate their publications and announcements at the 'Apostolic Court of the Temple' (*Cour apostolique du Temple*). They dated their documents from 'Magistropolis', according to a mystical calendar which commenced with the foundation of the Templar Order in 1118. After 1830 the officials of the Order assumed yet more pompous titles. Jean-Marie Ragon, a former member of the Masonic Rite des Trinosophes, was an official in the Ministry of the Interior. After 1831 he became 'Count Jean-Marie de Venise', Primatial Vicar of the French Catholic Church. Like most 'clergy' of sects of the Johannite kind, he gave lectures rather than sermons. Another prominent member of the group was the publisher, Guyot, the former editor of the *Manuel des Chevaliers de l'Ordre du Temple* (1825). The impression given by the Neo-Templar membership of this final period is that of a decorous, respectable, middle-class establishment, which still sought to maintain its connection with the Masonic nobles.

The alliance between Chatel and Fabré-Palaprat did not last long. Chatel soon tired of his Masonic friends, was expelled with ignominy from the Neo-Templar or Johannite flock, and was 'tried' for heresy in a synod in which, in true Masonic fashion, the guilty heretic was represented by a rag doll! This was not the end of the troubles of the new religion. In 1836 the noblemen in the Order who preferred the old tradition of Masonic chivalry to the new Johannite religion precipitated a schism, led once more by the Duc de Choiseul. Fabré-Palaprat defended the purity of his new religion, and expelled the former Grand-Chancellor of the Order, Louis-Théodore Juge. He reinforced the noble element in the Johannite congregation by admitting the retired British admiral, Sir William Sydney Smith, whose connection with the chivalric Masonic orders in Paris had been long and close. After Fabré-Palaprat's death in 1838 Smith was elected Regent of the Order, which he then led back to reunion with the Templar rump. The Johannite religion faded entirely from view, and the Neo-Templar Order tottered slowly towards its natural and final death in the early 1840s, under the direction of a small group of French and Belgian noblemen.

The Johannite religion lacked enthusiasm: it was more like one of the other nineteenth-century religions of 'progress' which sociologists classify as 'manipulative' than it was like the excitable ecstasies of the Saint-Simonians in their worship of Père Enfantin. The source of the *Levitikon* manuscript on which the religion was founded is obscure. It was almost certainly of relatively recent composition, and its claim to antiquity is no more convincing than that of the other Masonic-Templar monuments. Yet the Johannite creed asks for some attention as almost the only occasion on which Masonry emerged from the shelter of the lodges to put on a Church attire. It suffered from crippling disadvantages as a religion. Partly because it had remained faithful to the old Masonic idea of a 'high initiation', partly because it had grown in the half-noble, half-bourgeois atmosphere of the chivalrous lodges, it had no popular appeal whatsoever. The reports on the final schism of 1836 make it plain that only a handful of people were interested either in the Neo-Templars or in the *Levitikon*.

Many imaginative writers were aware of the recent history of Templarism, some vaguely, others less so. In 1836 Balzac wrote his *Études Philosophiques sur Catherine de Médicis*, in which two fictitious esoteric adepts, Lorenzo and Cosimo Ruggieri, in 1573 are granted an interview with the French King Charles IX and with his mistress. Lorenzo addresses the king in grandiloquent fashion, telling him about the wisdom and the omniscience of the masters of hidden knowledge. This Lorenzo is termed 'Grand Master of the New Templars', a title which seems to suggest a reference to the Parisian Neo-Templars of the 1830s, though poor Fabré-Palaprat does not measure up to the dignified and powerful magus described by Balzac. The Templars are brought into the discussion in a way which is quite in accordance with Masonic lore on the matter; this is hardly surprising, since Balzac's knowledge of Freemasonry was considerable, and *Louis Lambert*, for example, is virtually a Masonic novel. Ruggieri in *Catherine de Médicis* claims to the king that from Chaldea, India, Persia, Egypt, Greece, and Morocco, the sciences of the magi, the highest form of secret knowledge, have been transmitted secretly from one generation to another, and principally through intermediaries of the Order of the Temple. Philip the Fair had burned the bodies of the Templars but their mysteries had continued to be transmitted, and the eventual rebuilding of the Temple was to be the task of a body of men whose identity was at present unknown. These are the old stories, though it is a little worrying that Lorenzo ends, after his royal guest has left, by joyfully exclaiming to his companion that they have led the king by the nose! Balzac hints at charlatanism, as well as at hidden knowledge.

Balzac was in his way an initiate who was aware of many of the current theosophical ideas. In a strange, short novel, *Séraphita* (1835), he uses the doctrine of the Swedish mystic, Swedenborg, to describe an androgynous being who is the product of spiritual illumination. The delicate, fiery, Séraphitus-Séraphita, mystically entranced in the beautiful Norwegian landscape, is far from the ugly, brutal, Gnostic-pagan androgynous creatures of Hammer's *Mystery of Baphomet Revealed*. Yet they are spiritual cousins.

Sir Walter Scott was no initiate, but he was passionately interested in the chronicles of witchcraft. Though intellectually sceptical, he saw superstition as one of the keys to the understanding of past history, and also as a kind of emotional catalyst. Nor was he immune to the charms of the picturesque Gothic style, which is not surprising for the heir to the Gothic tale. 'Superstition, when not arrayed in her full horror, but laying a gentle hand only on her suppliant's head, had charms which we fail not to regret.'[48] He portrayed the Templars as representatives of the more sinister side of the Middle Ages. In *Ivanhoe* the Templar Grand Master is a severe fanatic, determined to clear his Order of the imputation of magic and heresy, who stops at nothing to get the Jewish girl condemned for heresy. Two of his Templar knights are faithless to their vows, and one is without religion or morals. These men are very different from the just, sensitive Templar Grand Master whom Lessing had depicted in *Nathan der Weise* a generation earlier. In *The Talisman* (1825) Scott showed himself well aware of the precarious state of Templar reputation. The Grand Master is 'at the head of that singular body, to whom their order was everything and their individuality nothing –seeking the advancement of its power, even at the hazard of that very religion which the fraternity were originally associated to protect – accused of heresy and witchcraft, although by their character Christian priests – suspected of secret league with the Soldan, though by oath devoted to the protection of the Holy Temple, or its recovery – the whole order, and the whole personal character of its commander, or Grand Master, was a riddle, at the exposition of which most men shuddered.' Small wonder, either, that the Grand Master in *The Talisman* proves a monster of faithlessness and treachery, or that Joseph Hammer should have thoroughly approved of Scott's views on the Templars and should have gone out of his way, in *The Mystery of Baphomet Revealed*, to quote *Ivanhoe*.

In the next generation of Romantic writers Gérard de Nerval was the poet of the flight to the East, the historian of the mystical Illuminists, whose aim was to pour out visionary experience into real life. He was also the friend and companion of contemporary occultists.[49] In *Cagliostro* (1850) he adopted what he called the 'supernaturalism' of a wisdom claiming to be based on that of the Essenes and the Gnostics, which purported to draw on the doctrine of the oriental Assassins, and also on that of the Druses of Syria. He saw the Templars of crusading times as trying to bridge the gap between their culture and that of the subject oriental populations by making a synthesis of Catholicism with the wisdom of the Levantine sects. This synthesis, according to de Nerval, was the origin of Freemasonry. In his *Voyage en*

Orient (1851) he described his own imaginary romance with the daughter of a Druse sheikh, and said that he had successfully claimed brotherhood in Masonry with the Druse. 'The Druse', he wrote, 'are the Freemasons of the East. There is no other way to explain their ancient claim to descend from Crusader knights. During the two centuries of their occupation of the Lebanon, the Templar knights laid the foundation of a long-lived institution.' According to de Nerval the Druse were so penetrated by the ideas of 'Scottish' Freemasonry that they spoke of their co-religionaries in Europe in the Djebel El-Scouzia, the Scottish mountains! He also claimed that the Druse recognize one another by showing a 'black stone', which is the Bohomet or Baphomet of the Templar Order.

Although de Nerval had visited the East on one occasion in person, his *Voyage en Orient* belongs to the tradition of imaginary journeys like those of *Gulliver's Travels*. In writing about the Templars he adopted the same line as a writer of the late Enlightenment like Condorcet, who had identified the Order with the spirit of resistance to clerical tyranny. De Nerval claimed that the thoughtful and intelligent people of the Middle Ages sided with the Templars against clerical and feudal abuse, and that this trend was the equivalent of mid-nineteenth-century radicalism, or of what was called in his day 'the Opposition'. The identification was fanciful, and typical of de Nerval's tendency to play the sorcerer's apprentice and to imagine a real world like that of his occultist reading. But it also pointed towards a new trend, towards the popularization of esoteric Masonry and to the use of these ideas in the service of a radical political point of view.

In the mid-nineteenth century chivalrous Masonry was not dead; in fact it was about to experience a revival in the United States through the ideas of the eccentric Civil War General, Albert Pike. But both in Europe and America chivalrous Masonry was henceforth confined to the discretion and secrecy of the lodges; its active role in the general current of ideas was over. On the other hand, Masonic Templar tradition had percolated into the substratum of magical lore which was the general patrimony of Romantic and Post-Romantic writers.[50] Once out of the hands of professed Masons, the Templar myth was used even more wildly and indistinctly. Templarist speculation ceased to be respectable, and could be used by radical satanists. Perhaps the most important element in this new milieu was to be the idea that the Templars had in the Middle Ages been some sort of mystical ruler–guardians, who had been free from the clerical contâgion of orthodox Catholic society.

The most distinguished convert of the Romantic period to the idea that the Templars may have been magicians was the great French historian, Jules Michelet, the editor of the manuscript of the Templar trial. His attitude was cautious and qualified, but he conceded that the Templars might, as Hammer claimed, have been influenced by oriental sects.[51] Yet at other points he was at once more reserved about the magical accusations and bolder in their interpretation. Michelet himself had in his youth been deeply affected by eighteenth-century Illuminism. In middle age, towards the end of the Orleanist monarchy and the beginning of the Second Empire, his disappointment in the decline of Revolutionary ideals led him to take a more radical stance. The Middle Ages, whose charm he had recognized as a young man, now seemed to him too profoundly marked by brutality, too deeply hostile to liberty. The idea of Templar rebellion against the oppressive orthodoxy of the Church and the cruel tyranny of the State attracted him, but though he was looking for medieval heretics who rebelled against the social order, the Templars were not the kind of heretic he wanted. Michelet was a democrat, and strongly attracted to contemporary feminist ideas. The secretive élitism of the Templars, their expressed hostility to all contact with women, and their possible addiction to sodomy, were all unacceptable to his liberal conscience. To Michelet it seemed that the real God of the Templars was the Order itself. They adored the Temple, and their Templar leaders, as living temples, not in the Masonic sense of temples of the Most High but in a bad sense. They symbolized their complete abandonment of their own personal wills by disgusting and vile ceremonies. He thought that the Order had in this way fallen into a strange kind of self-worship, into satanic egotism; and that this egotism was the logical conclusion of diabolism. It was an extremely orthodox theory for one as heterodox as Michelet.

Michelet's views on witchcraft were not very suitable for

application to the Templar trials. He saw witchcraft as being of little significance to the upper classes, whose libertinism and idle curiosity often induced them to turn to occult knowledge, but to whom the thing was no more than a pastime. To him the true meaning of witchcraft was its function as an indicator of the rebellious despair of the common people, and especially of the women. The immense amount of effort he must have expended on the edition of the Templar trials must have seemed to him so much time lost on a sad and irrelevant business, and, indeed, this period (1837–51) coincided with a period of depression and frustration in his life. His judgement on the evidence given by Templars at the trials was that so much of it was consistent from one Templar to another, and yet that so many differing circumstantial accounts were given of the acts to which these Templars confessed, that some of the charges – at the minimum the charge of renouncing and reviling the cross – must have been well founded. He thought that he could interpret the renunciation of the cross as a symbolic ceremony which had at first been conceived by orthodox Templars, either as a version of the renunciation of Christ by Peter or as a reflection of the sacred comedies of the Feast of Fools. This symbolism was then wilfully misunderstood by the accusers of the Templars, and used by them as the foundation of a successful propaganda which made all Christian men turn from the Templars in revulsion.

All in all, Michelet's judgements on the Templars showed a reasonable respect for the evidence – evidence which he knew better than anyone else at that time, since he had edited so much of it – and a willingness to consider contemporary theories on their heresy, including the wilder ones of Hammer. He did not wish to act as the accuser of the Templars; in spite of the brutality which he imputed to them he felt that they had already expiated this, and any other crimes, during the horrors of their examination and trial. Perhaps, he felt, their despair after the loss of the Holy Land had pushed them into rash doctrines. He was willing, in fact, to consider a number of possibilities without deciding definitely for any one of them. In effect he left the matter open, and this tolerant scepticism of his has been very influential on the judgements of subsequent historians down to our own day. When his contemporary, the great German historian Leopold von Ranke, came to the Templars in his 'World History', he took an attitude of prudent scepticism very like that of Michelet.[52] The tacit refusal of these respected authorities to defend Templar innocence was important. Where the great figures of nineteenth-century critical history reserved judgement, speculation could flourish.

8

THE POLITICS OF THE MARVELLOUS

The Templar myth was in part a literary invention in the Gothic taste, in part an offshoot of theosophical religious experience. It had been born in the same eighteenth-century milieu which had produced the Gothic tale, and contained most of the magical and sexual thrills which the Gothic story-tellers cherished. Like the abbot and the nuns in Matthew Lewis's *The Monk*, published in 1795, the Templars could be seen as guilty of blasphemy, sexual misconduct and perversion, and diabolism. The torture inflicted on the Templars during the judicial inquiries, and the executions by burning, could also be treated so as to pander to the sadistic tendencies to be found in Lewis and in many subsequent Gothic-horror novelists. Orientalism and the fable of hidden knowledge stored in the East are staple ingredients of the Gothic tale from the time of its first appearance.

Like all the Gothic tales, the Templar myth was rooted in romance. And romance, in its turn, was rooted in the medieval tales of knighthood. The historical novels written specifically about the Templars were indifferent ones,[53] but more important than any such works was the vague conviction which began to grow on the common reader of the early nineteenth century that the Templars were a sinister, teasingly interesting topic which was bound up in some way with the origins of medieval knighthood. The knight with knowledge of mysteries had been one of the staples of romance from its medieval beginnings. But in the earlier, Masonic stages of the Templar myth there had been no connecting link by which people interested in medieval romance could connect the esoteric speculations of the Masonic lodges with the common patrimony of romantic literature. This link was supplied by Jospeh Hammer. At the sources of all romantic literature lay the Arthurian legend and the Grail myth. When Hammer, in *The Mystery of Baphomet Revealed*, wove the Templar myth into the Grail legend, he unwittingly ended the convention which until that time had preserved the Templar legend for the private contemplation of the few. A dissertation written in Latin and published in Vienna in a periodical entitled *Fundgrube des Orients* may seem an unlikely vehicle for popularization; and Hammer has, indeed, been more frequently cited than read. But the basic idea he conveyed, that the Grail knights and the Templar knights were all secret Manichees, fell in easily with many other ideas which were current in Hammer's time. His work became generally known through a summary in French which Raynouard had composed in order to refute its arguments, and which was republished in the 1820s in the widely read *Histoire des Croisades* of Michaud.[54] In this way Hammer's thesis about the Gnostic Templars was brought into a book likely to be read by most people who shared the fashionable interest in the Middle Ages. Such people might not have been knowledgeable about Freemasonry: their interests were likely to be in chivalry, or in the wider subject of the persistence of pre-Christian beliefs in medieval Christian Europe.

Thus Templarism was brought to the attention of the students of the medieval romances, and also to early theorists of the anthropology of the Christian Middle Ages. But it also formed part of the stock-in-trade of the theorists of political conspiracy, who were now to be found among the political propagandists of both the Left and the Right. The Abbé Barruel had done his work so well that not only had many conservatives come to believe in the importance of radical secret societies, but so also had many of the radicals themselves. In some cases, as with the Italian revolutionary conspirator, Filippo Buonarroti, radicals came to accept the mythical, secret Illuminist groups as models which influenced both their political vocabulary and the way in which they organized their own conspiratorial groups.[55] Another figure who played, in his youth, with the revolutionary secret societies, later became an influential imaginative writer. This was Charles Nodier, the youthful activist of the abortive Philadelphian conspiracy, who in middle age published colourful and romanticized accounts of the secret societies of the Directory and Napoleonic periods.[56] It is inconceivable that anyone as wildly unpractical as Nodier can ever have been of real importance to genuine revolutionary organizations, but he certainly played a part in making the idea of mystically inspired secret conspiracies fashionable and acceptable.

By the fourth and fifth decades of the nineteenth century the Templars had come to symbolize, to many people who thought themselves informed and enlightened, the notion of persecution by authority on account of the possession of hidden and powerful knowledge. The knowledge supposed to have been guarded by the Templars could be interpreted as working for good or ill, according to the way people read the conspiracy-theory literature. Most of this literature had originated with men who believed in the need to respect the principles of absolute monarchy, and who believed the conspiracies to have been the work of wicked men. In conservative circles in France and Germany there was plenty of support for such points of view, at least until the 1830s. But it was always possible to read the conspiracy-theory literature in a sense opposite to that which Barruel had intended. Hammer's *Mystery of Baphomet Revealed* is an example of how the conspiracy literature could be turned inside out. If Hammer was read in a conservative sense, then the Templars were wicked and seditious Manichees who had plotted against Christian civilization. But, perhaps because of a latent radicalism in Hammer's own text, fewer and fewer people came to read it in a conservative way, and more and more came to read it as a manifesto for a secret revolutionary group which had possessed hidden knowledge fatal to orthodox Christianity, and which pointed forwards to the establishment of a new, enlightened society.

The contempt expressed by Marx for anyone who lamented the medieval feudal order has obscured from us the nostalgia which many radicals and socialists of the early nineteenth century felt for the Middle Ages. The conservatives were not the only ones to hanker after the Gothic world. Many radicals looked back wistfully to the organic society and the supposed social harmony of the world of the medieval craftsmen: this was a feeling which long pre-dated the *News from Nowhere* of William Morris. On the other hand, the radicals were repelled by the clericalism and feudalism of the Middle Ages, and in order to construct a picture of medieval times with which they could feel genuine sympathy they looked for an 'opposition' to the medieval governing class, comparable to their own opposition to the modern social order. Medieval peasant revolts met this requirement only to a limited extent, since the socialist theorists sought in medieval society for some equivalent to a radical intellectual class with a theory of social revolution. To meet this need, some radicals convinced themselves of the existence of secret revolutionary societies during the Middle Ages. Borrowing from the right-wing conspiracy fantasies of Barruel and Hammer, they imagined such groups to have stood for free thought and for opposition to clerical tyranny, and to have ensured the transmission of their principles by clandestine means. The evidence that such people existed at all in the Middle Ages is meagre in the extreme. If they were to be found anywhere at that period then it must have been among such heretical bodies as the Cathars (Albigensians). But the Cathars were unsatisfactory in that, even if they had had principles of free thought and of anticlerical revolt, there was no tradition which assured that they had handed these principles on to subsequent generations. The Cathars had, apparently, been wiped out except for a few stray survivors by the end of the thirteenth century. But the Templar myth as transmitted through Barruel and Hammer seemed to offer an alternative medieval 'opposition'.

This new legend was not adopted by all radicals. The professional historian, Michelet, was indeed a radical, but one who found it impossible to represent the Templars as having been other than the reactionary and élitist body that they were, even though he allowed the possibility that they might have deviated from the Catholic faith. Michelet's vision of popular fraternity was an ideal which he found impossible to apply to the Templars. But there were plenty of radicals who were quite untroubled by any great burden of knowledge about the Middle Ages, who were only too willing to adopt the Templars as the putative leaders of a reformist enlightenment which had been rooted in secret conspiracy.

The first of such radicals to weave a new theory in which the Templars played a major part was the Italian exile in England (father of the poet and painter), Gabriele Rossetti. Rossetti took refuge in England in the 1820s, and in 1832 published an extravagant, fanciful book on the currents of opposition to the Papacy in the Middle Ages which later led to the Reformation (*Sullo spirito antipapale che produsse la Riforma*). He based his arguments on a strange interpretation of Dante's *Divine Comedy*, and he took the idea of a medieval opposition to the Roman Catholic Church to extreme lengths. He knew hardly anything of the heresies which had in fact existed in the Middle Ages but he made up for this by inventing new ones on a generous scale. As he saw it, Dante had been inspired by principles almost identical with those of the Freemasons, but the great poet had also supported very similar principles which he had found among the Cathars and the Templars. Both the Cathars and the Templars were co-workers in their sectarian opposition to the Church of their time. Rossetti was perhaps not a true esoteric thinker, and his knowledge of Freemasonry sometimes seems as inaccurate and confused as that of Barruel. He turned the arguments upside-down, so that the Templar–Masonic villains of Barruel became his heroes. It is a muddle; it is not surprising that their father's 'mystic books' used to make the Rossetti children groan with boredom. Rossetti composed another book which was never published in a regular fashion in England since his friends feared that its unorthodox views about religion might lose him his teaching post in London. The later work was influenced by Hammer as well as by Barruel, and suggested that the Templars were Cathar and Grail knights as well as Masonic revolutionaries. Dante was a party, he thought, to these medieval conspiracies. Dante's injunction to his readers to look for the concealed meaning of his verses rather than the literal one was acted upon by Rossetti with a wildness which bordered on mania.[57]

By mid-century the idea of a continuous Manichaean–Gnostic opposition to the Christian faith of the Middle Ages, an opposition which anticipated that of the nineteenth-century radicals, had become almost a commonplace. But the hopes of the Left continued to be stigmatized as the fears of the Right. Conservatives continued to come to conclusions about Gnostic–revolutionary secret societies which differed hardly at all from those of the Left, and which encouraged rather than discouraged the left-wing secret society fantasies. The 'Gnostic coffers' which Hammer had examined twenty years earlier were taken out of the cupboard, and their message was again said to be Manichaean and disturbing, concerned with sinister androgynous beings.[58] The aged Hammer himself returned to the controversy in 1854, after Michelet had published the documents of the

Templar case, which Hammer claimed as further proof of his earlier assertions of Templar guilt. One pleasingly bizarre suggestion was that Templar devotion to St John the Baptist should be explained by the Arabic slang meaning of 'Janbetif' (John Baptist), which was, according to Hammer, 'anus'![59]

Rossetti's ideas about a medieval Gnostic opposition which included the Cathars, the Templars, and Dante were diffused with frenetic enthusiasm by the French politician and writer, Eugène Aroux, who portrayed the Middle Ages as having been penetrated by a vast Manichaean conspiracy. The main agents of this plot had been the knightly class, and the courts of love had been the committee meetings of this secret society. The knights of the Holy Grail, the 'Massenie du Saint Graal', had been Manichaean missionaries, precursors of the Freemasons. In this way the Cathars or Albigensians had protested against the tyranny and injustice of their time; when they were bloodily suppressed by the Inquisition their doctrine had passed to the Templars, who were then put down in their turn.[60] At this period of the nineteenth century the black tyranny of the Middle Ages was being denounced by well-known writers of radical tendency such as Victor Hugo and the historian Michelet, whose disillusion with the Middle Ages was now complete. Fanciful interpretations of medieval history such as these were inspired by the idea (to be found in Condorcet) that the human spirit will not, even in times of apparent ignorance and obscurantism, submit without protest to oppression and tyranny. These fantasies found a readier acceptance in an atmosphere in which the conservative writers were equally willing to consent to a picture of the Middle Ages in which secret societies played a subversive part. Thus the great medievalist architect, Viollet-le-Duc, the friend of the family of the Emperor Napoleon III, wrote in his *Dictionary of Medieval Architecture* that Templar buildings were inspired by number mysticism, that the plans of some of their chapels were determined by a mystic scheme of two interpenetrating equilateral triangles, and that their chapels were adapted for chapter meetings which normally took place only at night.[61]

The concept of a great medieval alliance of Manichaean groups, in which the Templars made common cause with Albigensians, Vaudois, and other heretics, reached a peak with the publication in 1877 of the last major Templarist forgeries. A

German Masonic specialist called Merzdorf claimed to have found among other Masonic manuscripts a Latin 'Rule' of the Templars purporting to date from the thirteenth century. The forgery was probably executed at some time after the mid-nineteenth century, when interest in Cathars (Albigensians) became general and when Michelet's documents of the Templar trial had been published. The Rules supposed to have been newly discovered were two, that of the 'chosen brothers' and that of the 'consoled brothers'. The first is written in the spirit of Aroux, describing the medieval Church as the 'Synagogue of Anti-Christ' and stipulating an Elect reception ceremony with various ritual kisses, including one on the male member, though by a misunderstanding of the medieval texts of the trial the Rule makes the aspirant receive the kiss instead of give it. Both Rules emphasize that the Grand Master of the Templar Order is never to be an initiate of the hidden mysteries: this fits with the older Masonic idea that the nominal Grand Masters of the Order had not been the real ones. Both Rules, but especially the second, imply that the Templars shared the doctrine of the Cathars, including that of the *consolamentum* or mystical baptism. There is also a strong suggestion that medieval operative Masons were already in possession of occult secrets; the initiates are told to seek 'great buildings' in order to find other heretical groups. The last are detailed by name in a list taken from histories of medieval heresy. The suggestion is that all these groups – Poor Men of Lyons, Cathars, Bagnolenses, Bulgars, Beguins – were in active correspondence with one another, a notion which would make a modern historian of these matters smile. A peculiarly nineteenth-century addition, perhaps taken from de Nerval, is the idea that the Druses of the Lebanon were another corresponding heretical sect which ought to be fraternally welcomed by the others. Finally, the 'Rule of the Consoled' stipulates a bizarre ceremony in which the opening verse of the Koran is to be recited (though why monotheist Islam is thus imported into dualist heresy is hard to see), the aspirant receives the consoling 'baptism of fire', the idol of Baphomet is taken from its coffer to be adored, and the congregation cry 'Yah-Allah!'

What distinguishes the Merzdorf Templar 'Rules' from earlier Templarist forgeries is that they were documents concocted to be read, not rites concocted to be enacted. The earlier

Masons had invented all sorts of Templarist fictions with the intention of inventing or strengthening Orders or Degrees; the aim was that brothers should actually assemble to 'work' one rite or another. But the Merzdorf forgeries are literary inventions whose eventual target is the reading public, not the restricted Masonic circle. The guise under which the Rules were presented was historical: in fact the text of the historical Rule of the Templars, by then well known, was prefaced by Merzdorf to the other two. The primary aim of Templarism was no longer ritualistic but literary.

From the beginning the Templar myth had been marked by ambiguity of purpose. Was its intention religious or political? The Templars had been represented as having formed a secret society, but was that society an assembly of wise and benevolent men or a wicked conspiracy? The rites inspired by the Templar myth were solemn and imposing, but was their practice the enactment of a serious parable or a trivial piece of play-acting? These ambiguities were never better illustrated than in the career of the French Catholic deacon, the Abbé Alphonse-Louis Constant, who later wrote under the name of Eliphas Lévi.[62] Constant was a writer and artist, in minor Catholic orders, who was one of the main 'Communists' in French radical circles in the 1840s. As a journalist and propagandist Constant was not negligible. He was the friend, adviser, and, eventually, editor of the feminist socialist writer, Flora Tristan. He was also the friend of similar figures who dabbled in left-wing politics and mysticism, such as the Marquis Sarrazin de Montferrier, the former chief-priest of the Neo-Templars. Sarrazin for a time owned a newspaper which printed Constant's articles, but he later occasioned scandal when Constant's wife left her husband on his account.

In this environment Constant encountered the Templar myth in its radical form as a story of enlightened, benign conspirators who transmitted doctrines of wisdom and power and opposed clerical tyranny. Constant remained a 'Communist' of some sort into the period of the Revolution of 1848, in the course of which he edited a short-lived journal, the *Tribun du Peuple*. But he became disillusioned with politics shortly afterwards, and his last socialist work appeared in July 1848. From that point onwards the mystical strain in his work became more important than the political. It is possible that his conversion to the role of an esoteric seer happened under the influence of Sarrazin's brother-in-law, the Polish polymath, Hoene-Wronskí.

Constant turned to magical doctrines, hoping to combine the heritages of eighteenth-century Illuminism and of Renaissance Cabbalism in a single 'scientific' theory. The idea that all esoteric learning could be combined in a single synthesis of hidden knowledge was far from new, but Constant acted on it in a particulary wholesale way, and in a sense he was among the first of modern 'occultists', who purport to deal with all such knowledge, whereas the older esoteric studies had concerned themselves with single and discrete occult sciences. Constant was in fact quite unequal to the demands of the task he had set himself, and much of his work is a dreadful jumble. Politics having ceased to be his dominant interest, his political views became infuriatingly equivocal. He drifted away from socialism, but did not renounce it. In 1855, some time after he had turned towards occultism, he was imprisoned for a short time for lampooning the Emperor Napoleon III; though it would be fair to add that he secured his release by addressing a conciliatory poem to the ruler whose police he had offended.

In his history of magic Constant assigned the Templars a bloodcurdling conspiratorial role, in the tradition of Barruel. They had been 'des conspirateurs terribles'. Though he dismissed the Neo-Templars of the 1830s as amateurs, Constant adopted the essentials of their doctrine, in a very embroidered form. Following the *Levitikon* of Fabré-Palaprat, Constant made the Templars into 'Johannites' who had inherited the mystic gospel of the priests of Osiris in Egypt through Jesus and the apostle John. Like the Englishman William Blake (but in spite of the Catholicism he affected to retain), Constant thought that 'The morning blushed fiery red/Mary was found in adulterous bed'. Jesus, instead of repudiating his mother, had adopted the myths of her virginity and of his divinity. The Johannite doctrine of Gnostic Cabbalism had been passed to the Templars, under whom according to Constant it had degenerated into a kind of pantheistic nature-worship. This transformation had persuaded the Templars to render divine honours to the idol 'Baphomet', on the lines of the adoration accorded to the Golden Calf by the

Hebrews. But this did not exhaust Constant's ideas on the Templars, to whom he gave a central place in his magical explanation of the world. He thought the Baphomet figure to have been the symbol of ultimate wisdom, of Azoth, of the philosopher's stone; it was also, because it continued traditions of primeval wisdom, to be agglomerated with the Egyptian goat-god, Mendes. The real crime of the Templars had been their betrayal of this great secret to the profane, through the organization of the proto-Masonic lodges by the last Templar Grand Master.

Constant's pretensions to scientific understanding, though they may have deceived some, were a thin covering for a mind whose real talent was for the invention of poetic parables. There is a parallel between his elaboration of the Templar myth and his invention of the idea of a correspondence between the 'triumph' cards of the card game of Tarot and a fictitious system of 'Egyptian' symbolism. Piling fresh inventions on those to be found in the book of the late-eighteenth-century Freemason, Court de Gébelin, Constant fabricated a magical relationship between the Hebrew Cabbala and the Tarot pack which is strikingly similar in nature to his fantasies about 'Baphomet'.[63] In both cases his own talent as an artist was pressed into service to illustrate his supposed discoveries: he executed a representation of 'Isis enthroned' in the so-called primitive Egyptian Tarot, and this figure is an equivalent to an equally imaginative engraving of 'Baphomet' in the same book, in which he endows Baphomet with ancient Egyptian characteristics.

When Constant came to the political implications of Templarism he adopted an outwardly conservative and Barruelist line, accepting the notion that the Templars had set up Masonic lodges which had persisted into the modern period, and which had been dedicated to the overthrow of Christian society. According to Constant the eighteenth-century French Masonic nobles had been guilty of a sort of mass social suicide: impelled by egalitarian fury, the nobles had themselves corrupted the people. The French Revolution had indeed been the revenge of Jacques de Molay; it had proceeded from 'a secret and irresistible impulse to destroy a decadent civilization'. Thus the theories of liberal historians about the part played by the nobility in the Revolution were woven into a magical explanation of history. But what were the political implications of Constant's position? No doubt he continued to see the French Revolution of 1789 as a liberation from dead institutions and ideas. This was not a politically unorthodox position under Napoleon III. But he also strongly suggested that the powers of the Templars and of the secret societies had been real, because based on true knowledge of the nature of things. He thus supplied a basis on which another generation of occultist politicians could once more take up the Templar myth, and use it in a different way.

The radicals had maintained the Templars to have been an early form of enlightened opposition to Church and State. They had had this idea from the conservatives, who condemned as diabolical what their opponents hailed as inspired by secret truth. But the nature of the Templar and of the secret-society myths was so amorphous that it was quite easy to adapt their message and to turn it from the radical Left to the radical Right. When a new, anti-clerical, and romantic Right emerged in the 1890s, some of its members could adopt the Templars as a secret élite who were the custodians of superior knowledge. Later, this was destined to confer on its adepts the supreme power in modern society. When Constant (in his guise as 'Eliphas Lévi') acquired readers and disciples in the France of the Third Republic, these post-1870 followers incorporated much of his magical doctrine, including Templarism, into the new theory of aristocratic politics. It was no accident that one of Constant's first important supporters, when he began to preach magical lore, had been the Englishman Bulwer Lytton, later the author of *The Future Race*. Lytton predicted the dissolution of decadent democracy and the rule of an enlightened ruler-class called the Vril: he was typical, in this, of many of Constant's readers in the last part of the century.

Behind most romantic fantasies of the Templar type lay the idea of a pre-Christian, profound wisdom, preserved through the period of orthodox Catholic belief by means of some form of secret society. Belief in the pre-Christian origin of the secret societies was widely enough diffused to attract a mention in Disraeli's novel, *Lothair*. Often connected with this was the belief in the persistence of primitive linguistic traditions. The Druid and the Celtic myths were in many respects parallel to the Templar myth. Folklorists were therefore in many ways the natural allies of Templarists, especially as the idea of primitive pre-Christian survivals in peasant custom was fundamental to the ideas of the 'Germanist' party among the folklore students. Hammer's suggestion that the Templars had been the custodians of a phallic cult originating in much earlier times was an idea which fitted in well with this mode of thought. In 1865 the distinguished antiquary, Thomas Wright, with two others contributed an essay 'On the worship of the generative powers during the Middle Ages in Western Europe' to Richard Knight's *A Discourse on the Worship of Priapus and its connection with the mystic theology of the Ancients*. Wright and his co-writers (Witt and Tennent) depended for their argument on the thesis of Michelet in *La Sorcière* that the peasantry turned to priapic rites as a form of social protest. But they added that the upper classes of society cultivated the priapic beliefs in a higher form through the medium of secret societies, and they instanced the Templars as an example.[64]

The idea of a Templar phallic cult in the Middle Ages, though strongly pressed by Hammer and repeated by Wright, was not the argument which proved most interesting to the folklorists, though the concept of a fertility cult was not far from their minds. Two elements in the Grail legend seemed to point towards a connection with the Templars, both of them most strongly emphasized in a poem by Wolfram of Eschenbach. One was the poet's mention of a body of Grail knights called *Templeisen*, though it was not clear that these knights actually were Templars. It seemed, however, to some writers, that the term demonstrated that there had been a connection between the Grail and the Templar Order. Allied with this possibility was the suggestion that the Fisher King of the Grail story who was mutilated in the genitals belonged to a tradition that the reproductive forces of nature were affected by the sexual potency of the ruler. The charge against the Templars that their idol made the trees grow and the plants flower seemed to connect them with a vegetation cult of this sort.[65]

The British folklorist Alfred Nutt was deeply committed to the idea of a tradition of pre-Christian myth which was present in Christian peasant society. He interpreted the 'Grail Church' of the medieval romances as not only reminiscent of but modelled on the principles of the Knights Templar. To him the Grail stood behind a 'knightly priesthood' which claimed to be equal if not superior to the Catholic priesthood. According to Nutt the 'Templar knights' had stood out against 'ultramontanism' or Catholic orthodoxy; strikingly, he employed the language of theological controversy of the 1870s and 1880s to describe these medieval matters.[66] Though rejected by some mystical folklorists, Nutt's thesis was enthusiastically embraced by his disciple in the Folklore Society and in the study of supposed Arthurian tradition, Miss Jessie L. Weston. Embroidering on Nutt's thesis, she returned to the Hammer thesis of continuity between third-century Gnosticism (she decided, for obscure reasons, in favour of a sect called the Naassenes) and the Templars. Had the Templars come into contact with a survival of the Naassene tradition during their crusading service in the East, she asked? It seemed to her to be exceedingly probable. If this had been so, it would explain the 'puzzling connection' of the Templars with the Knights of the Grail and it would also explain the doom which fell upon the Templar Order. By a further jump in the argument, which is particularly hard to follow, she purported to see that Templar knowledge of Grail secrets made them into no ordinary heretics but into the possessors of a doctrine which criticized Christianity in such a fundamental and radical way that at the time of the Templar trial the existence of the Grail heresy had to be hushed up, so as not to imperil the very survival of the Christian faith!

Jessie Weston, whose work on a related subject was later to be drawn on by T. S. Eliot for *The Waste Land*, was yet another writer whose speculations were poetic parables rather than scholarly investigations. Wolfram of Eschenbach may have allowed the name of the Templars, as another body of devoted Christian knights, to have influenced him when he called his Grail knights *Templeisen*, but that does not in the least mean that he identified one set of knights with another, or that the Templars were in any way related to the Grail story. Jessie Weston's Gnostic story, and her assertion that the Templars possessed knowledge so lethal to the Christian faith that its existence had to be suppressed, were typical instances of the secret-society mania which was if anything rather more pervasive at the end of the nineteenth century than thirty or forty years earlier. Darwinism had for a time made mystical explanations unfashionable, but by the 1890s they were flooding back. In itself Jessie Weston's Templar story is negligible: it is logically absurd in that it explains nothing about the Templars which cannot be explained in other, far more satisfactory, ways. Its interest lies in its having carried the old Masonic, secret-society myths into fields of anthropological and literary studies which at least seemed to be serious and 'scientific'.

Popular science was, indeed, the milieu into which a great deal of theosophical and occultist activity was moved during the late nineteenth century. Eliphas Lévi (Alphonse-Louis Constant) and many similar writers pretended that their theories expressed some kind of 'natural supernaturalism' which was a true expression of modern 'scientific' thought. Other theories of the same sort asserted such pseudo-scientific theories as 'animal magnetism'. There was also a tendency, strongly evident in Constant's magical books, to merge all the occultist, mystical theories in a single complex source. Templars and Tarot, Masons and Cabbala, all came together in a single magical mish-mash. Esoteric Egyptology, Indian religion, occultist versions of medieval chivalrous epics, tales of the pre-history of Stonehenge and of the supposed tradition of the Druids and of Atlantis, doctrines of 'Johannine' Gnosticism, all began to flow in and out of one another in a crazy tradition of immemorial 'wisdom', which also purported to be a form of science.

Anthropologists and folklorists contributed, if indirectly, to this dubious tradition. Sir James Frazer's *The Golden Bough*, the most influential of all texts dealing with vegetation cults and their survival, was published in 1890. His ideas were picked over in Paris in the milieu of the 'Salon de la Rose†Croix', the group of artist–magicians round Joséphin Péladan ('Sâr' Péladan') and Stanislas de Guaita. De Guaita was a magician of the school of Constant; Péladan was an esoteric writer obsessed by the theme of bisexuality, who wrote tedious novels about the 'androgyne' in the tradition of Balzac's *Séraphita*. Hammer's *Mystery of Baphomet Revealed* had identified the god of the Templars as an androgynous deity, and the figures of ancient gods on the 'caskets' which he associated with the Templars were also bisexual; their worship was supposed to have been marked by orgiastic rites. This aspect of Hammer's doctrine was about to come in to its own. The period was that of an esoteric, élitist decadentism in which the magical arts held an important place.

It was in this charged, *fin-de-siècle* atmosphere that the Templar myth was transformed, for some of its devotees at least, from a tale of speculative mystics to a tale of abandoned Satanists. The key man in this process was a German journalist, Theodor Reuss. Reuss was an occultist connected with the fringes of British Freemasonry; he had at an earlier stage been in touch with British socialist groups, and perhaps with the esoteric circle around Mme Blavatsky. He was also interested in Yoga, which with other Eastern esoteric matters had become very fashionable at the end of the century: Reuss was especially interested in the sexual techniques of Yoga. In the late 1890s he met an Austrian industrialist called Karl Kellner; the latter proposed to launch a new 'Masonic Academy', but later abandoned this in favour of an 'Order of Oriental Templars'. Reuss appears to have done nothing about this for some years, in the course of which he became an enterprising promoter of esoteric Masonic orders, rather in the style of the Masonic charlatans of the eighteenth century. One of these 'Orders' was an attempt to revive the Illuminati of Bavaria, though doubtless in a form which had little to do with its original.

By 1906 Reuss had milked the German Masons of all the money he was likely to get from them, and he transferred his operations to England. By this time he was describing himself, in addition to many other grandiloquent titles, as 'Sovereign Grand Master of the Order of the Temple of the Orient'. He claimed to have proofs of the connection of his Order of the Temple with the original Order of medieval Templars, but these proofs were naturally of so secret a nature that it had never been possible to commit them to writing, and they could be communicated only to the initiated. Reuss's interests at this time were strongly towards the study of phallic or sexual religious practices, and it seems possible that the O.T.O. (Order of the Temple of the Orient) had been endowed with a doctrine which similarly emphasized these matters. But in 1912 Reuss met a magus more powerful than himself, whom he recognized as 'The Most Holy, Most Illustrious, Most Illuminated and Most Puissant Baphomet, X°, Rex Summus Sanctissimus, 33°, 90°,

96°, Past Grand Master of the United States of America, Grand Master of Ireland, Iona, etc.'[67] In this typically modest manner the British magician, Aleister Crowley, took up the cause of the Templars.

The nature of the rituals conducted in the O.T.O. under the magistracy of Aleister Crowley is mercifully rather obscure: Crowley on one occasion referred moderately to the O.T.O. as 'a training of the Masonic type'. On the other hand, reports of the 'Paris working' of 1914, which was closely connected with the O.T.O., refer to the ritual sodomizing of the unfortunate Victor Neuburg.[68] I cannot think that H.R.H. the Duke of Connaught, then Grand Master of the Masonic Order of the Temple, would have approved of these proceedings. Two things seem clear: first, that a large part of the preoccupations of the O.T.O. were with 'sexual magic'; second, that the historical origins which Crowley imagined for the Order were mostly fictitious. A long litany of predecessors was recited – Cagliostro, Mesmer, but above all the Bavarian Illuminati of Weishaupt –whose connection with the Templars was merely mythical. It is hard to know where the Templars fitted into the O.T.O.; there is no role for celibate zealots in a philosophy which emphasizes all sorts of odd sexual practices.

The myth of the secret societies, as diffused in the early nineteenth century in the writings of Barruel and Hammer, had represented the Templarists as wicked radicals. In the mid-nineteenth century, by a strange process of fusion through repulsion, the Templarist myth for a time became part of the radical socialist dream. But from the late nineteenth century onwards Templarism drifted back to a place in the imagination of the Right. It is true that 'spiritualism' of various kinds still kept a certain grip on some socialist circles as late as the turn of the century, not only in the milieu of Shaw and Mrs Besant, but in humbler parts of the Labour Movement like the Plebeian Spiritualists.[69] But the mainstream of *fin-de-siècle* magicians, particularly such groups as the Order of the Golden Dawn, with which Aleister Crowley was closely connected, professed an aristocratic philosophy of social selection and personal will. They opposed their anti-Christian mysteries, which were revealed to and understood by the few, to the vulgar conformism of the masses. Enlightenment came from personal instruction imparted by the master to the disciple. Inevitably, the political outlook linked with such doctrines was fiercely élitist. Crowley never referred to democracy with anything but contempt. His former admirer, the British soldier and military theorist, Major-General J. F. C. Fuller, gave his support in the 1930s to the British Union of Fascists.[70]

In France the connection between the later Templarist myths and the Right is much easier to follow. Its initiator was Joseph Alexandre Saint-Yves d'Alveydre, a mystical conservative of the 1880s. Saint-Yves d'Alveydre was in some respects a clericalist; he claimed to hold a title of nobility granted him by the pope. But he belonged to the chaotically romantic conservatives. Part of the inspiration for the doctrine he professed came from Aroux's ideas on the Templars as a secret society which had dominated the medieval world through the covert operation of their wealth and technical ability. Other aspects of his doctrine (one hesitates to call it 'thought') were drawn from the fashionable oriental fantasies of Louis Jacolliot (1837–90), and from the usual Masonic and occultist witches' brew. Saint-Yves d'Alveydre added a kind of Saint-Simonian emphasis on the importance of the Templars as managerial ruler-technocrats; and from this he produced the theory of theocratic 'synarchy' or joint rule, which aimed at the oligarchy of a chosen band of initiates who exercised their rule through bodies which represented the various orders of society.[71] The historical justification offered for this idea was that the Templars had been the hidden rulers of Europe, or virtually so, during the Middle Ages. Their ubiquitous presence throughout Europe and the Levant, and their possession of secret wisdom acquired in the East, led them to aim at the domination not only of Europe but of the continents of Africa and Asia, including the holy cities of Jerusalem and Mecca. Like Aroux and Rossetti, Saint-Yves d'Alveydre applied secret-society mania retrospectively to the Middle Ages: the fresh historical embroidery came from his imagination, or from Jacolliot.

Saint-Yves d'Alveydre also maintained that the Templars had been the true inspirers of the Estates General, the meeting of the three estates of clergy, commons, and nobles which had been a kind of representative institution under the French monarchy of the later Middle Ages. The implication was that the fall of the

Templars deprived the Estates General of their effectiveness, a doctrine which would surprise the historian who has recently maintained that Philip the Fair devoted much effort to securing the consent of nobles and commons to his measures.[72] To Saint-Yves d'Alveydre the Templars stood for a policy of federation and universal peace which went back to the Carolingians of the early Middle Ages. Like many French conservative thinkers, including (many years after him) Charles de Gaulle, he felt that the *ancien régime* in France had taken a wrong turning, responsible for its later catastrophe, which he could identify. Unfortunately his choice of the Templars as a solution to the supposed riddle of the French monarchy was wrong; they had performed none of the functions that he attributed to them, and his speculations about them were daydreams added to the old fantasies of Aroux.

His strange version of medieval history brought no fame to Saint-Yves d'Alveydre in his lifetime. But during and after the Second World War it gave rise to a new secret-society myth, which we may call the myth of the synarchists. The conditions under which the Vichy regime of 1940 was established and conducted were very favourable to the spread of myths. The regime included socialists as well as conservatives, and no one was sure what ideology it represented. The Vichy regime legislated against Freemasonry, and co-operated with the Germans in identifying and acting against Masons. But, even within the regime itself, people were very doubtful that Freemasonry had genuinely been banished. In the so-called 'Chavin Report', which seems to have originated from within or near government circles, allegations were made that a large number of people in responsible positions belonged to Masonic political groups called 'synarchist' which had been in existence since the 1920s. These synarchists were supposed to have been inspired in part by the doctrine of Saint-Yves d'Alveydre. They were represented as a group of influential politicians, businessmen, and so-called 'technocrats' who had been plotting to seize power ever since a reputed 'Synarchist Revolutionary Pact' of 1922. The heart of this synarchist group was made out to be the ministers round Pierre Pucheu in the Darlan government.[73] Pucheu was the first Vichy minister to be executed, so subsequent checking of the allegations was difficult.

It is more than likely that, in spite of the ban, there were still many Freemasons in the Vichy regime. Vichy represented the interests of a *grande bourgeoisie* in which Freemasonry had always been strong. It is even possible that a few of these Vichy Freemasons had at some time interested themselves in branches of esoteric Masonry in which the ideas of synarchy were discussed. But there is no proof that synarchy played any political role whatsoever in the Vichy regime. The idea was a secret-society smear which could have originated either among the left-wing elements of Vichy or from Gaullist sources outside France. It may have been inspired by the apparently parallel case of the 'X-Crise' Club of Jean Coutrot, an organization which had publicized the ideas of technocratic planning during the Popular Front period of the mid-1930s. X-Crise had been a sort of left-wing plan for an oligarchy of technocrats; synarchy seems to have been thought of as a sort of Masonic right-wing plan for an oligarchy of technocrats. As in all secret-society mythology, the secret society was said to exist, but was also said to be too secret to be proved to exist. The allegations are far from surprising. The *Revue internationale des sociétés secrètes* had continued the Barruel tradition of the 'exposure' of subversive groups down to the Second World War. Templarism was not forgotten by the Second World War propagandists; one of the main writers to denounce 'synarchy' was Raoul Husson, who wrote his pamphlet under the pseudonym of Geoffroy de Charnay, the name of the Templar Preceptor of Normandy who was burned in 1314.[74]

But if the influence of Saint-Yves d'Alveydre on practical politics was nil, his influence on the dreamers was great, and is shown by virtually all subsequent French writers on esoteric subjects who tried to deal with Templarism. Victor-Émile Michelet, a former collaborator of the Symbolist poet Guillaume Apollinaire and a survivor of the esoteric groups of the 1890s, swallowed the fables of Saint-Yves d'Alveydre with the same enthusiasm that he swallowed those of Constant. Michelet was full of Eliphas Lévi fantasies, including those about the 'Baphomet', which he described picturesquely as 'the Kheroub of Assyria and Israel, the Arabic Kharouf, the Egyptian and Greek Sphinx, the *pantacle* [a favourite word of the Constant jargon, meaning an occult symbolic design] which combines the four animals of the Apocalypse', and so on. The 'Johannite' Templars, arbiters of medieval Christendom by virtue of their control of finance and industry, founders of the Estates General of France, are taken by Michelet more or less as he found them in the text of Saint-Yves d'Alveydre. However, Michelet added one or two pleasingly original touches, such as the casual assertion that the Hanseatic ports of medieval Germany were run by the Druids!

From the Second World War onwards, Michelet was in turn adopted more or less literally by most French popular writers on esoteric subjects. V.-E. Michelet had been a cultivated man, a poet if of the second rank. Although inspired by a frenzy for extravagant poetic parables, he knew that these were metaphors and not sober facts.[75] But his successors were credulous and literal-minded, and the myth of the Templars was divulged to the French public with scarcely a hint of its metaphorical nature.[76] Other, even wilder, writers extended the boundaries of the Templar dream to the shores of delirium. Louis Charpentier, for example, in two books not remarkable for the clarity of their ideas, claimed that the Templars were despatched to the Holy Land by St Bernard to fetch the Ark of the Temple of Solomon back to Europe. His evidence that they were successful in this enterprise is the building of the Gothic cathedrals of Europe, which the Templars financed partly with silver produced by the practice of alchemy, partly with more silver which (three centuries before Columbus) they imported from the Americas, and disembarked at La Rochelle![77] The dreams of Templar treasure returned, as in the eighteenth century, to make men pretend that they had occult knowledge of its whereabouts.[78] Both in France and Britain the luxuriant growth of Templar fantasy spilled over on to the television screen. Ideas of the Templars as mysterious, mystical guardians, probably connected with the Holy Grail, also led to their being represented as the custodians of a mysterious object, the Holy Shroud of Turin.[79] In France, but also to some extent in Britain, the old material of Templarist dreams has been re-worked, and has given rise to a minor journalistic industry.

All these fresh Templar fantasies, though absurd, have been very innocent. In spite of occasional attempts by the secret-society maniacs to represent it as such, Templarism is not and has never been a wicked and destructive fantasy of the type of the Protocols of the Elders of Zion, or like the old witchcraft hysteria. It has proved to be an eccentric but harmless theosophical dream, sometimes exploited by charlatans to the detriment of the credulous, but not used to encompass evil ends. Recent imaginative writers have on the whole used the Templar myth in ways which implicitly accept its theosophical premises. The British novelist Lawrence Durrell in *Monsieur* has used the Templar myth in a very traditional form, employing the reference to Gnostic cults of Valentinianism and Ophitism, and even using the explanations of Nicolai and Hammer for the etymology of 'Baphomet'. Templarism may lie in the background of the secret-society lore displayed in Thomas Pynchon's *The Crying of Lot 49*; it is drawn upon in a very crude and sensationalist way in Robert Shea's and Robert Anton Wilson's *Illuminatus!* On the other hand, the Italian novelist Italo Calvino, who is knowledgeable about eighteenth-century Illuminism, in *Il cavaliere inesistente* ('The non-existent knight') treats the Templar myth with considerable scepticism, mocks the mystical Templars for their pompous mumbo-jumbo, and treats them as examples of bigoted egotism.

No serious political use of Templarism has been made since the 'synarchy' stories of the period of Vichy and of the Liberation of France. There was some mention of synarchy in the trials of some of the political leaders of Vichy, and then the term dropped into obscurity. There has been, however, some confirmation that the political effects of dabbling or showing interest in Templarism and things of this nature can only be negative. From the secret-society panics of French Revolutionary times to the 'Lodge P2' scandals of modern Italy, the history of Freemasonry has shown that once secret-society mythology has been used, it can never be washed from the hands of the user. French journalists have been rather reckless about political Templarism. It has been asserted that the sordid murder in 1981 of Jacques Massié, a supposed official of the *Service d'Action Civile*, was connected with his membership of the Masonic Templars.

Anyone who dwells on supposed connections between esoteric organizations and political life has to pay a penalty. For example, ideas of the pervasive influence of secret societies and of the past importance of doctrines of the synarchy kind have for years been professed by a well-known contemporary French journalist, M. Louis Pauwels. M. Pauwels was the co-author of a best-selling book on esoteric and para-scientific traditions, and later the editor of a magazine, *Planète*, in which he constantly hinted at the existence of some sort of alternative culture which he thought could be offered as a substitute for scientific rationalism.[80] He was the general editor of a series of books on secret societies and mysterious persons, two of which concerned Templarism and synarchy respectively. Having worked for some years as a prominent journalist for the conservative newspaper, *Le Figaro*, M. Pauwels has recently sought to distance himself from the charges of conspiratorial extremism which tend to be brought against some sections of the French Right. In disowning extremism M. Pauwels is no doubt sincere; to a British reader he appears to be (if such a thing is imaginable) a sort of anti-Catholic G. K. Chesterton. But he has been hoist with his own petard. Having associated himself for so long with the notion that secretly acquired knowledge is a vital factor in human affairs, M. Pauwels now finds it impossible to convince people that he is saying all that he knows or thinks.[81]

Secret-society myths are usually concerned to suggest the existence of small, powerful groups which work invisibly. But the political importance of such myths is their effect on the general currents and atmosphere of public opinion. It can be shown from the history of Templarism that small, private groups of people who profess esoteric doctrines with a political flavour, and sometimes practice eccentric rituals, do from time to time exist. So far as Templarism is concerned, the political and social effect of such groups has been negligible. What matters to society is the vague, disquieting effects either of propagandists who spread alarming reports of secret-society conspiracies or of esoteric publicists who diffuse ideas of the miraculous and the marvellous, and give the impression that social change can easily be effected by the performers of wonders. This second group, it is sometimes thought, may prepare the ground for revolutions even if they do not profess explicitly revolutionary ideas. There is an anxiety that superstitious and irrational novelties may dispose men's minds towards the acceptance of greater novelties, and so facilitate great and undesirable political changes. From the disillusioned Jacobin, Cadet de Gassicourt, onwards, the feeling that such people as Mesmerists and Templarists threaten rational political life has periodically come to the surface. In so far as this anxiety extends to the whole gamut of superstitious and esoteric beliefs in a society, it is too general to be meaningful. We may sympathize with someone like the German journalist, Rudolf Olden, who wrote a rather despairing preface to a book on superstitious and occult beliefs in Germany, published a few months before Hitler came to power in 1933. At that fateful moment Olden was appalled by the defencelessness of human personality when choices were made into which the 'marvellous' entered, whether the choice was sexual, or of a 'star' in the cinema, or of Adolf Hitler.[82] We may sympathize, with a little more imaginative effort, with the Byzantine intellectuals who were cut down in the magical purge of the Emperor Valens in AD 374. But the sad fact is that most societies are pervaded at some levels by superstitious and occult beliefs for most of the time, and a generalized concern about the bad effects of these beliefs gets us nowhere. What we can usefully do is to identify so far as we can the nature of such groups as Mesmerists or Templarists, and try to assess both the immediate political effects (if there were any) and the effects on the wider circles of public opinion and political discourse.

As James Billington has pointed out, the occult language adopted by one or two early social revolutionaries such as Buonarroti has had an incalculable effect on the later linguistic usage and perhaps on the organization of more modern revolutionary groups. But we must beware of thinking that occultism in itself has any power to direct men Left, Right, or Centre. Charles Nodier, of whose activities as an occultist 'Philadelphian' revolutionary Billington speaks at length, later in life adopted a much more pessimistic position about his dreams. Nodier's later view was that fantasy reconciles men to their fate. Fantasy and the taste for chimeras, he wrote, are symptoms of a time of political decay and transition, when the unpleasant realities of political life are too hard to bear. They serve a useful purpose in that they give men hope when scepticism and disillusion would otherwise drive them to despair.[83] Like Constant, in middle age Nodier turned to an esoteric position which was implicitly conservative.

Templarism is not dead. The Masonic Templars continue their lodges, which in Great Britain have several times in this century been presided over by a member of the reigning dynasty. In the United States the Masonic Templar 'encampments' still pitch their tents. On the continent of Europe there are many Templar organizations, some of which, if they sound bizarre and eccentric, are no more so than other Templar organizations which have been recorded in this book. The note of bizarre play-acting has never been absent from Templarism, and, indeed, in this lack of 'seriousness' some of its crazy charm lies. One of the more innocent attractions of esotericism is that it can be an irreverent and cheeky game, which by implication makes fun of established patterns of behaviour, especially those influenced by religion. It seems to the initiates that they go by rules and myths which the inspirers of the other rules and myths could not possibly know or understand, and that this is a game which they may play but which is forbidden to others. Who cannot remember from childhood the attractions of the game in which we would not allow the less favoured children to take part? One of the comments made by its early critics on Freemasonry was that the Masons were like children who wanted to 'faire la chapelle', which has the meaning of 'playing at church' just as children 'play at doctors'. A lot of the Templarist literature written for the popular market conveys this feeling of play: tales of buried treasure in Norman castles and Pyrenean hills, of astrological grids which lead us to the hidden places of the Holy Grail deep in the Forest of the East, are all so many reversions to the world of the fairy-tales of Charles Nodier. And Charles Nodier himself had begun as a radical and mystical Freemason, expert in the Masonic myths.

The shifting history of Templarism, with its movements from one interpretation of the Templar story to an opposite one, reflects the original Masonic confusion between the parable and the truth the parable was supposed to represent. But it also reveals the way in which men fulfil their spiritual needs in a manner which broadly corresponds to an earlier pattern, but which is nevertheless made in their image. Nothing is more misleading than the claim that there is an immemorial esoteric tradition which places antique and prehistoric wisdom at the disposal of the adept. It is true that some esoteric principles derive from a philosophical tradition of great antiquity. But students of the supposed hidden truths are also men of their times, and they have employed esoteric ideas in the service of interests and concepts which have changed from one generation to another. The tradition as applied to the Templar myth has proved to be Protean in its mutability. The Templars have been benign, rational sages for one generation, demonic Satanists for another, wise, wealthy technocrats for a third.

The unromantic truth is that the Templars of the Middle Ages made not the slightest attempt to build the Temple of Wisdom, unless that Temple is defined as that of the Catholic Church. The end of the Templars arose not from the operation of demonic forces but as a result of their own mediocrity and lack of nerve. A handful of them measured up to the terrible challenge which confronted them, but most, including their leaders, at the moment of trial proved to have nothing much to say. In the Holy Land the Templars had been brave soldiers but rather short-sighted politicians, who in no way conformed to the high standards which their nineteenth-century admirers ascribed to them. The most striking characteristic of the medieval Templars was their ordinariness; they represent the common man, and not the uncommon visionary. Mozart's noble Masonic opera, *The Magic Flute*, holds out the vision of a Temple of Reason and Nature presided over by the ruler-seer, Sarastro. If the Temple of Sarastro is ever to be built, and if man is to live in some state of Mozartian harmony, it may be on principles in which the Freemason ideal has had a part, but it will not be based on the ideals of the medieval Templars.

NOTES

Part I. The Templars

1. See H. Grundmann, *Ausgewählte Schriften*, i (*Schriften der Monumenta Germaniae Historica*, xxv, 1976), p. 131; and A. Murray, *Reason and Society in the Middle Ages* (Oxford, 1978), pp. 374–82.

2. St Bernard, *Sermo exhortatorius ad milites Templi*, cap. v. This passage is often assumed to concern the Templars alone, but at a time when they were so few the mention of a 'vast throng' and of a 'torrent' of crusading warriors in the passage makes it more likely that the reference is to crusading knights in general.

3. B. A. Lees, *Records of the Templars in England in the Twelfth Century* (London, 1935), pp. lxii, 38. The best discussion of the privileges of the Military Orders is in J. Riley-Smith, *The Knights of St John in Jerusalem and Cyprus c. 1050–1310* (London, 1967), pp. 375–89.

4. E. Lambert, *L'Architecture des Templiers* (Paris, 1955). Opinion is divided whether the circular churches imitated the rotunda of the Church of the Holy Sepulchre or the Dome of the Rock. Cf. C. Enlart, *Les monuments des croisés dans le royaume de Jérusalem*, ii (Paris, 1928), p. 209.

5. H. de Curzon, *La règle du Temple* (Paris, 1886), pp. 23–4. I cannot agree with the idea that these knights had been excommunicated for heresy. Heretic knights would not receive the absolution from the bishop which the statute contemplates.

6. A. J. Forey, *The Templars in the Corona de Aragón* (London, 1973), pp. 281–2, 288.

7. Curzon, *La règle*, pp. 313–14.

8. M. L. Bulst-Thiele, 'Templer in königlichen und päpstlichen Dienst', *Festschrift Percy Ernst Schramm*, i (Wiesbaden, 1964), pp. 289–308.

9. S. Schein, '*Gesta dei per Mongolos*: the genesis of a non-event', *English Historical Review*, xciv (1979), pp. 805–19. For Innocent III see R. W. Southern, *Western Views of Islam in the Middle Ages* (Cambridge, Mass., 1962), p. 42; and see also N. Daniel, *The Arabs and Mediaeval Europe* (London, 1975).

10. M. L. Bulst-Thiele, *Sacrae Domus Militiae Templi Hierosolymitani Magistri. Untersuchungen zur Geschichte des Templerordens 1118/19 – 1314* (Göttingen, 1974) [henceforth, Bulst-Thiele, *SDMTHM*], pp. 159 ff.

11. R. C. Smail, *Crusading Warfare, 1097–1193* (Cambridge, 1956); idem, *The Crusaders* (London, 1973); J. Riley-Smith, *The Knights of St John in Jerusalem and Cyprus c. 1050–1310* (London, 1967); P. Deschamps, *Les Châteaux des*

Croisés en Terre Sainte (Paris, 1934–9); T. S. R. Boase, *Castles and Churches of the Crusading Kingdom* (London, 1967); M. Benvenist, *The Crusaders in the Holy Land* (Jerusalem, 1970); Bulst-Thiele, *SDMTHM*, pp. 351 ff.

12. Riley-Smith, *Knights of St John*, pp. 127 ff. For Templar-Hospitaller disputes, ibid. pp. 151 ff., 443 ff.; M. L. Bulst, 'Zur Geschichte der Ritterorden . . .', *Deutsches Archiv*, xxii (1966), pp. 197–226, esp. pp. 207 ff.

13. 1,100,000 besants, worth about £25,000 sterling of the period, or roughly five-sixths of the ordinary annual revenue of the English king.

14. Burton Annals, *Annales Monastici* (ed. H. R. Luard, *Rolls Series*, 1864), i, pp. 491–5. Cf. Bulst-Thiele, *SDMTHM*, pp. 238–9.

15. L. Delisle, 'Mémoire sur les opérations financières des Templiers', *Mémoires de l'Institut National de France. Académie des Inscriptions et Belles-lettres*, xxxiii, pt. 2 (1888), esp. pp. 32–7.

16. F. Lundgreen, *Wilhelm von Tyrus und der Templerorden* (Berlin, 1911); Bulst–Thiele, *SDMTHM*, pp. 55, 89, 93–4. The main texts are in Guillelmus Tyrensis archiepiscopus, *Historia rerum in transmarinis partibus gestarum*, in *Receuil des historiens des croisades: Historiens occidentaux*, i–ii (Paris, 1844), bk. xvii, 27; bk. xviii, 9; bk. xx, 29, 30. For Rachid ed-din-Sinan (below) see B. Lewis, *Arabica*, xiii (1966), pp. 225–67, and also S. Runciman, *A History of the Crusades* (Cambridge, 1952), ii, pp. 396–8.

17. F. Tupper and M. B. Ogle, *Master Walter Map's Book, De Nugis Curialium* (1924), p. 41.

18. Bulst, articles quoted above in *Deutsches Archiv*; R. Vaughan, *Matthew Paris* (Cambridge, 1958); Bulst-Thiele, *SDMTHM*, pp. 222–3. The 'cancelled' passage in Matthew Paris is in his *Historia Anglorum*, ii (*Rolls Series*, ed. F. Madden), p. 312, n. For what follows see also Matthew Paris, *Chronica Majora* (*Rolls Series*, ed. H. R. Luard), iv, pp. 25, 138–9, 167–8, 524–6; ibid. v, pp. 133, 147–51; idem, *Historia Anglorum*, iii, p. 259. The battles of Hattin and Mansourah are discussed in Runciman, *A History of the Crusades*, ii–iii, and in R. Grousset, *Histoire des Croisades et du royaume franc de Jérusalem* (Paris, 1934–6), ii–iii.

19. J. Michelet, *Le Procès des Templiers* (Paris, 1841–51), i, p. 44 Joinville's version is in his *Histoire de Saint Louis* (ed. N. de Wailly, Paris, 1890), pp. 91–2. Joinville wrote this account in old age, after the arrest and examination of the Templars had already begun.

20. The bull is in Migne, *Patrologia Latina*, ccxv, cols. 1217–18. There is a free and rather misleading translation of part of the text in H. C. Lea, *A History of the Inquisition in the Middle Ages*, iii (New York, 1889), p. 243. For the general question of authorized Templar violation of ecclesiastical interdict, see above, p. 12. For a typical modern misunderstanding of what the bull is about, see M. Ruthven, *Torture: the grand conspiracy* (London, 1978), p. 99. The bull was not concerned principally with Templar pride in the abstract, as N. Cohn, *Europe's Inner Demons* (St Albans, 1976), p. 79, and M. Barber, *The Trial of the Templars* (Cambridge, 1978), pp. 12–13, seem to imply. Its so-called title, 'De Insolentia Templariorum', was conferred on it by the scribe who wrote the rubrics, not by the pope. The theological

point at issue in the bull concerns those who cause scandal in the Church.

21. *Les Registres de Clément IV* (Paris, ed. E. Jordan), no. 836. Cf. Bulst-Thiele, *SDMTHM*, p. 245.

22. See H. E. Mayer, *The Crusades* (London, 1972); J. S. C. Riley-Smith *What were the Crusades?* (London, 1971); K. M. Setton, *The Papacy and the Levant (1204–1571)*, i (Philadelphia, 1976); J. R. Strayer, 'The Political Crusades of the Thirteenth Century', in *A History of the Crusades*, ii (ed. R. L. Wolff and H. W. Hazard, Philadelphia, 1962); P. Throop, *Criticism of the Crusade. A study of public opinion and crusade propaganda* (Amsterdam, 1940).

23. Song of the Second Crusade, translated by R. W. Southern in *The Making of the Middle Ages* (London, 1953), p. 55.

24. *Ottonis Episcopi Frisingensis Chronica sive historia de duabus civitatibus* (ed. A. Hofmeister, Hanover-Leipzig, 1912), pp. 320–1.

25. V. de Bartholomaeis, *Poesie provenzali storiche relative all'Italia*, ii (Rome, 1931), pp. 222–4. The poem is ascribed to Ricaut Bonomel. For 'Baphomet', see below, p. 68.

26. E. Stickel, *Der Fall von Akkon: Untersuchungen zum Abklingen des Kreuzzugsgedankens am Ende des 13. Jahrhunderts* (Bern–Frankfurt/M, 1975), pp. 190–211.

27. P. Meyer, 'Les derniers troubadours de la Provence', *Bibliothèque de l'Ecole des Chartes*, 6th ser., v (1869), pp. 484–5, 497–8.

28. S. Baluzius, *Vitae Paparum Avenionensium*, iii (ed. G. Mollat, Paris, 1921), pp. 145–54. Cf. Riley–Smith, *Knights of St John*, pp. 198–226; Setton, *The Papacy and the Levant*, pp. 163 ff.; Bulst-Thiele, *SDMTHM*, pp. 305 ff.; Barber, *Trial of the Templars*, pp. 14–15. Barber reads '50,000 foot-soldiers' for five thousand foot soldiers (Baluzius, ed. Mollat, p. 148).

29. G. H. Ladner, '*Homo Viator*: Mediaeval Ideas on Alienation and Order', *Speculum*, xlii (1967), pp. 233–59; for what follows see also Stickel, *Der Fall von Akkon*.

30. J. N. Hillgarth, *Ramon Lull and Lullism in Fourteenth Century France* (Oxford, 1971); E. W. Platzeck, *Raimund Lull* (Düsseldorf, 1962). For Lull's attitude to the Temple after the trial had begun, see below, pp. 89–90.

31. Cohn, *Europe's Inner Demons*, pp. 10–11; W. H. C. Frend, *Martyrdom and Persecution in the Early Church* (Oxford, 1965), pp. 109–12, 162–3. For what follows, see Ammianus Marcellinus, *Res Gestae* (ed. J. C. Rolfe, Cambridge, Mass., and London, 1958), iii, bk. xxix, 2, pp. 215 ff.

32. C. Vogel, 'Pratiques superstitieuses au début du XIe siècle d'après le *Corrector sive medicus* de Burchard évêque de Worms', *Etudes de civilisation médiévale . . . offertes a E.-R. Labande (n.d.)*, pp. 751–61. Vogel quotes earlier parallel texts.

33. P. Brown, *Religion and Society in the Age of St Augustine* (1972); idem, 'The rise and function of the holy man in late Antiquity', *Journal of Roman Studies*, lxi (1971), pp. 80–101; H. Chadwick, *Priscillian of Avila: the occult and the charismatic in the early Church* (Oxford, 1976); E. R. Dodds, *Pagan and Christian in an Age of Anxiety* (1965); A. Momigliano, *Essays in Ancient and Modern*

Historiography (Oxford, 1977), p. 142.

34. M. Douglas (ed.), *Witchcraft Confessions and Accusations* (London, 1970); M. Marwick, *Witchcraft and Sorcery: Selected Readings* (Harmondsworth, 1970); L. Mair, *Witchcraft* (London, 1969); J. C. Baroja, *The World of the Witches* (London, 1968); J. B. Russell, *Witchcraft in the Middle Ages* (Ithaca and London, 1972); R. Kieckhefer, *European Witch Trials: their foundations in popular and learned culture 1300–1500* (Berkeley and Los Angeles, 1976); E. Peters, *The Magician, the Witch and the Law* (Philadelphia and London, 1978).

35. Grundmann, *Ausgewählte Aufsätze*, i, pp. 315 ff., 338 ff. It is a pity that J. B. Russell did not take more account of these classic essays in his *Witchcraft in the Middle Ages* (cited above).

36. For the awe-inspiring problem of the distinction between magic and religion I found especially helpful J. Goody, 'Religion and Ritual: the definitional problem', *British Journal of Sociology*, xii (1961), pp. 142–64: and from a different point of view C. Geertz, 'Religion as a cultural system', *Anthropological Approaches to the study of Religion* (ed. M. Banton, 1966), pp. 1–46. See also K. V. Thomas, *Religion and the Decline of Magic* (London, 1971), pp. 41, 267–77, 636–40; and E. E. Evans-Pritchard, *Theories of Primitive Religion* (Oxford, 1965).

37. Douglas (ed.), *Witchcraft Confessions and Accusations*, p. 178; E. E. Evans-Pritchard, *Witchcraft, Oracles and Magic among the Azande* (Oxford, 1937). For what follows, Cohn, *Europe's Inner Demons*, pp. 180 ff.; T. S. R. Boase, *Boniface VIII* (1933), pp. 281, 372 ff.; P. Partner, *The Lands of St Peter* (London, Berkeley and Los Angeles, 1972), pp. 288–96; Russell, *Witchcraft in the Middle Ages*, pp. 172–3, 193–4, 330–1; D. P. Walker, *Spiritual and Demonic Magic* (London, 1958).

38. A. Beardwood, 'The trial of Walter Langton, Bishop of Lichfield, 1307–12', *Transactions of the American Philosophical Society*, n.s., liv, pt. 3 (1964).

39. R. Holtzmann, *Wilhelm von Nogaret* (Freiburg i.B., 1898) is the standard biography.

40. G. Gifford, *A Discourse of the Subtill Practises of Devilles by Witches and Sorcerers* (1587), quoted by A. Macfarlane, *Witchcraft in Tudor and Stuart England* (London, 1970), p. 188.

41. Printed in Holtzmann, *Nogaret*, pp. 353–5.

42. F. Pegues, *The Lawyers of the Last Capetians* (Princeton, 1962); Cohn, *Europe's Inner Demons*, pp. 185–92.

43. J. Favier, *Un conseiller de Philippe le Bel: Enguerran de Marigny* (Paris, 1963).

44. Some are listed by Russell, *Witchcraft in the Middle Ages* (p. 194), and others by P. S. Lewis, *Later Mediaeval France: the Polity* (London, 1968). English examples are the magical charges brought by Henry V against his stepmother, and those against the Countess of Gloucester (1441) and the dowager Duchess of Bedford (1470). W. R. Jones, 'Political Uses of Sorcery in Medieval Europe', *The Historian*, xxxiv (1972), pp. 670–87.

45. Quoted by Partner, *Lands of St Peter*, pp. 316–17. For John XXII and magic see, besides Russell and Cohn, G. Mollat, *The Popes at Avignon* (London, 1963), pp. 12–13.

46. G. Franceschini, *I Montefeltro* (1970), pp. 201–20.

47. A.-M. Michel, 'Le procès de Matteo et de Galeazzo Visconti', *Mélanges d'archéologie et d'histoire de l'Ecole française de Rome*, xxix (1909), p. 292, in note. Cf. Russell, *Witchcraft in the Middle Ages*, p. 173.

48. S. Lukes, 'Some problems about rationality', reprinted in *Rationality* (ed. B. R. Wilson, Oxford, 1970); cf. S. Anglo (ed.), *The Damned Art* (London, 1977). I cannot agree with the line taken by S. Clark, in 'Inversion, Misrule and the Meaning of Witchcraft', *Past and Present*, no. 87 (1980), pp. 98–127.

49. The papal estimate of Templar numbers is to be found in H. Finke, *Papsttum und Untergang des Templerordens* (Münster-i-W, 1907), ii, p. 114. G. Mollat, *The Popes at Avignon 1305-1378* (Engl. trs. London, 1963), at p. 232, erroneously takes this figure to indicate two thousand *knights*, a gross mistake in which he has been followed by others. For a dubious claim that between one and two thousand Templars avoided capture, and in 1310 were congregated near Lyons and hoping to defend the Order, see the text cited by Barber, *Trial*, p. 224. For numbers of Templar knights, see also Bulst-Thiele, *SDMTHM*, pp. 137 n., 340. For the royal statement to the University about the numbers confessing, see G. Lizerand, *Le Dossier de l'affaire des Templiers* (Paris, 1923), pp. 58–9. For Templar fugitives see Barber, pp. 46–7.

50. C. R. Cheney, 'The Downfall of the Templars and a letter in their defence', in *Medieval Miscellany Presented to Eugène Vinaver* (Manchester, 1965).

51. Riley-Smith, *Knights of St John*, pp. 198 ff.; Setton, *The Papacy and the Levant*, i, pp. 163 ff.; Hillgarth, *Ramon Lull and Lullism*, pp. 72 ff. For Philip's guarantees to the Order in 1303–4, see Bulst-Thiele, *SDMTHM*, pp. 296–7.

52. Finke, *Papsttum und Untergang des Templerordens*, ii, p. 51. Discussed by Hillgarth, *Ramon Lull and Lullism*, pp. 93 ff. Spinola suggests that King Philip was acting in concert with the pope, which is unlikely.

53. Riley-Smith, *Knights of St John*, p. 225; A. Luttrell, 'The Crusade in the Fourteenth Century', in *Europe in the Late Middle Ages* (ed. J. R. Hale, J. R. L. Highfield, and B. Smalley, London, 1965), pp. 122-54.

54. I follow Hillgarth's pioneering book, incomprehensibly neglected by Barber. For Lull's apparent acceptance of the guilt of the Templars, see Hillgarth, p. 104. For the MS. from which he quotes, which has been published only in a very scarce Spanish periodical, ibid. p. 84, note 138.

55. Finke, ii, p. 339; cf. Barber, *Trial*, p. 101. There is a pleasingly confused account of this document in G. de Sède, *Les Templiers sont parmi nous ou l'énigme de Gisors* (Paris, 1976), p. 146. De Sède went to the trouble of examining the original of this document in the Vatican, but this did not enable him to read it accurately. Jean de Folhac, a Templar priest, referred

to 150,000 gold florins which he said the Grand Master brought from the East to France, K. Schottmüller, *Der Untergang des Templerordens* (Berlin, 1887), ii, pp. 37–8. But he was an unreliable witness; see Barber, pp. 52, 64, 143–4.

56. Cf. H. C. E. Midelfort, *Witch Hunting in Southwestern Germany 1562–1684; the social and intellectual foundations* (Stanford, 1972), p. 105. It should in fairness be noted that Michelet, who edited the main Templar documents, thought the variants in the confessions so striking that they indicated Templar guilt (*Procès*, i, p. v; ibid. ii, pp. vii–viii). But the uniformities are equally striking.

57. R.-H. Bautier, 'Diplomatique et histoire politique: ce que la critique diplomatique nous apprend sur la personnalité de Philippe le Bel', *Revue Historique*, cclix (1978), pp. 3–27. Cf. Holtzmann, *Nogaret*, p. 144.

58. This is Holtzmann's view, *W. von Nogaret*, pp. 54, 137. For the general difficulty of identifying responsibilities in such governments, see O. A. Ranum, *Richelieu and the Councillors of Louis XIII* (Oxford, 1963), pp. 2–3. The extreme view of Philip IV as a cipher is in the recent article of Bautier cited in the preceding note. See also J. A. McNamara, *Gilles Aycelin, the servant of two masters* (Syracuse, 1973); F. Pegues, *The Lawyers of the Last Capetians*; J. R. Strayer, *The Reign of Philip the Fair* (Princeton, 1980), Barber, *Trial*, pp. 29–30. There is a good résumé of the problem in J. Favier, *Philippe le Bel* (Paris, 1978), pp. 39–46.

59. Cf. E. F. Jacob, 'Verborum florida venustas', *Essays in the Conciliar Epoch* (Manchester, 1953), pp. 185–206; J. H. Mundy, *Europe in the High Middle Ages* (London and New York, 1973), pp. 583–4.

60. R. Scholz, *Die Publizistik zur Zeit Philipps des Schönen und Bonifaz VIII* (Stuttgart, 1903), p. 439.

61. Scholz, *Die Publizistik*, p. 516.

62. A. K. Wildermann, *Die Beurteilung des Templerprozesses bis zum 17. Jahrhundert* (Freiburg, 1971).

63. Cf. McNamara, *Gilles Aycelin*, pp. 163–4, 172–3; for the general question of papal policy, Finke, i, pp. 268–70.

64. N. Daniel, *Islam and the West, the Making of an Image* (Edinburgh, 1966); E. W. Said, *Orientalism* (London and New York, 1978).

65. Barber, pp. 185–8, develops at some length (after Reinach) the background of two magical stories told in the trial evidence about the Templar idol-head; the stories derive from the Perseus legend. But we cannot know whether the original story of a Templar 'Baphomet' idol-head was invented because the fabricators of the charge were acquainted with the Perseus legend, or whether the oriental Perseus tales were produced in evidence at the trial as a sort of explanation of the idolatry charge. The main witness on the point was not a Templar but an Italian notary called Antonio Sici of Vercelli (*Procès*, i. pp. 619, 641 ff.) who entered his own separate 'roll' of evidence. Sici's contribution is more like a literary essay than a piece of criminal evidence. His 'roll' was subsequently referred to by a Templar knight called Hugues de Faure (ibid. ii, pp. 220, 223), but Faure offered no

independent evidence.

66. Michelet, *Procès*, ii, pp. 398–400; ibid. i, pp. 588–91. For de Gonneville, who was an important and able man, in spite of his claim to be illiterate, see also *Procès*, i, pp. 88, 119–20, 514–15; also Bulst-Thiele, *SDMTHM*, pp. 249, 309. His interrogation before the cardinals is in Finke, ii, p. 326.

67. See below, p. 161–3.

68. *Procès*, ii, p. 434. For the allegation by the royal official that there was a secret Rule, see Barber, *Trial*, pp. 144–5. The prohibition against a Templar brother holding a copy of the Rule without permission is in Curzon, *La règle du Temple*, p. 189, para. 326.

69. D. Wilkins, *Concilia Magnae Britanniae et Hiberniae*, ii (London, 1737), p. 338.

70. Barber, *Trial*, pp. 202–3.

71. Cf. Partner, *The Lands of St Peter*, pp. 301–3; Barber, *Trial*, pp. 226–9.

72. Finke, *Papsttum und Untergang des Templerordens*, i, pp. 326 ff. Some distinguished historians have in their *obiter dicta* implied that they accept a degree of moral turpitude in the Templar Order, e.g. H. Jedin, *Kleine Konziliengeschichte* (Freiburg, Basle, and Vienna, 1960), p. 58; S. Runciman, *A History of the Crusades*, iii (1954), pp. 435–6, and n.

73. Barber, *Trial of the Templars* (1978); Cohn, *Europe's Inner Demons* (1976).

Part II. The Myth

1. Wildermann, *Die Beurteilung des Templerprozesses bis zum 17. Jahr.* (1971). Barber, *Trial of the Templars*, does not mention the full and interesting chronicle of Geffroi de Paris (ed. A. Diverres, Paris, 1956).

2. Hillgarth, *Ramon Lull and Lullism* (1971), pp. 66–125, esp. p. 104.

3. Wildermann, op. cit., is helpful but incomplete. See, e.g., Blondii Flavii Forliviensis, *Historiarum ab inclinato Rom. imperio Decades III* (Basle, 1531), ii, 9, fo. 340; *Commentariorum Urbanorum Raphael. Volaterrani* (Basle, 1544), p. 256: O. Rainaldi, *Annales Ecclesiastici post Baronum* (Lucca, 1747–56), ad annum 1311; A. Ciaconii, *Vitae et res gestae pontificum Romanorum et S.R.E. cardinalium*, ed. Oldoin, ii (Rome, 1677), col. 358.

4. T. Wright, *Political Poems and Songs relating to British History*, i (Rolls Series, 1859), p. 267 (spelling modernized).

5. C. G. Nauert, *Agrippa and the Crisis of Renaissance Thought* (Urbana, 1965), p. 243. See Agrippa's claims for the book in his letter to Trithemius, Ep. i, 23, in *Opera* (Lyons, n.d.), ii, p. 72. See also P. Zambelli, 'Agrippa von Nettesheim in den neuren kritischen Studien und in den Handschriften', *Archiv für Kulturgeschichte*, li (1969), pp. 264–95.

6. *De occulta philosophia libri tres* (Cologne, 1533), lib. i, cap. 39, p. xlv. Cf. Nauert, op. cit., pp. 60, 246; F. A. Yates, *Giordano Bruno and the Hermetic Tradition* (London and Chicago, 1964), p. 133. I am indebted to Miss Yates's book for the reference, which is not to be found in Wildermann. I have also consulted a photocopy of the Würzburg MS. of the Agrippa text

which is held by the Warburg Institute. In this MS. the passage is in lib. i, cap. 31; the text does not differ significantly.

7. Cohn, *Europe's Inner Demons*, pp. 18–19, 42–59.

8. *Chronique de Savoye* (Lyons, 1552), pp. 248–50.

9. *Six livres de la République* (Lyons, 1580), bk. iii, ch. 7, p. 347; *The Six Bookes of a Commonweale* (tr. R. Knolles, London, 1606), pp. 382–3, 389. It is not clear to what German authors Bodin referred; he may have intended Naucler.

10. M. Del-Rio, *Disquisitionum magicarum libri sex* (Cologne, 1679), pp. 651–2. For Bodin's method of approaching witchcraft, see C. Baxter, 'Jean Bodin's "De la Démonomanie des Sorciers": the logic of persecution', in S. Anglo (ed.), *The Damned Art* (London, 1977), pp. 76–105.

11. *The Third Universitie of England, or a Treatise of the Foundations of all the Colledges, auncient Scooles of Priviledge, and of houses of Learning, and Liberall Arts, within and about the most famous Cittie of London* (1615), in John Stow, *Annales or a Generall Chronicle of England* (London, 1631). Cf. Wildermann, p. 144. The rather ambiguous seventeenth-century attitude to medieval chivalry is discussed by N. Edelman, *Attitudes of Seventeenth-Century France towards the Middle Ages* (New York, 1946).

12. F. A. Yates, *The Rosicrucian Enlightenment* (London and Boston, 1972); R. S. Westman and J. E. McGuire, *Hermeticism and the Scientific Revolution* (Los Angeles, 1977); C. H. Josten, *Elias Ashmole* (Oxford, 1966). For Buonnani (below), see his *Ordinum Equestrium et Militarium Catalogus* (Rome, 1711). The Templar is illustrated on plate 115, where the Italian commentary refers to the Templars as 'this most noble Order'.

13. *Traittez concernant l'histoire de France, scavoir la condemnation des Templiers* . . . (1654). I have used the editions of 1700 (Paris) and 1751 (Brussels). See also Wildermann, pp. 163–73; Edelman, *Attitudes of Seventeenth-Century France towards the Middle Ages*, pp. 50, 67.

14. E. Baluze, *Vitae Paparum Avenionensium*, (Paris, 1693), col. 590; *Histoire Génealogique de la Maison d'Auvergne* (Paris, 1707), i, pp. 174–5.

15. H.-J. Martin, *Livres, pouvoir et société à Paris au XVIIème siècle* (Geneva, 1969), especially ii, pp. 845–6; *Livre et société dans la France du XVIIIe siècle* (Paris and The Hague, 1965–70), especially J. L. and L. M. Flandrin, 'La circulation du livre dans la société du 18e siècle: un sondage à travers quelques sources', ibid, ii, pp. 40–72.

16. P. Chevalier, *Histoire de la Franc-Maçonnerie Française* (Paris, 1974–5); C. Francovich, *Storia della Massoneria in Italia dalle origini alla rivoluzione francese* (Florence, 1974); J. M. Roberts, *The Mythology of the Secret Societies* (London, 1972); D. Roche, *Le siècle des lumières en province: académies et académiciens provinciaux, 1680–1789* (Paris and The Hague, 1978), i, pp. 257–80; J. Katz, *Jews and Freemasons in Europe 1723–1939* (Cambridge, Mass., 1970), especially pp. 204 ff.

17. Chevalier, i, pp. 16 ff.; A. Mellor, *Our separated brethren the Freemasons* (London, 1964). Text in A. Palou, *La Franc-Maçonnerie* (Paris, 1964), and G. A. Schiffmann, *Andreas Michael Ramsay* (Leipzig, 1878).

18. See *Hurd's Letters on Chivalry and Romance* (ed. E. J. Morley, London, 1911), pp. 56, 91, 151–2; L. Gossman, *Mediaevalism and the ideologies of the Enlightenment: the world and work of La Curne de Sainte-Palaye* (Baltimore, 1968).

19. R. le Forestier, *La Franc-Maçonnerie templière et occultiste au XVIIIe et XIXe siècle* (ed. A. Faivre, Paris, 1970) is exhaustive and reliable; his *Occultisme et la franc-maçonnerie écossaise* (Paris, 1928) is also to be consulted. K. Epstein, *The Genesis of German Conservatism* (Princeton, 1966), is important for the political background, as are the books of Roberts and Francovich quoted above.

20. The editors of the new Brussels edition of Dupuy (1751) were clearly much less confident about Templar guilt than he had been.

21. A. Viatte, *Les Sources occultes du Romantisme: Illuminisme-Théosophie 1770–1820* (Paris, 1927), ii, pp. 269–70. Cf. R. Darnton, *Mesmerism and the end of the Enlightenment in France* (Cambridge, Mass., 1968); C. Garrett, *Respectable Folly: Millenarians and the French Revolution in France and England* (Baltimore and London, 1975). K. S. Wilkins, 'Some aspects of the irrational in 18th-century France', *Studies on Voltaire and the Eighteenth Century*, cxl (1975), pp. 107–201, is diligent but not always critical.

22. A. O. Hirschman, *The Passions and the Interests: political arguments for Capitalism before its triumph* (Princeton, 1977), p. 133. Cf. H. H. Gerth and C. Wright Mills, *From Max Weber* (New York, 1946), p. 51.

23. H. A. Korff, *Geist der Goethezeit* (Leipzig, 1954–5); M. H. Abrams, *Natural Supernaturalism: tradition and revolution in Romantic literature* (London, 1971).

24. H. W. Coil, *A Comprehensive View of Freemasonry* (Richmond, Virginia, 1973), p. 167. The date usually given by modern 'Templar' Masons in England for the foundation of their Order is 1791.

25. See, for Freemasonry at this period, besides the works of Le Forestier, Roberts, Francovich, and Epstein: P. C. Ludz (ed.), *Geheime Gesellschaften* (Wolfenbütteler Studien zur Aufklärung in Auftrag der Lessing-Akademie herausgegeben von G. Schulz, vol. v, pt. 1, Heidelberg, 1979); E. A. Balázs, L. Hammermayer, H. Wagner, J. Wojtowicz (ed.), *Beförderer der Aufklärung im Mittel- und Osteuropa: Freimaurer, Gesellschaften und Clubs* (Studien zur Gesch. der Kulturbeziehungen im Mittel-und Osteuropa, v, Berlin, 1979); *Klasse en ideologie in de vrijmetsalarij*: Classes et idéologies dans la Franc-Maçonnerie (Tijdschrift voor de studie van de verlichtung, iv, Brussels, 1976); H. Möller, 'Wie aufgeklärt war Preussen?', in *Preussen im Rückblick* (ed. H. J. Puhle and H. U. Wehler, Göttingen, 1980), pp. 176–201; A Soboul, 'La franc-maçonnerie et la Révolution française', *Annales historiques de la Révolution française*, xlvi (1974), pp. 76–88.

26. G. Krüger, 'Johann A. Starck der Kleriker: ein Beitrag zur Geschichte der Theosophie im 18. Jahrhundert', *Festgabe von Fachgenossen und Freunden Karl Müller zum 70. Geburtstag dargebracht* (Tübingen, 1922), pp. 244–66.

27. J. A. Starck, *Über die alten und neuen Mysterien* (Berlin, 1782), pp. 290–1.

28. Francovich, pp. 271 ff.

29. R. van Dülmen, *Der Geheimbund der Illuminaten* (Stuttgart, 1977), especially pp. 107–12, 133–9. J. H. Billington, *Fire in the Minds of Men. Origins of the*

Revolutionary Faith (New York and London, 1980), pp. 93–7, is a great deal less cautious than van Dülmen about the Illuminati. See also J. Rogalla von Bieberstein, *Die These von der Verschwörung 1776–1945: Philosophen, Freimaurer gegen die Sozialordnung* (Bern and Frankfurt, 1976).

30. 'Des conspirations contre le peuple ou des proscriptions', in *Nouveaux Mélanges Philosophiques, Historiques, Critiques, &c. &c.*, pt. iv (1767), pp. 188–209. Cf. Wildermann, *Beurteilungen des Templerprozesses*, pp. 175–7, which seems to be taken straight from M. Dessubré, *Bibliographie de l'Ordre des Templiers* (Paris, 1928), pp. 273–5.

31. See Le Forestier, pp. 663–72. And cf. L. Hammermayer, *Der Wilhelmsbader Freimaurer-Konvent von 1782: ein Höhe und Wendepunkt in der Geschichte der deutschen und europäischen Geheimgesellschaften* (Wolfenbütteler Studien zur Aufklärung, vol. v, pt. 2, Heidelberg, 1980), esp. pp. 53–5.

32. F. Nicolai, *Versuch über die Beschuldigungen welche dem Tempelherrerorden gemacht worden und über dessen Geheimnis* (Berlin and Stettin, 1782), pt. i, pp. 124 ff. See also H. Möller, *Aufklärung in Preussen: Friedrich Nicolai* (Berlin, 1974), pp. 362–407; Epstein, *Genesis of German Conservatism*, pp. 38–41.

33. *Le tombeau de Jacques Molay ou le secret des conspirateurs, à ceux qui veulent tout savoir* (Paris, l'An IV). Cf. Roberts, pp. 180–1. The later editions, *Les initiés anciens et modernes, suite du tombeau de Jacques Molai* and *Le tombeau de Jacques Molai ou histoire secrète et abregée des initiés anciens et modernes* (Paris, l'An V) show important variations. Cadet de Gassicourt had had closer connections with the Jacobins than he confessed to; see his speech commemorating Marat, *Discours prononcé par le citoyen Cadet-Gassicourt à l'inauguration des bustes de Marat et le Pelletier, faite le 12 Frimaire, à la section de Mont-Blanc*. The other publicist to denounce Orléans was Ventre de la Touloubre ('Montjoie'), *Histoire de la Conjuration de Louis-Philippe-Joseph d'Orléans* (Paris, 1794); see vol. i, p. 56, for the 'vengeance' of the Masons. For de Bonneville, see Darnton, *Mesmerism and the end of the Enlightenment*, pp. 33–5, and Billington, *Fire in the Minds of Men*, pp. 35–44, 101–3.

34. *Mémoires pour servir à l'histoire du Jacobinisme* (London, 1797–8). See Roberts, pp. 188–202; Rogalla von Bieberstein, *passim*; J. Godechot, *The Counter-Revolution: doctrine and action 1789–1804* (London, 1972). Much the best introduction to Barruel, however, is Thomas de Quincey's essay, 'Secret Societies' (in *Works*, Edinburgh, 1863, vol. vi).

35. Robert Darnton, *Mesmerism and the end of the Enlightenment in France* (1968).

36. *Mémoires*, ii, pp. 363, 387–8.

37. The Neo-Templars are best dealt with by Le Forestier, *La Franc-maçonnerie templière et occultiste*, and by Chevalier, *Hist. de la Franc-maçonnerie française*, ii, pp. 9–99. See also Nodier, *Souvenirs de la Révolution et de l'Empire* (Paris, n.d.), ii, pp. 134–5. There are useful details in C.-H. Maillard de Chambure, *Règles et statuts secrets des Templiers* (Paris, 1840), and in E. L. Montagnac, *Histoire des chevaliers templiers et de leurs prétendus successeurs* (Paris, 1864).

38. See S. Bann, 'Historical text and historical object: the poetics of the Musée de Cluny', *History and Theory*, xvii (1978), pp. 251–66.

39. *Nouvelle Biographie Générale*, xiv (1862), cols. 773–8; the rest of Napoleon's criticism in *Correspondance de Napoléon I publié par ordre de l'Empereur Napoléon III*, xiv (Paris, 1863), p. 127. The researches of Raynouard (below) were published in his *Monumens historiques relatifs à la condamnation des Chevaliers du Temple et à l'abolition de leur ordre* (Paris, 1813). His play, *Les Templiers, tragédie*, was published in 1805.

40. See W. Bietak, *Gottes ist der Orient: Gottes ist der Okzident; eine Studie über Joseph von Hammer-Purgstall* (Vienna and Zurich, 1948). Hammer's main relevant works are 'Mysterium Baphometis revelatum', *Fundgruben des Orients*, vi (1818), pp. 1–120, 445–99; *Mémoire sur deux coffrets gnostiques du moyen age du cabinet de M. le Duc de Blacas* (Paris, 1832); 'Die Schuld der Templer', *Denkschriften der kaiserlichen Akademie der Wissenschaften, Philosophisch-historische Classe*, vi (Vienna, 1855); *Geschichte der Assassinen* (1818; English trs., London, 1835). See also J. Barrow, *Life and Correspondence of Admiral Sir William Sydney Smith*, i (London, 1848), pp. 425–8. Hammer's claim that he had learned about Freemasonry from books abandoned in Cairo by French Masons of the Egyptian expeditionary force is probably false: he learned about Freemasonry from Smith.

41. B. Lewis, *The Assassins* (London, 1967), p. 12, describes Hammer's book on the Assassins as 'a tract for the times'.

42. Cf. R. M. Grant, *Gnosticism and early Christianity* (New York and London, 1966); S. Benko, 'The Libertine Gnostic Sect of the Phibionites according to Epiphanius', *Vigiliae Christianae*, xxi (1967), pp. 103–19. The Ophites are not mentioned by the authors who accuse the Gnostics of sexual depravity. See also W. Foerster, *Gnosis* (Oxford, 1972), pp. 84–99, 313–25, and cf. pp. 261–82, ibid.

43. A. L. Owen, *The Famous Druids* (Oxford, 1962).

44. Bietak, pp. 16–17.

45. Quoted by Korff, *Geist der Goethezeit*, iv, p. 179.

46. H. B. Grégoire, *Histoire des Sectes Religieuses*, ii (Paris, 1828), p. 404. I have been unable to ascertain if he is correct in saying that the Hospitallers in exile made advances to the Neo-Templars (loc. cit.).

47. D. G. Charlton, *Secular Religions in France, 1815–1870* (London, 1963). For a modern doctrine in some ways comparable to the Johannite one see R. Ambelain, *Jésus ou le mortel secret des Templiers* (Paris, 1970). For 'manipulationist' sects see B. Wilson, *Religious Sects* (London, 1970); and cf. T. W. Adorno, *The Authoritarian Personality* (New York, 1950), p. 767.

48. Quoted by C. O. Parsons, *Witchcraft and Demonology in Scott's Fiction* (Edinburgh and London, 1964), p. 151.

49. Such as Henri Delaage, author of *Le monde occulte* (1851) and *Doctrine des Sociétés Secrètes* (1852). See also J. Richer, *Gérard de Nerval et les doctrines esotériques* (Paris, 1947).

50. M. Praz, *The Romantic Agony* (London and New York, 1951). See also Northrop Frye, *Fables of Identity: studies in poetic mythology* (New York, 1963).

51. *Histoire de France*, iii (Paris, 1872), pp. 362–3. There is no significant change

from the earlier editions, and Michelet's laconic prefaces to his editions of the *Procès des Templiers* (1841–51) add nothing. For recent judgements of his work see J. A. Dakyns, *The Middle Ages in French Literature 1851–1900* (London, 1973); H. White, *Metahistory: the historical imagination in nineteenth-century Europe* (Baltimore and London, 1973); O. Chadwick, *The Secularization of the European Mind in the Nineteenth Century* (Cambridge, 1975), pp. 198–202.

52. *Weltgeschichte*, viii (Leipzig, 1898), pp. 621–2.

53. e.g. E. L. de Lamothe-Langon, *Les mystères de la Tour de Saint-Jean ou les Chevaliers du Temple* (1818); (P. Leicester), *The Templars: an historical novel* (1830). For Lamothe-Langon, see Cohn, *Europe's Inner Demons*, pp. 132–3.

54. Raynouard's original review was published in *Journal des Savants* (1819), pp. 151–61, 221–9. In the 6th edn. of Michaud (1841) it is summarized in vol. v, pp. 428–35. Michelet also printed an extract from Raynouard's review of Hammer in the notes to his *Histoire de France*.

55. This is the main thesis of J. H. Billington, *Fire in the Minds of Men*. For Buonarroti see Billington, pp. 87 ff., 114–16.

56. Billington, pp. 110–14; P.-G. Castex, *Le Conte Fantastique en France de Nodier à Maupassant* (Paris, 1951), pp. 121–67.

57. R. D. Waller, *The Rossetti Family, 1824–1854* (Manchester, 1932); E. R. Vincent, *Gabriele Rossetti in England* (London, 1936); M. Wicks, *The Italian Exiles in London* (Manchester, 1937).

58. Mignard, *Monographie du Coffret de M. le Duc de Blacas* (Paris, 1852); *Suite de la monographie . . . ou preuves du Manichéisme de l'Ordre du Temple* (Paris, 1853). For Hammer's earlier examination of the coffer, see note 40 above. An example of the 'Manichaean' interpretation of the Templars being treated as commonplace is the school book of F.-R. de Chateaubriand, *Analyse Raisonnée de l'Histoire de France* (Paris, 1845), pp. 76–7.

59. *Denkschriften der k. Akademie der Wissenschaften*, vi (1855), p. 209. It no longer has this meaning in Arabic. If the meaning has disappeared after only a century, it seems foolish to suppose that it had existed since the thirteenth century. But the list of Hammer's absurdities is endless.

60. E. Aroux, *Dante hérétique, révolutionnaire et socialiste* (Paris, 1854); idem, *Les mystères de la chevalerie et de l'amour platonique au moyen age* (Paris, 1858); see also Dakyns, *The Middle Ages in French Literature*, pp. 100 ff.

61. *Dictionnaire raisonné de l'architecture française du XIe au XVIe siècle*, ix (Paris, 1868), p. 16.

62. For his biography see P. Chacornac, *Eliphas Lévi* (Paris, 1925), and for the connection with Flora Tristan, J. Puech, *La vie et l'oeuvre de Flora Tristan 1830–1844 (L'Union ouvrière)* (Paris, 1925); and see also Billington, *Fire in the Minds of Men*, pp. 487–8. There is a somewhat severe analysis of Constant in M. Dummett, *The Game of Tarot from Ferrara to Salt Lake City* (London, 1980), pp. 113–20. The main passages in Constant relating to the Templars are in his *Histoire de la Magie* (Paris, 1860), pp. 273–80, 441 ff., but see also his *Dogme et Rituel de la Haute Magie* (2nd edn., Paris, 1861).

63. See Dummett, *The Game of Tarot.*

64. The eccentric but not uninteresting book by G. Legman, *The Guilt of the Templars* (New York, 1966), reproduces Wright's essay. For Wright see R. M. Dorson, *The British Folklorists: a History* (London, 1968), which is also useful for other folklorists interested in Templars. Legman dedicated his book to the memory of Joseph Hammer, but I could not find much evidence that he had read him.

65. *Procès*, i, pp. 89–96; cf. Barber, pp. 178, 249.

66. A. Nutt, *The Legends of the Holy Grail* (London, 1902); cf. Dorson, *British Folklorists*, pp. 229 ff. For Nutt's pupil Jessie Weston, see her *From Ritual to Romance* (Garden City, N.Y., 1957) and *The Quest of the Holy Grail* (reprint, 1964).

67. E. Howe and H. Möller, 'Theodor Reuss: irregular Freemasonry in Germany, 1900–1923', *Transactions of the Quattuor Coronati Lodge*, xci (1978), pp. 28–42.

68. J. O. Fuller, *The magical dilemma of Victor Neuburg* (London, 1965), pp. 195–217. For the O.T.O. see also Crowley's *Magick without Tears* (Hampton, N.J., 1954); I have not been diligent in consulting Crowley's works.

69. See L. Barrow, 'Socialism in Eternity: the ideology of the Plebeian Spiritualists, 1853–1913', *History Workshop Journal*, Spring 1980, pp. 37–69.

70. A. J. Trythall, *'Boney' Fuller: the intellectual General* (London, 1977). For the Order of the Golden Dawn see E. Howe, *The Magicians of the Golden Dawn* (London, 1972); Dummett, *The Game of Tarot*, pp. 148 ff.

71. Saint-Yves d'Alveydre, *La France Vraie* (Paris, 1887); idem, *Mission actuelle des Souverains par l'un d'eux* (Paris, 1882). J. Weiss, *La synarchie d'après l'oeuvre de Saint-Yves d'Alveydre* (Paris, 1976) is useless.

72. Cf. Strayer, *The Reign of Philip the Fair*, pp. 384–423. J. Favier, *Philippe le Bel*, pp. 183 ff., is more sceptical.

73. J. Saunier, *La Synarchie* (Paris, 1971). A. Ulmann and H. Azeau, *Synarchie et pouvoir* (Paris, 1968); H. Coston, *Les technocrates et la synarchie* (Paris, 1962) is a deliriously right-wing view. P. Farmer, *Vichy: political dilemma* (New York, 1977), pp. 265–6, adds nothing to the matter. R. Mousnier, *Les Hiérarchies sociales de 1450 à nos jours* (Paris, 1969), pp. 174–5, refers to 'les groupes synarques de Vichy en 1942', but without offering any explanation of why he thought they existed.

74. G. de Charnay, *Synarchie: panorama de 25 années d'activité occulte* (Paris, 1946). The identification of the author with Raoul Husson is asserted by Ulmann and Azeau, *Synarchie et pouvoir*, p. 337.

75. V.-E. Michelet, *Le secret de la chevalerie* (Paris, 1930), p. 5.

76. The basic post-war books are those of J. Charpentier, *L'Ordre des Templiers* (Paris, 1944; 2nd edn., 1961); and J.-H. Probst-Biraben, *Les mystères des Templiers* (Nice, 1947; 2nd edn., Paris, 1973). There are scores of others.

77. *Les mystères de la cathédrale de Chartres* (Paris, 1966; English trs., 1972); *Les mystères Templiers* (Paris, 1967).

78. See G. de Sède, *Les Templiers sont parmi nous* (Paris, 1962; 2nd edn., 1976), who locates the Templar treasure at Gisors. There are much wilder speculations in Maurice Guingand and Béatrice Lanne, *L'Or des Templiers: Gisors ou Tomar?* (Paris, 1973). De Sède's theories have been followed and elaborated by the British writer for television, Henry Lincoln.

79. By I. Wilson, in *The Turin Shroud* (Harmondsworth, 1979). This author seems to have been influenced by the stories about Grail-Templar knights (pp. 182, 205). His argument for Templar custody of the Shroud rests on its having been in the possession in 1356 of Geoffroy de Charnay, who has the same name as one of the Templar leaders burned in 1314. There is, however, no proof of a collateral relationship between the two.

80. See L. Pauwels and J. Bergier, *Le Matin des Magiciens* (Paris, 1960; English trs. 1963 and 1971), *Le meilleur de Planète: principaux articles, illustrations et aujourd'hui* (Paris, 1978).
    L. Pauwels, *Ce que je crois* (Paris, 1974); idem, *Le droit de parler* (Paris, 1981). And see also J.-P. Apparu (ed.), *La Droite aujourd'hui* (Paris, 1978).

81. See *Le droit de parler*, especially at pp. 238–47.

82. R. Olden (ed.), *Das Wunderbare oder die Versauberten* (Berlin, 1932).

83. C. Nodier, *Oeuvres* (reprint, Geneva, 1968, of Paris edn. 1832–7), v, pp. 77–9. For the changes in the political views of Nodier in later life, see J. Larat, *La tradition et l'exotisme dans l'oeuvre de Charles Nodier* (Paris, 1923), pp. 292–8.

BIBLIOGRAPHY OF
WORKS CITED

Abrams, M. H., *Natural Supernaturalism: tradition and revolution in Romantic litera-ture*, London, 1971.

Adorno, T. W., *The Authoritarian Personality*, New York, 1950.

Agrippa, H. Cornelius ab Nettesheim, *Opera*, 2 vol., Lyons, n.d.

—— *De occulta philosophia libri tres*, Cologne, 1533.

Ambelain, R., *Jésus ou le mortel secret des Templiers*, Paris, 1970.

Anglo, S., ed., *The Damned Art*, London, 1977.

Apparu, J.-P., ed., *La Droite aujourd'hui*, Paris, 1978.

Aroux, E., *Dante hérétique, révolutionnaire et socialiste*, Paris, 1854.

—— *Les mystères de la chevalerie et de l'amour platonique au moyen age*, Paris, 1858.

Ashmole, Elias, *Institutions, Laws and Ceremonies of the most noble Order of the Garter*, 2 vol., London, 1672.

Balázs, E. A., Hammermayer, L., Wagner, H., Wojtowicz, J. (ed.), *Beförderer der Aufklärung im Mittel- und Osteuropa: Freimaurer, Gesellschaften und Clubs* (Studien zur Gesch. der Kulturbeziehungen im Mittel- und Osteuropa, v, Berlin, 1979).

Baluze, S., *Vitae Paparum Avenionensium*, 2 vol., Paris, 1693; also ed. G. Mollat, 4 vol., Paris, 1914–27.

—— *Histoire Généalogique de la Maison d'Auvergne*, 2 vol., Paris, 1707.

Bann, S., 'Historical text and historical object: the poetics of the Musée de Cluny', *History and Theory*, xvii (1978), pp. 251–66.

Barber, M., *The Trial of the Templars*, Cambridge, 1978.

Barrow, J., *Life and Correspondence of Admiral Sir William Sidney Smith*, 2 vol., London, 1848.

Barrow, L., 'Socialism in Eternity: the ideology of the Plebeian Spiritualists, 1853–1913', *History Workshop Journal*, Spring 1980.

Bautier, R.-H., 'Diplomatique et histoire politique: ce que la critique diplo-matique nous apprend sur la personnalité de Philippe le Bel', *Revue His-torique*, cclix (1978), pp. 3–27.

Barruel, A. de, *Mémoires pour servir à l'histoire du Jacobinisme*, 3 vol., London, 1797–8.

Baxter, C., 'Jean Bodin's "De la Démonomanie des Sorciers": the logic of persecution', in S. Anglo, ed., *The Damned Art*, London, 1977, pp. 76–105.

Beardwood, A., 'The trial of Walter Langton, Bishop of Lichfield, 1307–12', *Transactions of the American Philosophical Society*, n.s., liv, pt. 3 (1964).

Benko, S., 'The Libertine Gnostic Sect of the Phibionites according to Epiphanius', *Vigiliae Christianae*, xxi (1967), pp. 103–19.

Bernard, St, 'Liber ad milites Templi de laude novae militiae', in *Sancti*

Bernardi Opera, ed. J. Leclercq, iii, Rome, 1963.

Bietak, W., *Gottes ist der Orient: Gottes ist der Okzident: eine Studie über Joseph von Hammer-Purgstall*, Vienna and Zurich, 1948.

Billington, James H., *Fire in the Minds of Men: origins of the revolutionary faith*, New York and London, 1980.

Biondo, Flavio, *Historiarum ab inclinato Rom. imperio Decades III*, Basle, 1531.

Boase, T. S. R., *Boniface VIII*, London, 1933.

Bodin, Jean, *Six livres de la République*, Lyons, 1580 (Engl. trs. by R. Knolles, *The Six Bookes of a Commonweale*, London, 1606).

Brown, Peter, *Religion and Society in the Age of Augustine*, London, 1972.

—— 'The rise and function of the holy man in antiquity', *Journal of Roman Studies*, lxi (1971), pp. 80–101.

Buc, George, 'The Third Universitie of England', in John Stow, *Annales or a Generall Chronicle of England*, London, 1631.

Bulst, M. L. (later Bulst-Thiele), 'Zur Geschichte der Ritterorden und des Königreichs Jerusalem im 13. Jahrhundert', *Deutsches Archiv*, xxii (1966), pp. 197–226.

—— 'Templer in königlichen und päpstlichen Dienst', *Festschrift Percy Ernst Schramm*, i (Wiesbaden, 1964), pp. 289–308.

—— *Sacrae Domus Militiae Templi Hierosolymitani Magistri. Untersuchungen zur Geschichte des Templerordens 1118/19–1314*, Göttingen, 1974 (*Abhandlungen der Akademie der Wissenschaften, Phil. Hist. Klasse*, Folge iii, n. 86).

Buonanni, Filippo, *Ordinum equestrium et militarium catalogus imaginibus expositus*, Rome, 1711.

Burton Annals, in *Annales Monastici*, ed. H. R. Luard, i (*Rolls Series*, 1864).

Cadet de Gassicourt, Charles Louis, *Le tombeau de Jacques Molay ou le secret des conspirateurs, à ceux qui veulent tout savoir*, Paris, l'an IV (1796).

—— *Les initiés anciens et modernes, suite du Tombeau de Jacques Molay*, n.d., but probably 1796.

—— *Les Franc-Maçons ou les Jacobins démasqués: fragmens pour l'histoire*, n.d.

—— *Discours prononcé par le citoyen Cadet-Gassicourt à l'inauguration des bustes de Marat et le Pelletier, faite le 12 Frimaire, à la section de Mont-Blanc*, n.d.

Carr, H., ed., *The Early French Exposures*, London, 1971.

Castex, P.-G., *Le Conte Fantastique en France de Nodier à Maupassant*, Paris, 1851.

Chacornac, P., *Eliphas Lévi*, Paris, 1925.

Chadwick, H., *Priscillian of Avila: the occult and the charismatic in the early Church*, Oxford, 1976.

Chadwick, O., *The Secularization of the European Mind in the Nineteenth Century*, Cambridge, 1975.

Charpentier, John, *L'Ordre des Templiers*, Paris, 1962.

Charpentier, Louis, *Les mystères de la Cathédrale de Chartres*, Paris, 1966 (Engl. trs. 1972).

—— *Les mystères Templiers*, Paris, 1967.

Charlton, Donald G., *Secular Religions in France, 1815–1870*, London, 1963.

Cheney, O. R., 'The Downfall of the Templars and a letter in their defence', in *Medieval Miscellany presented to Eugène Vinaver*, Manchester, 1965.

Chevalier, P., *Histoire de la Franc-Maçonnerie Française*, 3 vol., Paris, 1974–5.

Ciaconius, A. (Chacon, Alonso), *Vitae et res gestae pontificum Romanorum et S. R. E. cardinalium*, ed. Oldoin, 4 vol., Rome, 1677.

Clark, S., 'Inversion, Misrule and the Meaning of Witchcraft', *Past and Present*, no. 87 (1980), pp. 98–127.

Cohn, Norman, *Europe's Inner Demons*, St Albans, 1976.

Coil, H. W., *A Comprehensive View of Freemasonry*, Richmond, Virginia, 1973.

Coston, H., *Les technocrates et la synarchie*, Paris, 1962.

Crowley, Aleister, *Magick without Tears*, Hampton, N.J., 1954.

Curne de Sainte Palaye, J. B. la, *Mémoires sur l'ancienne Chevalerie considérée comme un établissement politique et militaire*, 3 vol., Paris, 1781.

Curzon, H. de, ed., *La règle du Temple*, Paris, 1886.

Dakyns, J. A., *The Middle Ages in French Literature 1851–1900*, London, 1973.

Daniel, N., *Islam and the West, the making of an image*, Edinburgh, 1966.

Darnton, R., *Mesmerism and the end of the Enlightenment in France*, Cambridge, Mass., 1968.

De Bartholomaeis, V., ed., *Poesie provenzali storiche relative all'Italia*, 2 vol., Rome, 1931 *(Fonti per la Storia d'Italia)*.

De Bonneville, N., *La Maçonnerie écossoise comparée avec les trois professions et le secret des Templiers du 14e siècle*, Orient de Londres (i.e. Paris), 1788.

—— *Les Jésuites chassés de la maçonnerie et leur poignard brisé par les maçons*, (Paris), 1788.

'De Charnay, Geoffroy' (pseud.), *Synarchie: panorama de 25 années d'activité occulte*, Paris, 1946.

De Guaita, Stanislas, *Essais de Sciences Maudites: ii, Le serpent de la Genèse, bk. i, Le Temple de Satan*, Paris, 1891.

Delisle, L., 'Mémoire sur les opérations financières des Templiers', *Mémoires de l'Institut National de France. Académie des Inscriptions et Belles-Lettres*, xxxiii (1888), pt. 2.

Del-Rio, M., *Disquisitionum magicarum libri sex*, Cologne, 1679.

Deschamps, P., *Les Châteaux des Croisés en Terre Sainte*, 2 vol., Paris, 1934–9.

De Sède, Gérard, *Les Templiers sont parmi nous*, Paris, 1962 (2nd edn. 1976).

Dessubré, M., *Bibliographie de l'Ordre des Templiers*, Paris, 1928.

Dodds, E. R., *Pagan and Christian in an Age of Anxiety*, London, 1965.

Dorson, R. M., *The British Folklorists: a history*, London, 1968.

Douglas, M., ed., *Witchcraft and Sorcery: Selected Readings*, Harmondsworth, 1970.

Dummett, M., *The Game of Tarot from Ferrara to Salt Lake City*, London, 1980.

Dupuy, Pierre, *Traitez concernant l'histoire de France, scavoir la condemnation des Templiers . . .* , Paris, 1700 and Brussels, 1751.

Edelman, Nathan, *Attitudes of Seventeenth-Century France towards the Middle Ages*, New York, 1946.

Epstein, K., *The Genesis of German Conservatism*, Princeton, 1966.

Evans-Pritchard, E. E., *Theories of Primitive Religion*, Oxford, 1966.

—— *Witchcraft, Oracles and Magic among the Azande*, Oxford, 1937.

Fabré-Palaprat, B.-R., *Esquisse du mouvement héroique du peuple de Paris dans les journées immortelles des 26, 27, 28 et 29 juillet 1830*, Paris, 1830.

—— *Levitikon, ou exposé des principes fondamentaux de la doctrine des chrétiens catholiques primitifs*, Paris, 1831.

—— *Recherches historiques sur les Templiers et sur leurs croyances religieuses par J.P.*, Paris, 1835.

Farmer, P., *Vichy: political dilemma*, New York, 1977.

Favier, J., *Un conseiller de Philippe le Bel: Enguerran de Marigny*, Paris, 1963.

—— *Philippe le Bel*, Paris, 1978.

Finke, H., *Papsttum und Untergang des Templerordens*, 2 vol., Münster-i-W, 1907.

Flandrin, J. L. and L. M., 'La circulation du livre dans la société du 18e siècle: un sondage à travers quelques sources', in *Livre et société dans la France du XVIIIe siècle*, 2 vol. (Paris and the Hague, 1965–70), ii, pp. 40–72.

Foerster, W., *Gnosis*, Oxford, 1972.

Forey, A. J., *The Templars in the Corona de Aragón*, London, 1973.

Franceschini, G., *I Montefeltro*, Varese, 1970.

Francovich, C., *Storia della Massoneria in Italia dalle origini alla rivoluzione francese*, Florence, 1974.

Frend, W. H. C., *Martyrdom and Persecution in the Early Church*, Oxford, 1965.

Fuller, J. O., *The Magical Dilemma of Victor Neuburg*, London, 1965.

Garrett, C., *Respectable Folly: Millenarians and the French Revolution in France and England*, Baltimore and London, 1975.

Geertz, C., 'Religion as a cultural system', in *Anthropological Approaches to the study of Religion*, ed. M. Banton, 1966, pp. 1–46.

Gifford, G., *A Discourse of the Subtill Practises of Devilles by Witches and Sorcerers*, 1587; reprint, 1931.

Godechot, J., *The Counter-Revolution: doctrine and action 1789–1804*, London, 1972.

Goody, J., 'Religion and Ritual: the definitional problem', *British Journal of Sociology*, xii (1961), pp. 142–64.

Gossman, L., *Mediaevalism and the Ideologies of the Enlightenment: the world and work of La Curne de Sainte-Palaye*, Baltimore, 1968.

Grant, R. M., *Gnosticism and Early Christianity*, New York and London, 1966.

Grégoire, H. B., *Histoire des Sectes Religieuses*, 6 vol., Paris, 1828–45.

Grousset, R., *Histoires des Croisades et du royaume franc de Jérusalem*, 3 vol., Paris, 1934–6.

Grundmann, H., 'Der Typus des Ketzers', in *Ausgewählte Schriften*, i (*Schriften der Monumenta Germaniae Historica*, xxv, 1976), pp. 313–27.

Guingand, M., and Lanne, B., *L'Or des Templiers: Gisors ou Tomar?*, Paris, 1973.

Hammer-Purgstall, J. von, 'Mysterium Baphometis revelatum', *Fundgruben des Orients*, vi (1818), pp. 1–120, 445–99.

—— *Mémoire sur deux coffrets gnostiques du moyen age du cabinet de M. le Duc de Blacas*, Paris, 1832.

—— 'Die Schuld der Templer', *Denkschriften der kaiserlichen Akademie der Wissenschaften, Philosophisch-historische Classe*, vi (Vienna, 1855).

—— *Geschichte der Assassinen*, 1818 (English trs. 1835).

Hammermayer, L., *Der Wilhelmsbader Freimaurer-Konvent von 1782: ein Höhe und Wendepunkt in der Geschichte der deutschen und europäischen Geheimgesellschaften* (Wolfenbütteler Studien zur Aufklärung im Auftrag der Lessing-Akademie herausgegeben von G. Schulz, vol. v, pt. 2, Heidelberg, 1980).

Hillgarth, J. N., *Ramon Lull and Lullism in Fourteenth-Century France*, Oxford, 1971.

Hirschman, A. O., *The Passions and the Interests: political arguments for Capitalism before its triumph*, Princeton, 1977.

Holtzmann, R., *Wilhelm von Nogaret*, Freiburg-i-B., 1898.

Howe, E., *The Magicians of the Golden Dawn*, London, 1972.

—— and Möller, H., 'Theodor Reuss: irregular Freemasonry in Germany, 1900–23', *Transactions of the Quattuor Coronati Lodge*, xci (1978), pp. 28–42.

Hurd, Richard, *Hurd's Letters on Chivalry and Romance*, ed. E. J. Morley, London, 1911.

Innocent III, Pope, Letters, in Migne, *Patrologia Latina*, ccxiv–ccxvi.

Joinville, Histoire de Saint Louis, ed. N. de Wailly, Paris, 1890.

Jones, W. R., 'Political Uses of Sorcery in Medieval Europe', *The Historian*, xxiv (1972), pp. 670–87.

Josten, C. H., *Elias Ashmole*, Oxford, 1966.

Katz, J., *Jews and Freemasons in Europe 1732–1939*, Cambridge, Mass., 1970.

Klasse en ideologie in de vrijmetselarij: Classes et idéologies dans la Franc-Maçonnerie (Tijdschrift voor de studie van de verlichting, iv, Brussels, 1976).

Kieckhefer, R., *European Witch Trials: their foundations in popular and learned culture*, Berkeley and Los Angeles, 1976.

Korff, H. A., *Geist der Goethezeit*, 4 vol., Leipzig, 1923–55.

Krüger, G., 'Johann A. Starck der Kleriker: ein Beitrag zur Geschichte der Theosophie im 18. Jahrhundert', in *Festgabe von Fachgenossen und Freunden Karl Müller zum 70. Geburtstag dargebracht* (Tübingen, 1922), pp. 244–66.

Ladner, G. H., '*Homo Viator*: Mediaeval Ideas on Alienation and Order', *Speculum*, xlii (1967), pp. 233–59.

Lambert, E., *L'Architecture des Templiers*, Paris, 1955.

Lees, B. A., ed., *Records of the Templars in England in the Twelfth Century*, London, 1935.

Le Cour, Paul, *L'Évangile esotérique de Saint-Jean*, Paris, 1950.

Le Forestier, R., *La Franc-Maçonnerie templière et occultiste au XVIIIe et XIXe siècle*, ed. A. Faivre, Paris, 1970.

—— *Occultisme et la franc-maçonnerie écossaise*, Paris, 1928.

Le Meilleur de Planète: principaux articles, illustrations et photographes publiés dans les numéros introuvables du no. 1 au no. 12, Paris, 1966.

Legman, G., *The Guilt of the Templars*, New York, 1966.

Lévi, Eliphas, *Histoire de la Magie*, Paris, 1860.

—— *Dogme et Rituel de la Haute Magie*, 2 vol., 2nd edn., Paris, 1861.

Lewis, B., 'Kamal al-Din's biography of Rasid al-Din Sinan', *Arabica*, xiii (1966), pp. 225–67.

—— *The Assassins*, London, 1967.

Lewis, P. S., *Later Mediaeval France: the Polity*, London, 1968.

Livre et Société dans la France du XVIIIe siècle, 2 vol., Paris and The Hague, 1965–70.

Lizerand, G., *Le Dossier de l'affaire des Templiers*, Paris, 1923.

Ludz, P. C. (ed.), *Geheime Gesellschaften* (Wolfenbütteler Studien zur Aufklärung im Auftrag der Lessing-Akademie herausgegeben von G. Schulz, vol. v, pt. 1, Heidelberg, 1979).

Lukes, S., 'Some problems about rationality', in *Rationality*, ed. B. R. Wilson, Oxford, 1970.

Lundgreen, F., *Wilhelm von Tyrus und der Templerorden*, Berlin, 1911.

Luttrell, A., 'The Crusade in the Fourteenth Century', in *Europe in the Late Middle Ages*, ed. J. R. Hale, J. R. L. Highfield, B. Smalley, London, 1965.

Macfarlane, A., *Witchcraft in Tudor and Stuart England*, London, 1970.

McNamara, J. A., *Gilles Aycelin, the Servant of Two Masters*, Syracuse, 1973.

Maillard de Chambure, C.-H., *Règles et statuts secrets des Templiers*, Paris, 1840.

Mair, L., *Witchcraft*, London, 1969.

Map, Walter, *Master Walter Map's Book, De nugis curialium*, ed. F. Tupper and M. B. Ogle, London, 1924.

Marcellinus, Ammianus, ed. J. C. Rolfe, Cambridge, Mass. and London, 3 vol., 1935–9.

Martin, H.-J., *Livres, pouvoir et société à Paris au XVIIème siècle*, 2 vol., Geneva, 1969.

Marwick, M., ed., *Witchcraft and Sorcery: Selected Readings*, Harmondsworth, 1970.

Matthew Paris, *Chronica Majora*, ed. H. R. Luard, 7 vol., 1872–83 (Rolls Series).

—— *Historia Anglorum*, ed. F. Madden, 3 vol., 1866–9 (Rolls Series).

Mayer, H. E., *The Crusades*, London, 1972.

Mellor, A., *Our Separated Brethren the Freemasons*, London, 1964.

Merzdorf, J. F. L. T., *Die Geheimstatuten des Ordens der Tempelherren . . . zum ersten Mal herausgegeben*, Halle, 1877.

Meyer, P., 'Les derniers troubadours de la Provence', *Bibliothèque de l'École des Chartes*, 6th ser., v (1869), pp. 484–98.

Michelet, J., *La Sorcière*, Paris, 1862.

—— *Histoire de France*, 17 vol., Paris, 1835–67; new edn., 19 vol., Paris, 1879.

—— ed., *Le procès des Templiers*, 2 vol., Paris, 1841–51.

Michelet, V.-E., *Le secret de la chevalerie*, Paris, 1930.

Midelfort, H. C. E., *Witch Hunting in Southwestern Germany 1562–1684: the social and intellectual foundations*, Stanford, 1972.

Mignard, *Monographie du Coffret de M. le Duc de Blacas*, Paris, 1852.

—— *Suite de la monographie . . . ou preuves du Manichéisme de l'Ordre du Temple*, Paris, 1853.

Mollat, G., *The Popes at Avignon, 1305–1378*, English trs., London, 1963.

Möller, H., *Aufklärung in Preussen: Friedrich Nicolai*, Berlin, 1974.

—— 'Wie aufgeklärt war Preussen?' in *Preussen im Rückblick*, ed. H. J. Puhle and H. V. Wehler, Göttingen, 1980.

Momigliano, A., *Essays in Ancient and Modern Historiography*, Oxford, 1977.

Montagnac, E. L., *Histoire des chevaliers templiers et de leurs prétendus successeurs*, Paris, 1864.

Mousnier, R., *Les Hiérarchies sociales de 1450 à nos jours*, Paris, 1969.

Mundy, J. H., *Europe in the High Middle Ages*, London and New York, 1973.

Murray, A., *Reason and Society in the Middle Ages*, Oxford, 1978.

Napoleon I, *Correspondance de Napoléon I publié par ordre de l'Empereur Napoléon III*, 32 vol., Paris, 1858–69.

Nauert, C. G., *Agrippa and the Crisis of Renaissance Thought*, Urbana, 1965.

Nicolai, F., *Versuch über die Beschuldigungen welche dem Tempelherrerorden gemacht worden und über dessen Geheimniss*, Berlin and Stettin, 1782.

Nodier, Charles, *Oeuvres Complètes*, 11 vol., Paris, 1832–7 (reprint, Geneva, 1968).

—— *Souvenirs de la Révolution et de l'Empire*, 2 vol., Paris, n.d.

Nutt, A., *The Legends of the Holy Grail*, London, 1902.

Olden, R., *Das Wunderbare oder die Verzauberten*, Berlin, 1932.

Otto of Freising, *Ottonis episcopi Frisingensis Chronica sive Historia de duabus civitatibus*, ed. A. Hofmeister, Hanover and Leipzig, 1912.

Owen, A. L., *The Famous Druids*, Oxford, 1962.

Palou, A., *La Franc-Maçonnerie*, Paris, 1964.

Paradin, Guillaume, *Chronique de Savoye*, Lyons, 1552.

Parsons, C. O., *Witchcraft and Demonology in Scott's Fiction*, Edinburgh and London, 1964.

Partner, Peter D., *The Lands of St Peter*, London, Berkeley and Los Angeles, 1972.

Pauwels, L., *Ce que je crois*, Paris, 1974.

—— *Le droit de parler*, Paris, 1981.

—— and Bergier, J., *Le Matin des Magiciens*, Paris, 1960 (English trs., *The Dawn of Magic*, London, 1963 and *The Morning of the Magicians*, St Albans, 1971).

Pegues, F. J., *The Lawyers of the Last Capetians*, Princeton, 1962.

Peters, E., *The Magician, the Witch and the Law*, Philadelphia and London, 1978.

Platzeck, E. W., *Raimund Lull*, Düsseldorf, 1962.

Praz, M., *The Romantic Agony*, London and New York, 1951.

Probst-Biraben, J.-H., *Les mystères des Templiers*, Nice, 1947 (2nd edn., Paris, 1973).

Puech, J., *La vie et l'oeuvre de Flora Tristan 1830–1844 (L'Union ouvrière)*, Paris, 1925.

Ranke, L. von, *Weltgeschichte*, 9 vol., Leipzig, 1888.

Raynaldi, O, *Annales Ecclesiastici post Baronum*, Lucca, 1747–56.

Raynouard, F. J. M., *Les Templiers, tragédie*, Paris, 1805.

—— *Monumens historiques relatifs à la condamnation des chevaliers du Temple et à l'abolition de leur ordre*, Paris, 1813.

—— 'Étude sur "Mysterium Baphometi revelatum"', *Journal des Savants* (1819), pp. 151–61, 221–9.

Richer, J., *Gérard de Nerval et les doctrines esotériques*, Paris, 1947.

Riley-Smith, J., *The Knights of St John in Jerusalem and Cyprus c. 1050–1310*, London, 1967.

Roberts, J. M., *The Mythology of the Secret Societies*, London, 1972.

Roche, D., *Le siècle des lumières en province: académies et académiciens provinciaux, 1680–1789*, 2 vol., Paris and The Hague, 1978.

Rogalla von Bieberstein, J., *Die These von der Verschwörung 1776–1945: Philosophen, Freimaurer gegen die Suzialordnung*, Bern and Frankfurt, 1976.

Runciman, S., *A History of the Crusades*, 3 vol., Cambridge, 1951–4.

Russell, J. B., *Witchcraft in the Middle Ages*, Ithaca and London, 1972.

Ruthven, M., *Torture: the grand conspiracy*, London, 1978.

Saint-Yves d'Alveydre, J.-A., *La France Vraie*, Paris, 1887.

—— *Mission actuelle des Souverains par l'un d'eux*, Paris, 1882.

Saunier, J., *La Synarchie*, Paris, 1972.

Schein, S., '*Gesta dei per Mongolos*: the genesis of a non-event', *English Historical Review*, xciv (1979), pp. 805–19.

Schiffman, G. A. *Andreas Michael Ramsay*, Leipzig, 1878.

Scholz, R., *Die Publizistik zur Zeit Philipps des Schönen und Bonifaz VIII*, Stuttgart, 1903.

Schottmüller, K., *Der Untergang des Templerordens*, 2 vol., Berlin, 1887.

Setton, K. M., *The Papacy and the Levant 1204–1571*, 2 vol., Philadelphia, 1976–8.

Smail, R. C., *Crusading Warfare, 1097–1193*, Cambridge, 1956.

—— *The Crusaders*, London, 1973.

Soboul, A., 'La franc-maçonnerie et la Révolution française', *Annales historiques de la Révolution française*, xlvi (1974).

Southern, R. W., *The Making of the Middle Ages*, London, 1953.

Western Views of Islam in the Middle Ages, Cambridge, Mass., 1962.

Starck, J. A., *Über die alten und neuen Mysterien*, Berlin, 1782.

Stickel, E., *Der Fall von Akkon: Untersuchungen zum Abklingen des Kreuzzugsgedankens am ende des 13. Jahrhunderts*, Bern and Frankfurt-a-M., 1975.

Strayer, J. R., 'The Political Crusades of the Thirteenth Century', in *A History of the Crusades*, ed. R. L. Wolff and H. W. Hazard, ii, Philadelphia, 1962.

—— *The Reign of Philip the Fair*, Princeton, 1980.

Thomas, K. V., *Religion and the Decline of Magic*, London, 1971.

Throop, P., *Criticism of the Crusade: a Study of public opinion and crusade propaganda*, Amsterdam, 1940.

Trythall, A. J., *'Boney' Fuller: the intellectual General*, London, 1977.

Ulmann, A., and Azeau, H., *Synarchie et pouvoir*, Paris, 1968.

Van Dülmen, R., *Der Geheimbund der Illuminaten*, Stuttgart, 1977.

Ventre de la Touloubre ('Montjoie'), *Histoire de la Conjuration de Louis-Philippe-Joseph d'Orléans*, 2 vol., Paris, 1794.

Viatte, A., *Les Sources occultes du Romantisme: Illuminisme-Theosophie 1770–1820*, 2 vol., Paris, 1927.

Vincent, E. R., *Gabriele Rossetti in England*, London, 1936.

Viollet-le-Duc, E. M., *Dictionnaire Raisonné de l'architecture française du XIe au XVIe siècle*, 10 vol., 1858–68.

Vogel, C., 'Pratiques superstitieuses au début du XIe siècle d'après le *Corrector sive medicus* de Burchard éveque de Worms', *Études de civilisation médiévale . . . offertes à E.-R. Labande*, Poitiers, n.d., pp. 751–61.

Voltaire, F. M., 'Des conspirations contre les peuples ou des proscriptions', in *Nouveaux Mélanges Philosophiques, Historiques, Critiques, &c. &c.*, pt. iv, 1767, pp. 188–209.

Walker, D. P., *Spiritual and Demonic Magic*, London, 1958.

Waller, R. D., *The Rossetti Family, 1824–1854*, Manchester, 1932.

Weber, Max, *From Max Weber*, ed. H. H. Gerth and C. Wright Mills, New York, 1946.

Weston, J. L., *From Ritual to Romance*, Garden City, New York, 1957.

—— *The Quest of the Holy Grail*, London, 1964.

White, H., *Metahistory: the historical imagination in nineteenth-century Europe*, Baltimore and London, 1973.

Wicks, M., *The Italian Exiles in London*, Manchester, 1937.

Wildermann, A. K., *Die Beurteilung des Templerprozesses bis zum 17. Jahrhundert*, Freiburg, 1971.

Wilkins, D., *Concilia Magnae Britanniae et Hiberniae*, 4 vol., London, 1737.

William of Tyre, Guillelmus Tyrensis archiepiscopus, *Historia rerum in transmarinis partibus gestarum*, in *Receuil des historiens des croisades: Historiens occidentaux*, 5 vol., Paris, 1844–95.

Wilson, B., *Religious Sects*, London, 1970.

Wilson, I., *The Turin Shroud*, Harmondsworth, 1979.

Wright, T., ed., *Political Poems and Songs relating to British History*, 2 vol., 1858–9 (Rolls Series).

—— with George Witt and James Tennant, 'On the worship of the generative powers during the Middle Ages of Western Europe', in Richard P. Knight, *A discourse on the Worship of Priapus and its connection with the mystic theology of the ancients*, London, privately printed, 1865.

Yates, F. A., *Giordano Bruno and the Hermetic Tradition*, London and Chicago, 1964.

—— *The Rosicrucian Enlightenment*, London and Boston, 1972.

Zambelli, P., 'Agrippa von Nettesheim in den neueren kritischen Studien und in den Handschriften', *Archiv für Kulturgeschichte*, li (1969), pp. 264–95.

INDEX